Industrial Design and Artistic Expression

Art and Law

Volumes published in this Brill Research Perspectives title are listed at *brill.com/rpal*

Industrial Design and Artistic Expression

The Challenge of Legal Protection

By

Barbara Pasa

BRILL

LEIDEN | BOSTON

This paperback book edition is simultaneously published as issue 3.2–3 (2019) of *Art and Law*, DOI:10.1163/24684309-12340008

Library of Congress Control Number: 2020902299

Typeface for the Latin, Greek, and Cyrillic scripts: "Brill". See and download: brill.com/brill-typeface.

ISBN 978-90-04-43030-3 (paperback)
ISBN 978-90-04-43031-0 (e-book)

This journal is printed on acid-free paper and produced in a sustainable manner.

Contents

Industrial Design and Artistic Expression
The Challenge of Legal Protection 1
Barbara Pasa
Abstract 1
Keywords 1
Introduction. What Is Design: A First Approximation from Different Perspectives 1
Part 1: The Work 21
1 *The Thin Line of Artistic Speculation about Design Activity* 22
1.1 In Law 22
1.2 In Design 30
2 *Design as a Projection of the Identity of the Nation in Post-war States* 39
3 *Legal Requirements for Defining Protectable Design Works* 43
3.1 International Legal Requirements, or the Lack Thereof: A Very Broad Definition 43
3.2 European Legal Requirements: A Stricter Definition 47
3.3 The Lack of Definition in Design Studies: What Does It Matter for the Regulatory Framework? 49
3.3.1 *Categories of Goods: Objects, Artefacts, and Useful Articles* 50
3.3.2 *Features Solely Dictated by Technical Function* 53
3.3.3 *"Appearance": Canons and Styles* 58
4 *Parameters to Define Protectable Works* 62
4.1 The Courts Parameter: "Original Work" as "Author's Own Intellectual Creation" 62
4.2 The Parameters Available from Design Practice: "Original Work" as "Designer's Provenance of the Project" 68
5 *Protecting Works of Design Today: A Wide Variety of Legal Tools* 70
Part 2: The Author 74
6 *Who Is Protected* 75
6.1 The "Author" According to Law in the Design/Copyright Interface 75
6.1.1 *EU "Author's Own Intellectual Creation"* 78
6.1.2 *National Variances: The "Author" According to Different Courts* 86

6.1.3 *Low Threshold: German, Swiss, Dutch and Belgian Laws* 88
6.1.4 *France's Equal Treatment of All Intellectual Creative Endeavours* 96
6.1.5 *The High Thresholds of Italian and Portuguese Laws* 99
6.1.6 *The Eclectic UK Position: Periodic Swings in Protection* 110
6.2 The "Author": Common Usages and Design Practice 116
Conclusion 122
Acknowledgments 137

Industrial Design and Artistic Expression

The Challenge of Legal Protection

Barbara Pasa
Università Iuav di Venezia, Italy
bpasa@iuav.it

Abstract

The complex nature of industrial design, which combines functional and aesthetic elements, allows for different modes of protection, with cumulative, separate or partially overlapping regimes applicable according to different legal systems. The legal framework is rapidly changing, especially in Europe where the principle of cumulation of a special *sui generis* regime for protecting industrial design with copyright rules has been established. Over the last decade, the national courts of some Member States construed the "cumulative regime" with a peculiar meaning, while other courts enforced design rights in line with the interpretation given by the Court of Justice of the European Union. The copyright/design interface is presented here to a wider, non-specialist audience, taking as a starting point the notion of industrial design derived from design studies, on the borderline between art and science. Other challenges which will need to be confronted urgently over the coming years are also raised.

Keywords

copyright – design rights – industrial design – originality – intellectual property – patents – shape of configuration – unfair competition – utility models – work of applied art – work of art

Introduction. What Is Design: A First Approximation from Different Perspectives

My aim in this work is to engage experts from different fields – from lawyers and philosophers to designers, artists, and businesspeople – in an interdisciplinary

 | DOI:10.1163/9789004430310_002

inquiry through the maze of IP law. My focus will be on the overlapping legal protections afforded to mass produced goods through the copyright/design interface, with only tangential treatment provided of trademark/design, patent, and utility patent/design interfaces and the protection afforded by competition rules.

The complex nature of Industrial Design allows for at least two modes of protection, namely protection by a special *sui generis* regime and protection by copyright. Depending on whether the two systems are applied alternatively or simultaneously, three regimes can be conceived: a "cumulative" regime (fully overlapping one another, for instance in France), a "separate" regime (with special rules for industrial design, as in the USA and in China), and a "partially overlapping" regime (industrial design protection for the appearance of any utilitarian, industrial product, plus copyright protection only where the design can also be considered an original work, for instance in Nordic countries, Benelux and Germany, or as a work of applied art with strict artistic value and creative character, such as in Italy and Portugal). This legal framework, however, is rapidly changing especially in Europe, ever since EU lawmakers instructed that in the absence of the full harmonization of copyright law, it is important to establish the principle of "cumulative protection" under European design and copyright laws, whilst leaving Member States free to establish the extent of copyright protection and the conditions under which such protection is afforded. European Directive 98/71/EC of 13 October 1998 on the legal protection of designs and European Regulation No. 6/2002 of 12 December 2001 on Community designs together established the principle of cumulation with copyright, but left the conditions under which such cumulative protection is afforded – "including the level of originality required" – to be determined by each Member State, thus hampering lawful trade between countries and undermining their competitiveness. As we will see in the second part of this paper, the Court of Justice of the European Union has interpreted the level of originality required as meaning the "author's own intellectual creation," on the grounds of which the Court then challenged the high threshold required by Italian and Portuguese law, opting instead for an interpretation calibrated to the lower standard recently set by German, Dutch, and Belgian courts. However, neither the requirement of "artistic value" nor an "above-average level of creativity" would appear to be compatible with the European harmonization process and the competitive single market.

The growing ephemerality of hardware and software, witnessed in how technology today can be upgraded within the space of a few months, or in the monthly plans companies provide offering automatic subscription to the latest device, and in the greater value placed on user-generated content, is an issue I will only touch on in this work. The peculiarities of software design, user interface and environment design, and so on, are tied not so much to the device itself as to the investment they make in data, raising major privacy and security concerns for all the data collected through websites, mobile devices, social media networks, and the Internet of Things. The boom in documents and messages characterizing our digital age – the "*documedia* revolution,"[1] as it has been called – deserves more in-depth study than what can be developed here. It is an ongoing revolution which has been transforming, for the first time in world history, every kind of document (from maps to photographs, from messages to likes) into an actual or potential commodity, generating money from the billions of data that 4.4 billion Internet users[2] worldwide generate through the Web. The "design for the next 50 billion connected devices" and its guiding principles based on "calm technology"[3] will be the subject of another inquiry, bearing in mind what has been said on the relationship between the private sphere and the new technology as a reminder and a call: "future products must be designed with respect for our right to self-determination over personal data."[4]

As a final introductory note, my focus here will mainly concern "physical" artefacts designed to show beauty and give pleasure. The abundance of high-quality material goods which continue to be found in fields as far apart as furniture and sports, fashion and active-ageing, goes to show how the death knell of material culture has yet to sound. Indeed, on the contrary, we are witnessing its rebirth, as contemporary industrial design, just like art, seeks to stimulate an emotional bond between users and artefacts, to give pleasure and status, and maintain its value over time. Unlike art, however, industrial design demands functionality, technical reproducibility, standardization, sturdiness, and industrial feasibility.[5] Such a distinction is important, as it shapes the growing debate over how reasonable it is to extend copyright protection (pertaining

1 Ferraris, *From Fountain to Moleskine: The Work of Art in the Age of its Technological Producibility*, Leiden/Boston, 2019, pp. 65 ff.

2 On the amount of data created each day on the Internet (2019) see Schultz, *How Much Data is Created on the Internet Each Day?*, 08.06.2019, available at https://blog.microfocus.com (accessed 10.8.2019). See Floridi, *The Fourth Revolution. How the Infosphere is Reshaping Human Reality*, Oxford, 2014.

3 Weiser, "The Computer for the 21st Century," *Scientific American*, 265, 1991, pp. 66–75; Case, *Calm Technology: Principles and Patterns for Non-Intrusive Design*, Sebastopol, 2016.

4 Rodotà, *Il diritto di avere diritti*, Rome-Bari, 2015, Kindle ed., pos. 5564. In design studies see Costa, "Human-Data Experience Design: progettare con i personal data," *MD Journal* [2] 2016, pp. 12–23.

5 Bakker et al., *Products that Last*, Delf, 2014. See also Maldonado, "Cosa c'è di vero nella dematerializzazione?" *Alfabeta*, 1988, II–III.

to the traditional fields of literature, drama, art, and music) to all products of the creative mind – and, therefore, works of industrial design – to ensure an equitable return for creative endeavour.

Industrial Design, Multimedia Design, and Product & Visual Communication Design have emerged as leading fields in which creative and practical skills[6] are combined to create products that enhance user experience, while maximizing environmental and social sustainability, to develop print and digital communication projects for the marketing of artefacts, and to design systems and processes (integrated product-service systems) for public and private institutions. Industrial design today is recognized as a key element of the contemporary meaning of doing business. But what is industrial design? What does an industrial designer do? And what makes a product of industrial design qualify as a creative work and become eligible for copyright protection? How can industrial design be distinguished from the decorative arts, sculpture, drawing, and other creative endeavours? To understand how industrial design can be protected under a *sui generis* regime or copyright law, we need to turn to *le droit du design*, or design law, and set aside any preconceived notions we might have of what design is.

At the 29th General Assembly in Gwangju, South Korea (2015), the Professional Practice Committee of the World Design Organization (WDO, formerly known as the International Council of Societies of Industrial Design, ICSID) presented the following renewed definition of industrial design:

> Industrial Design is a strategic problem-solving process that drives innovation, builds business success, and leads to a better quality of life through innovative products, systems, services, and experiences. Industrial Design bridges the gap between what is and what's possible. It is a trans-disciplinary profession that harnesses creativity to resolve problems and co-create solutions with the intent of making a product, system, service, experience or a business, better. At its heart, Industrial Design provides a more optimistic way of looking at the future by reframing problems as opportunities. It links innovation, technology, research, business, and customers to provide new value and competitive advantage across economic, social, and environmental spheres.[7]

6 Maddalena, *The Philosophy of Gesture*, Montreal/London, 2015. In learning by doing, "doing" is not simply the execution of a routine, but has a decisive role in the invention of the new objects; "doing" is possible without understanding, as theorized with several examples by Dennett, *From Bacteria to Bach and Back: The Evolution of Minds*, London, 2017.

7 WDO, available at https://wdo.org/about/definition/ (accessed 6.8.2019).

Whether it is in manufacturing industries, professional, technical, scientific or service sectors, or in creative fields, the employment opportunities for industrial designers appear endless – in the technical offices, quality control teams, production layout and development units, and R&D labs of private enterprises, as well as in professional firms, national agencies, cultural institutions, museums, libraries, archives, and art galleries, to name but a few. The palette of tools that industrial designers can draw on is of extraordinary richness, building on their multidisciplinary and experimental approach and belief in shaping culture and society. Industrial design in all its forms – product, visual communication, interior, graphic, multimedia, fashion, Web, interaction, and information design – ties into a vast number of fields of study, from the arts and architecture, business and engineering, to marketing and decision theory, sociology, and computer science.

Another possible understanding of industrial design is given by management studies, which alludes to the great potential it has in spearheading innovation and driving change in markets, rather than simply adapting to them, and to the extraordinary ability of design-driven innovators to understand and influence how people give meaning to things for the production of goods or services that become part of users' sense of self.[8] Industrial design is evidently a strategic asset for enterprises of different sizes in different commodity sectors – especially in Italy for "Made in Italy" industries,[9] epitomized by the Brianza district near Milan and Milan itself, the city which in the 1970s launched the democratic message of "products for all" on an industrial scale,[10] a global capital of pret-a-porter fashion,[11] the place where most Italian designers have built their careers, and where the Italian design system as a whole was created. According to a recent green paper by the Italian Entrepreneurial Association, *Confindustria*, a first scenario forecasts that by 2023, thirty new markets[12] for Italian "BBF" imports (the acronym stands for "*bello e ben fatto*",

8 Verganti, *Design-Driven Innovation*, Harvard, 2009.

9 See the Italian law protecting textile, leather and footwear goods, *Legge 8 aprile 2010, n. 55, Disposizioni concernenti la commercializzazione di prodotti tessili, della pelletteria e calzaturieri*, GU, Serie Generale no. 92, 21.04.2010.

10 Branzi, *Una generazione esagerata*, Milan, 2014. Milan plays host to some of the biggest international trade fairs, including the *Salone Internazionale del Mobile* (furniture), Micam (shoes), Mido (eyewear), Mipel (bags), Mifur (furs), and Mipap (leather, fur and accessories).

11 See the exhibition *Italiana: Italy through the Lens of Fashion 1971–2001* at Palazzo Reale in Milan, curated by Maria Luisa Frisa and Stefano Tonchi (2018). See Pozzo, Jacometti (eds.), *Fashion Law*, Milan, 2016.

12 Algeria, Angola, Saudi Arabia, Argentina, Brazil, Chile, China, Colombia, Egypt, United Arab Emirates, Philippines, Ghana, India, Indonesia, Kazakstan, Kenya, Lebanon,

meaning "beautiful and well made")[13] will grow by +40% (from €10.4 billion in 2017 to €14.6 billion in 2023), almost double the aggregate growth estimated for advanced markets. The most ambitious scenario predicts growth of +75%, with an export value of €18.2 billion.[14]

A further understanding of industrial design is related to intellectual property rights and the legal framework. In Europe, design is defined as the outward appearance of a product or part of it, resulting from the lines, contours, colours, shape, texture, materials, and/or its ornamentation.[15] Accordingly, EU design law protects both two-dimensional and three-dimensional products in a vast array of conformations, including daily objects, fashion, packaging, graphic interfaces, logotypes, graphic symbols, computer icons, typefaces, maps, get-ups, and Web design. Therefore, design protection covers the appearance of any artefact, but it is excluded where the design is "predominantly or entirely functional" because it will fall under patent, or utility patent, or utility model protection.[16] The US Patent and Trademark Office (USPTO) has adopted an even stricter definition,[17] whereby design refers only to aesthetic, ornamental

---

Malaysia, Morocco, Mexico, Nigeria, Pakistan, Paraguay, Peru, Russia, South Africa, Thailand, Tunisia, Turkey, Vietnam.

13 The BBF sectors analyzed are: Food; Clothing and Home Textiles; Furniture; Footwear; Gold Jewellery; Eyewear.

14 See the Green Paper entitled *"Esportare la dolce vita"*, 9th ed., 2019. Available at https://www.assolombarda.it/centro-studi/esportare-la-dolce-vita-il-potenziale-di-mercato-per-il-bello-e-ben-fatto-italiano-nei-mercati-emergenti, (accessed 6.8.2019).

15 More details in the following pages. For an overview see Musker, *Community Design Law: Principles and Practice*, London, 2002; see also European Union, *Legal Review on Industrial Design Protection in Europe*, Luxembourg, 2016, available at http://ec.europa.eu/growth/tools-databases/newsroom/cf/itemdetail.cfm?item_id=8845 (accessed 6.8.2019).

16 Musker, "The Overlap between Patent and Design Protection" in Wilko, Basheer (eds.), *Overlapping Intellectual Property Rights*, Oxford, 2012, pp. 23–56; Bridges, "Navigating the Interface between Utility Patents and Copyrights" in Wilko, Basheer (eds.), *Overlapping Intellectual Property Rights*, Oxford, 2012, pp. 1–19; Harrison, "Patents and Utility Models" in Wilko, Basheer (eds.), *Overlapping Intellectual Property Rights*, Oxford, 2012, pp. 105–117. Cf Suthersanen, "Utility models: Do they really serve national innovation?" in Drexl, Sanders (eds.), *The Innovation Society and Intellectual Property*, Cheltenham, 2019, pp. 2–24.

17 USPTO, Design Patent Application Guide on line at https://www.uspto.gov/patents-getting-started/patent-basics/types-patent-applications/design-patent-application-guide#def_(accessed 6.8.2019). The statutes (United States Code) governing design patents are: 35 U.S.C. 171, 35 U.S.C. 172, 35 U.S.C. 173, 35 U.S.C. 102, 35 U.S.C. 103, 35 U.S.C. 112, 35 U.S.C. 132. The rules (Code of Federal Regulations) pertaining to the drawing disclosure of a design patent application are: 37 CFR § 1.84, 37 CFR § 1.152, 37 CFR § 1.121. *Cf* Suthersanen, *Design Law: European Union and United Stets of America*, 2nd ed., London, 2010; Du Mont, Janis, "The Origins of American Design Protection," *Indiana Law Journal* (on-line), Vol. 88, Iss. 3, Article 1, 2013, 837; Schickl, "Protection of Industrial Design

appearance, embodied in or applied to an article of manufacture, while functional aspects of products are considered pure inventions. Accordingly, a design patent protects only the appearance of the article, not structural, technical or functional features, which are protected by the patent system. The People's Republic of China, another big player in globalized markets, protects product design under patent law in terms of their shape, pattern, or the combination thereof, or the combination of the colour with shape and pattern, which should be rich in an aesthetic appeal and fit for industrial application.[18] Unlike the USA, China's legal system does not stress any sharp distinction between the shape, appearance, and function of industrial products.

On a closer look, according to US and European legal definitions (but not for China's), "design" is the shape, appearance, or configuration of an object, which is capable of being identified separately and independently from the functional aspects of the object in which it is embodied. Such a definition, however, is not fully satisfactory since the most successful designs purposefully combine, in a coherent unit, functional and aesthetic elements. As I will suggest in the following pages, the current legal framework, overzealous in its attempt to systematize and maintain coherence, does not match up to the complexity of the fields of product and communication design, and their processes. Any definition that turns on a sharp demarcation between "form" and "function" – a legacy of Modernism – is of little help today.[19] Non-purely-functional products, which are costly to design but not truly inventive, and therefore do not qualify for patent protection, should be protected as "a coherent unit" with the appearance of the object, because factories rely to a great extent on specific "design innovative abilities"[20] as an incentive for further investment. As such, it would be useful for legal theorists and practitioners to take account of what Tomás Maldonado has to say on industrial design:

---

in the United States and in the EU: Different Concepts or Different Labels?" *The Journal of World Intellectual Property*, 2013, pp. 15–38.

18 See Article 2 of Chinese patent law, amended after the third reform of Chinese patent law, promulgated on December 27, 2008 and in force since October 1, 2009 (followed by the Implementing Regulation issued on January 9, 2010, and the new version of the Guidelines for the examination of patent applications, which both entered into force on February 1, 2010). The text is available at http://english.www.gov.cn/archive/laws_regulations/2014/08/23/content_281474983043612.htm (accessed 6.8.2019). See Merges, Song, *Transnational Intellectual Property Law, Text and Cases*, Cheltenham, 2018.

19 In Italy, Auteri, *Industrial design* in Carnevali (ed.), *Dizionario del diritto privato*, Milan, 1981, p. 565; Floridia, "La protezione del diritto d'autore sulle opere dell'industrial design," *Riv. dir. ind.*, 1984, I, p. 375; Bergomi, "Industrial design," *Contr. e impr.*, 1987, p. 966; Franzosi, Magelli (eds.), *Design nozione e tutela*, Atti del Convegno di Parma, Bari, 1989.

20 See the British White Paper, Department of Trade and Industry (1986) Intellectual Property and Innovation, Cmnd 9712, London: HMSO.

> Industrial design is a creative activity whose aim is to determine the formal qualities of objects produced by industry. Those formal qualities are not only the external features but are principally the structural and functional relationships which convert a system into a coherent unity, both from the point of view of the producer and the user. Industrial design extends to embrace all aspects of the human environment which are conditioned by industrial production.[21]

As explained in a joint project between the European Patent Office and the European Union Intellectual Property Office, EU statistical data highlight the importance of protecting intellectual property rights in the most important design-intensive industries, even if, in all truth, the industries with a primary direct dependence on design and its legal protection account for only 13.4% of gross domestic product, although in more general terms, IPR-intensive industries all together generated more than 42% of total EU economic activity (GDP), worth €5.7 trillion, and generated 27.8% of all jobs in the EU.[22]

TABLE 1 Contribution of IPR-intensive industries to GDP. 2011–2013 average.

IPR-intensive industries	Value added/GDP (€ million)	Share of total EU GDP
Trade-mark-intensive	4,812,310	35.9%
Design-intensive	1,788,811	13.4%
Patent-intensive	2,035,478	15.2%
Copyright-intensive	914,612	6.8%
GI-intensive	18,109	0.1%
PVR-intensive	51,710	0.4%
All IPR-intensive	5,664,168	42.3%
Total EU GDP	13,387,988	

SOURCE: INTELLECTUAL PROPERTY RIGHTS (IPR) INTENSIVE INDUSTRIES AND ECONOMIC PERFORMANCE IN THE EUROPEAN UNION, INDUSTRY-LEVEL ANALYSIS REPORT, OCTOBER 2016

21 This is the definition proposed by Maldonado in 1969: *Disegno industriale: un riesame*, Milan, 1976; *cf* De Fusco, *Storia del design*, Rome-Bari, 2009.

22 See Intellectual Property Rights Intensive Industries and Economic Performance in the European Union, Industry-Level Analysis Report, 2nd ed, October 2016, available online (accessed 6.8.2019). The study covered the period 2011–2013, where IPR is used to refer to the six rights included in the analysis: patents, trademarks, registered designs, copyright, geographical indications, and plant variety rights.

TABLE 2 Direct and indirect contribution of IPR-intensive industries to employment. 2011–2013 average.

IPR-intensive industries	Employment (direct)	Share of total employment (direct)	Employment (direct+indirect)	Share of total employment (direct+indirect)
Trade-mark-intensive	45,789,224	21.2%	65,486,334	30.3%
Design-intensive	25,662,683	11.9%	38,673,508	17.9%
Patent-intensive	22,268,215	10.3%	36,021,154	16.7
Copyright-intensive	11,630,753	5.4%	15,240,509	7.1%
GI-intensive	n/a	n/a	399,815	0.2%
PVR-intensive	1,018,754	0.5%	1,220,410	0.6%
All IPR-intensive	60,032,200	27.8%	82,214,925	38.1%
Total EU employment			215,808,033	

SOURCE: INTELLECTUAL PROPERTY RIGHTS INTENSIVE INDUSTRIES AND ECONOMIC PERFORMANCE IN THE EUROPEAN UNION, INDUSTRY-LEVEL ANALYSIS REPORT, OCTOBER 2016

It is evident that intellectual property is a branch of law related to what is, in aggregate, a very significant part of the EU economy, encompassing for the most part the manufacturing sector, from watches and clocks to jewellery, sports goods to games and toys, household items and furniture to carpets and lightning equipment, clothes, and footwear. Protecting the position of those industries is, therefore, in the general economic interest.

In 2017, EUIPO (European Union Intellectual Property Office) statistics on Community design reported 26,047 applications in Europe,[23] with an increasing number of applications filed every year. In addition to design-intensive industries, the WIPO (World Intellectual Property Organization) also identifies three other groups of industries – interdependent industries (covering the manufacture, wholesale, and retail of TV sets, radios, CD-DVD-Blu-Ray players, electronic game equipment, and other similar equipment; computers and equipment; tablets and smartphones; musical instruments); partial industries (apparel, textiles, and footwear; furniture; jewellery and coins; household goods, china, and glass; wall coverings and carpets; toys and games; interior design;

23 EUIPO, Statistics of Community Designs, available from https://euipo.europa.eu/tunnel-web/secure/webdav/guest/document_library/contentPdfs/about_euipo/the_office/statistics-of-community-designs_en.pdf. *Cf* also World Intellectual Property Indicators 2018 on-line (accessed 8.8.2019).

TABLE 3 The 20 most design-intensive industries (based on design registrations filed in 2004–2006).

NACE code	NACE description	Designs/1000 employees
26.52	Manufacture of watches and clocks	90.68
77.40	Leasing of intellectual property and similar products, except copyrighted works	78.59
25.71	Manufacture of cutlery	70.23
23.41	Manufacture of ceramic household and ornamental articles	66.24
46.48	Wholesale of watches and jewellery	39.80
27.40	Manufacture of electric lighting equipment	39.18
28.24	Manufacture of power-driven hand tools	36.98
14.11	Manufacture of leather clothes	35.52
32.30	Manufacture of sports goods	30.79
27.51	Manufacture of electric domestic appliances	29.08
32.40	Manufacture of games and toys	26.25
28.14	Manufacture of other taps and valves	25.21
23.49	Manufacture of other ceramic products	24.36
32.99	Other manufacturing n.e.c.	23.70
23.42	Manufacture of ceramic sanitary fixtures	23.05
46.47	Wholesale of furniture, carpets and lighting equipment	22.17
30.99	Manufacture of other transport equipment n.e.c.	22.13
25.72	Manufacture of locks and hinges	21.57
46.42	Wholesale of clothing and footwear	19.66
17.22	Manufacture of household and sanitary goods and of toilet requisites	17.08

SOURCE: INTELLECTUAL PROPERTY RIGHTS INTENSIVE INDUSTRIES AND ECONOMIC PERFORMANCE IN THE EUROPEAN UNION, INDUSTRY-LEVEL ANALYSIS REPORT, OCTOBER 2016

museums); and non-dedicated support industries (general wholesale and retail; general transportation; information and communication) – which engage in activities relating to design and copyright protection to some degree, at different levels in the production, manufacture, sale, and retail of "creative works."[24]

24 WIPO, *Guide on Surveying the Economic Contribution of the Copyright Industries 2015 Revised Edition*, 59 ff available at https://www.wipo.int/edocs/pubdocs/en/copyright/893/wipo_pub_893.pdf (accessed 6.8.2019).

One new business sector that is shaping the contours of what design is more than any other is online auctioning. Online platforms for buying and selling design artefacts have grown significantly over the last ten years. While the vast amount of online business has lowered the quality of goods exchanged, on the other hand it has boosted competition and, in some cases, inflated prices staggeringly. Some online auctions are generalist in content, such as Catawiki[25] or Ebay;[26] others are specialized in certain sectors, such as seating, tables, storage, bedroom rugs, lighting, and mirrors, for Christie's, Phillips, and Sotheby's,[27] or *mode et bagagerie* for Cornette de Saint Cyr, Paris.[28] Of course there are also world-famous auction houses, such as the celebrated Phillips, and Richard Wright's latest Chicago auction house, an elegant 40,000-square-foot building in Chicago's West Loop neighbourhood, with a second location on Madison Avenue in New York City. Wright has handled more than 40,000 lots of twentieth and twenty-first century design since its founding in 2000, contributing to how we understand "design." In 2017, for instance, Wright presented "*Design in Motion: The Berkel Slicer Machine*," the first auction ever dedicated to vintage flywheel slicing machines, kitchen scales, and ephemera (Figure 1):[29]

> "One of the things I love about design is that there's something very democratic about it. People are feeling it, touching it, using it. Then, they give you their opinion," Wright says. "But most people will not look at a piece of art and tell you if they like it because they're intimidated. Maybe they don't know who it's by or are afraid they might sound ignorant. Design is different because people feel differently about their taste in it. That's the reason why these two markets are driven by two different things," he

25 Catawiki was founded in 2008 as an online community for collectors. Since 2011, the company has hosted weekly online auctions in various categories, from vintage comic books, model trains, coins, and watches, to art, jewellery, and classic cars: https://www.catawiki.com/a/th/955-design-auction-industrial. See *The Daily Telegraph*, 7 December 2015, "Internet auctioneer Catawiki launches in UK to capture biggest collectibles market"; see *La Stampa*, July 18, 2016, "Catawiki, le aste online per collezionisti" (accessed 8.8.2019).

26 *Van Groningen*, "'EBay of Antiques' CEO Predicts U.K. Sellers Benefit From Brexit," *Bloomberg News*, July 6, 2016 (accessed 8.8.2019).

27 It expanded into the interior design market with the relaunch and renaming of the retail website Viyet as Sotheby's Home: see https://sothebyshome.com/; Chesters, "Sotheby's expands into interior design market with relaunch of retail website," October 24, 2018, https://www.antiquestradegazette.com/news/2018/sotheby-s-expands-into-interior-design-market-with-relaunch-of-retail-website/ (accessed 8.8.2019).

28 Noe, "French Auction House Expands into Design Objects," January 29, 2013, https://www.core77.com/posts/24282/French-Auction-House-Expands-into-Design-Objects (accessed 8.8.2019).

29 Design in Motion, February 9, 2017, at https://www.wright20.com/auctions/2017/02/design-in-motion-the-berkel-slicer-machine/info (accessed 8.8.2019).

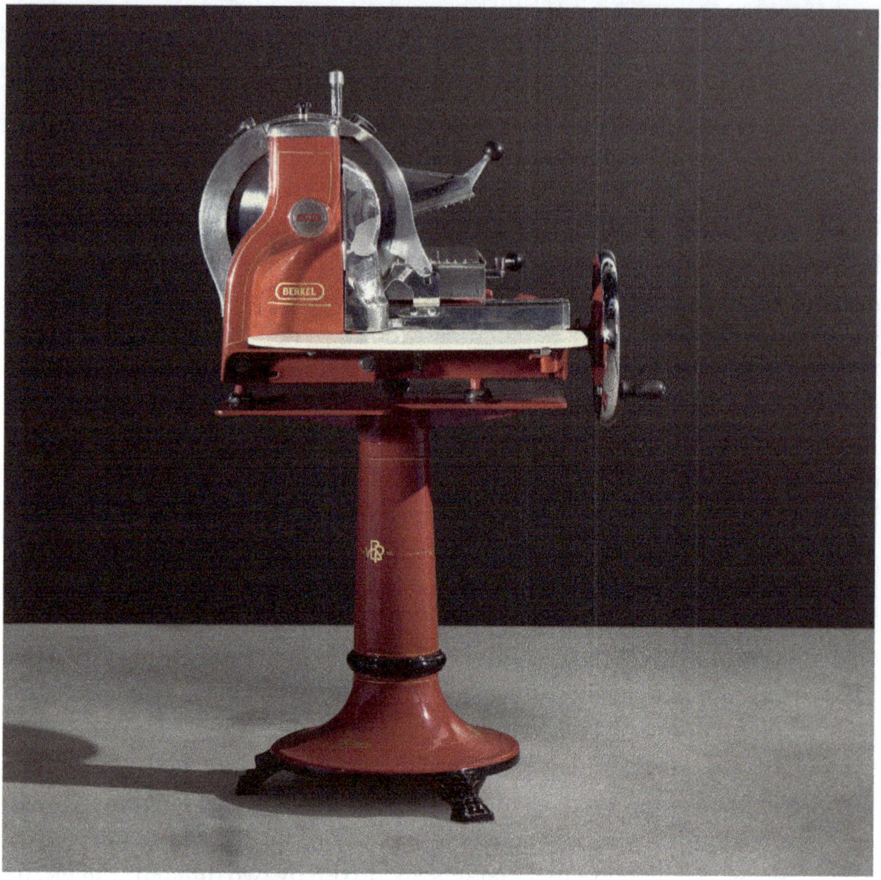

FIGURE 1 Berkel slicer machine
IMAGE AVAILABLE AT HTTPS://WWW.WRIGHT20.COM/ITEMS/INDEX/2000/105_1_DESIGN_IN_MOTION_THE_BERKEL_SLICER_MACHINE_FEBRUARY_2017_BERKEL_FLYWHEEL_SLICER_MODEL_115__WRIGHT_AUCTION.JPG?T=1485467403

explains. He's right. We tend to define ourselves by the objects we surround ourselves with in our intimate spaces. That's why design touches us in a way that is more direct and accessible. That's why we're so emotionally attached to possessions and why it's so hard to get rid of them, even if we never use them.[30]

It is in the realm of art, however, that *liaisons dangereuses* between works of art and works of applied art, as design pieces were called in the past, come to

30 Rigou, "The Design Trade: How Richard Wright created a world-class auction house," November 29, 2017, *Newcity Design on-line*, (accessed 8.8.2019).

light. In 1917, at the time of the October Revolution, Marcel Duchamp exhibited a urinal in a gallery, declaring it was a work of art entitled *Fountain*, signed R. Mutt. Half a century on, in 1964, when Lyndon B. Johnson began America's military escalation in Vietnam, Andy Warhol exhibited larger-scale reproductions of the Brillo soap pad box. By doing so, they rewrote the relationship of art with the audience, drafting a new contract with the final user where it was no longer a question of knowing whether a work was an original or a copy of a copy, but rather of determining how any object could, "by a stroke of magic" as it were, under certain conditions and regardless of any aesthetic consideration, become a work of art.[31] *Fountain* and the concept of the readymade were a breach of the contract in place between the artist and the audience under previous terms and conditions, where the first term breached was reproducibility (seriality), alongside the idea that works of art were identified by beauty; and the second term breached was repeatability, and the new relationship of the artist with it. On the other hand, *Brillo Box* and the Pop Art movement sought reconciliation with the pleasant world of commodities, the restoration of a fruitful dialogue with daily life, the social world, and industry. Whereas Duchamp, in exhibiting his readymade objects, such as the urinal, the bottle rack, and the bicycle wheel, went to the core of the canonical value of art, an entire legacy of respectability and of auraticity, Warhol highlighted how the artwork is above all "a thing," neither too big nor too small, and that a commodity is not the opposite of the work of art; it is the essence of it. "*In fact, the commodity is not just the hell of the market, as claimed by cheap moralists; it is also, and above all, a promise of happiness.*"[32] Still today, the Duchamp-Warhol effect echoes strongly, amplified by its critique of so many paradigms and principles strongly rooted in the Western understanding of art[33] and anchored to notions like those of "author," "aura," "originality," and "invention." Elaine Sturtevant's *Fountain* of 1973, Bruna Esposito's *Alla turca* of 1985, Alexander Kosolapov's *Russian Revolutionary Porcelain* of 1989–1990, Sherrie Levine's *After Marcel Duchamp* of 1991, Elaine Sturtevant's *Warhol Licorice Marilyn* of 2004, or Jeff Koons' *Birkin Bag (Shelf)* of 2014 (Figures 2–5), to name but a few, testify to the

31 Ferraris, op. cit, pp. 17 ff.

32 Ferraris, op. cit, p. 47.

33 See Michelson (ed.), *Andy Warhol*, Cambridge, MA 2002; Subrizi, "Effetti Duchamp: casi italiani per ripensare la storia" in Coltelli, Cossu (eds.), *Duchamp re-made in Italy*, Milan, 2013, pp. 149–172; Subrizi, *Introduzione a Duchamp*, Rome-Bari, 2016. See also the exhibition *Apariencia desnuda El deseo y el objeto en la obra de Marcel Duchamp y Jeff Koons, aun* (Appearance Stripped Bare: Desire and the Object in the Work of Marcel Duchamp and Jeff Koons, Even) which explores the work of both Marcel Duchamp and Jeff Koons, 19 May–29 September 2019, Museo Jumex, Mexico City. The presence of *Bottle Rack* in the Art Institute Chicago's galleries, acquired in 2018, pays tribute to Duchamp's pivotal role in modern and contemporary art.

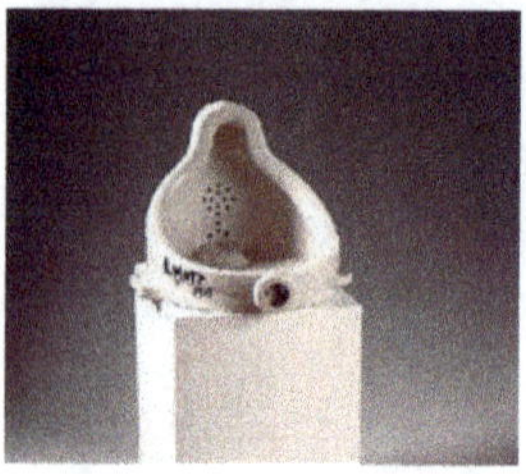

FIGURE 2 Elaine Sturtevant, *Fountain*, 1973
IMAGE AVAILABLE AT HTTP://WWW.ARTNET.COM

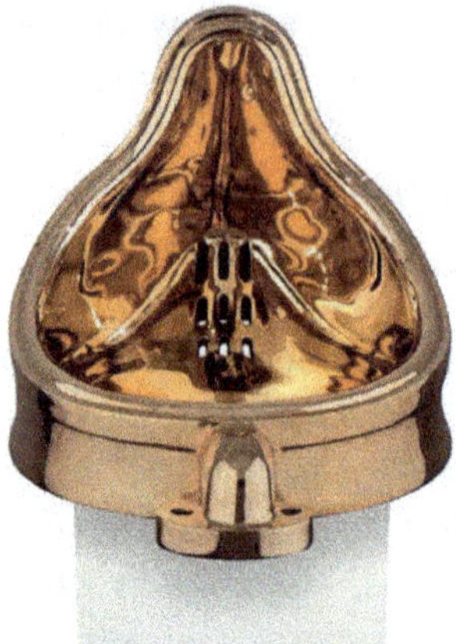

FIGURE 3 Sherrie Levine, *After Marcel Duchamp*, 1991
IMAGE AVAILABLE AT HTTP://WWW.ARTNET.COM

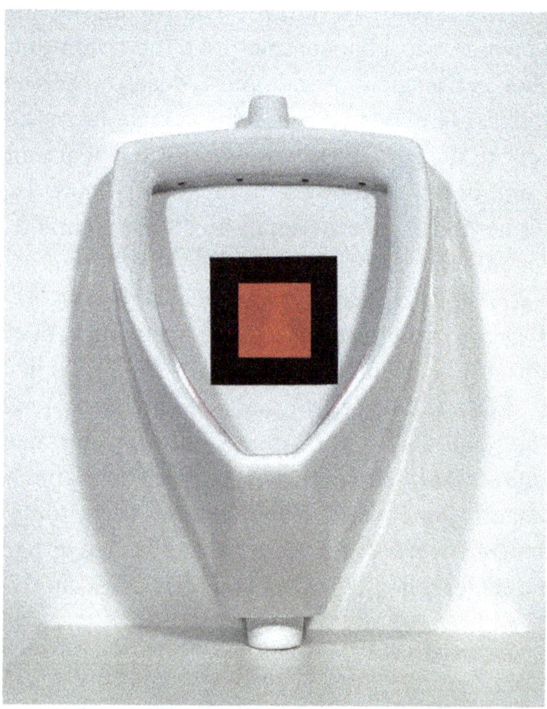

FIGURE 4 Alexander Kosolapov, *Russian Revolutionary Porcelain*, 1989–1990
IMAGE AVAILABLE AT HTTPS://WWW.SAATCHIGALLERY.COM

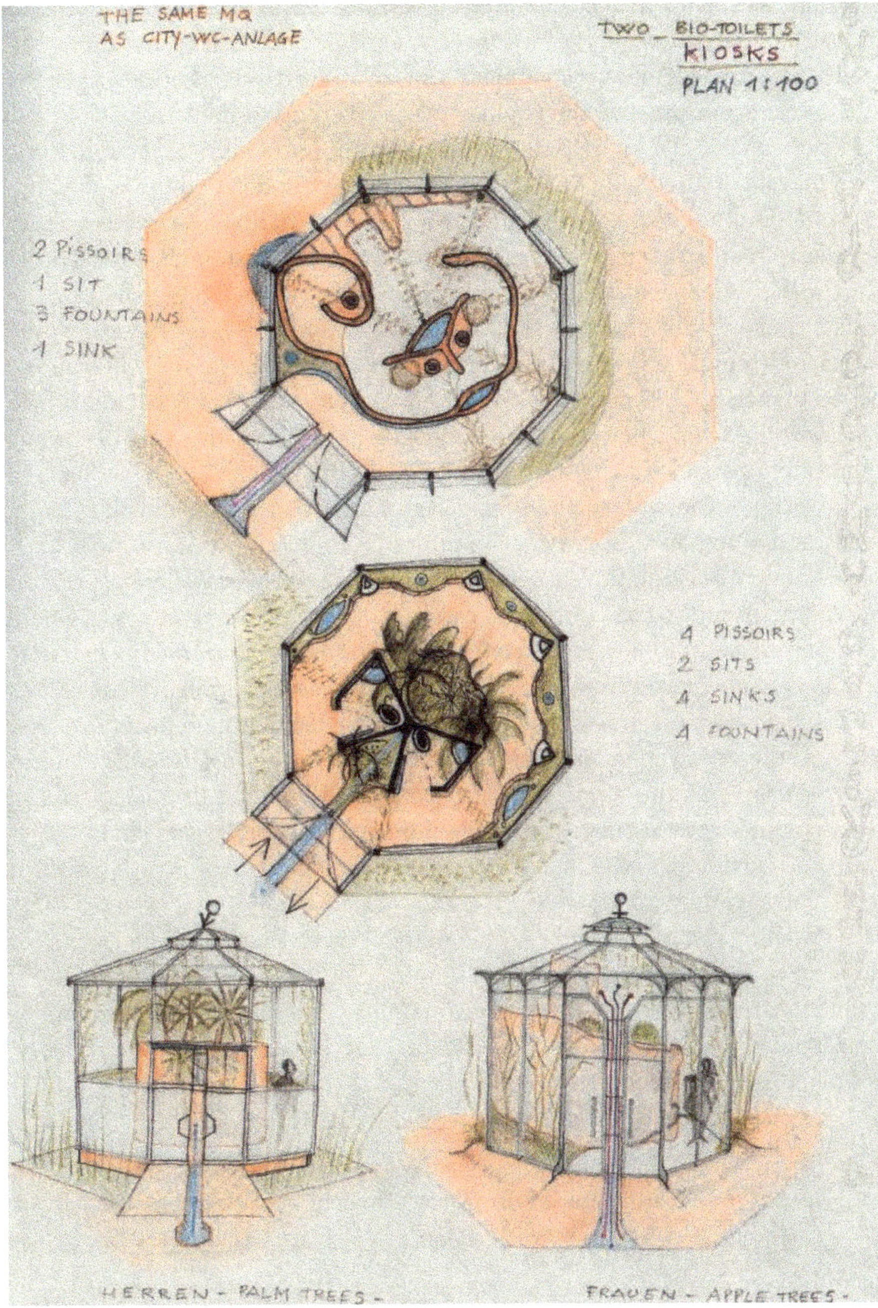

FIGURE 5 Bruna Esposito, *Alla turca*, 1985
IMAGE AVAILABLE AT HTTPS://WWW.EXIBART.COM

fact that the era in which Duchamp and Warhol lived, a society of standardized industrial production, marked by the centrality of commodities and characterized by the predominant role of marketing and advertising, is not over yet.

From this perspective, the challenge was taken up in the late 1960s by the first site-specific works, as Neil Armstrong and Buzz Aldrin became the first men to walk on the Moon during NASA's Apollo 11 mission and the Woodstock music festival rocked America. In those years, land artists and personalities such as Daniel Buren began to criticize art institutions, disputing, among other things, the function of the museum, which they considered a cemetery. The artists challenged the "art system," its alleged autonomy from the rest of the world, affirming the need to bring artistic practice back into daily life, and to contextualize it. For years now, artists have been bringing art back down to Earth, with artworks placed on the same level as the individual and becoming themselves part of the environment.[34] The German artist Tobias Rehberger, who works in the wider sphere of design and architecture, can thus claim today a new role for the designer in reinterpreting and transforming spaces, objects, and furnishing styles. Rehberger subjects industrial design to a critical re-reading, as for example in a work carried out with African craftsmen, where he asked each of them to rework a "classic" design chair, introducing dynamic temporal elements, destabilizing it, and inventing new a way to investigate elements of utility and superfluity. He received the Golden Lion award for Best Artist at the 2009 Venice Biennale for his work *Was du liebst, bringt dich auch zum weinen*,[35] for the "*Caffetteria la Biennale di Venezia, Giardini*" in Venice, which painted everything in the coffee shop, from the tables and chairs to the walls and furniture, in the "razzle dazzle" camouflage style of British warships in the First World War (Figure 6).

If anything can be a work of art today, the same cannot be said for works of design. For an object, the elevation to the status of "work of art" is something of a sanctification, while the status of "design object" is a somewhat lesser promotion, a mere beatification, if we like. That it is easier to be a saint than blessed is a paradox worth reflecting on.[36]

---

34 Detheridge, "Un drink al bar dell'artista", *Il Sole 24 Ore*, 17.05.2019, available at https://st.ilsole24ore.com/art/arteconomy/2009–05–19/un-drink-bar-artista 073626.shtml?uuid=AXj2MOo&refresh_ce=1 (accessed 9.8.2919).

35 Loosely translated as "*Everything you love makes you cry*".

36 Ferraris, op. cit., p. 48. Among beatified objects see: *Bocca* sofa by Studio 65 (1970) produced by GUFRAM; *Cactus* sofa by Galante, manufactured by Cerruti Baleri; tables by Garutti, manufactured by Design Gallery Milano; and the Panton chair by Panton, manufactured by Vitra. On this precise point, see the exhibition *Utopia* (till December 2019), in which Charles Zana turns Tornabuoni Art in Paris into a salon of "intimate conversations

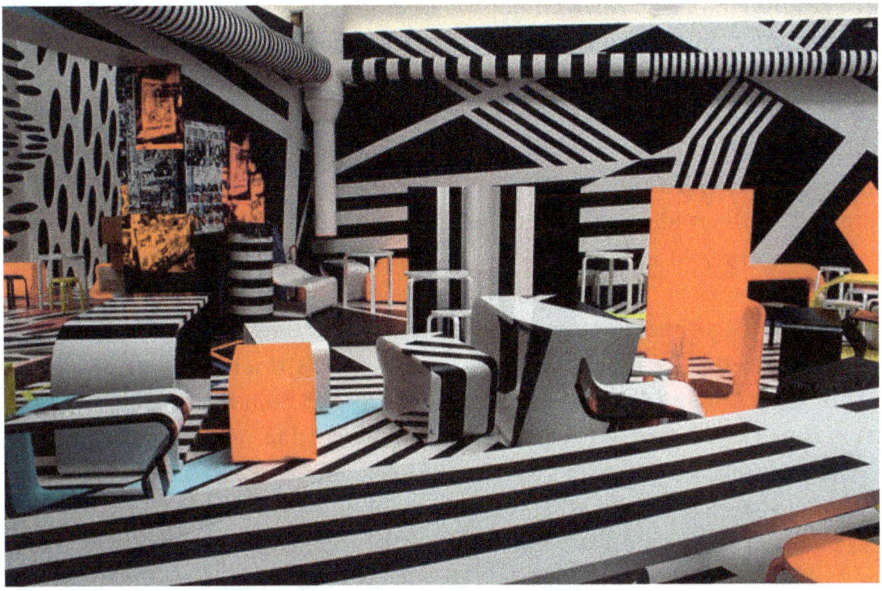

FIGURE 6 Caffetteria la Biennale di Venezia, Giardini, Venice
IMAGE AVAILABLE AT HTTPS://THECOOLHUNTER.NET/CAFETERIA-BY-TOBIAS-REHBERGER/

Against this backdrop, I would like to explore the issue raised by the "artification" of design, something particularly noticeable in the domain of law, where a *sui generis* design protection overlaps with copyright law. In order to do so, I will adopt a multidisciplinary approach for examining whether legal definitions and rules match with designers' own theories and practices, to better understand what form of legal protection the EU should promote and incentivize. In the absence of the full harmonization of copyright law, European lawmakers have stressed the importance of the principle of "cumulative protection" between design and copyright laws, leaving Member States free to establish the extent of copyright protection and the conditions under which such protection is afforded. But why would any rights-holder bear the cost of the design registration process when they could automatically obtain copyright protection? Is there a serious risk that copyright protection will serve as a back-door route to protection for designs that no longer qualify for registered

between Italy's greatest post-war artists and architects and designers" (Boetti, Pesce, Superstudio, Mendini, and Sottsass, beatified with their objects as well).

design protection?[37] It is well-known how copyright a double-edged sword, a potential weapon in the market place[38] which can be abused[39] to prevent or eliminate competition. In theory, copyright protection excludes the risk of becoming a monopoly right by requiring "copying" for its infringement, i.e., the artefact must be derived from the original work and its reproduction can be in any material form to qualify as infringement. National case law, however, shows how the traditional concept of "copying" can be stretched *to protect the copyright owner* in a number of cases that raise a variety of problems. They include the case of "reverse engineering," where the copyist works back from the designer's ultimate product to achieve the offending new product, and the case of "redesign," where a designer is presented a brief based on the original product and is asked to produce a new product from the brief rather than from the original product. Then there is the issue that projects by a designer are not simply sketches and drawings, but also incorporate "literary material," i.e., words and figures showing scales and dimensions, in which case the concept of "indirect copying" is involved, along with the subtle causal link that can be established between the original design and the ultimate product. On the other hand, national case law also shows how the traditional concept of "intellectual creation" can be narrowed *to protect the copyist.* Countries belonging to civil law traditions have shown a tendency to stress the personal relationship or personal input that an author puts into a work.[40] France, for instance, requires "proof of creation of a work possessing an original character bearing the mark of the personality of its author,"[41] Germany that "personal intellectual creations match exactly with a high threshold of originality" (although the German Supreme Court seems to have recently abandoned this doctrine),[42]

---

37 Bently, "The Return of Industrial Copyright," *European Intellectual Property Review*, 2012, pp. 654–672.

38 MacQueen, *Copyright, Competition and Industrial Design*, Hume Papers on Public Policy, Vol. 3, No. 2 Summer, 1995, p. 23. See the classic article by Zechariah Chafee Jr, "Reflections on the Law of Copyright," *Colum. L. Rev.* 1945, pp. 503 ff at 506.

39 Caron, *Abuse de droit a droit d'auteur*, Paris, 1998.

40 Goldstein, Hugenholtz, *International Copyright: Principles, Law, and Practice*, Oxford, 2013, pp. 192–193.

41 "*la preuve d'une creation d'une oeuvre possédant un caractère d'originalité portant le marque de la personalité de son auteur*" *Trib. Comm. Paris*, 14.09.2010, *Decotec v. La redoute*, inedit cit. in Mandel, Bootherstone, Massot, *Guide Pratique du droit du design*, 2 ed., Paris, 2015, at p. 22.

42 See *Geburtstagszug* [2013] I ZR 143/12; see Ohly, "The Case for Partial Cumulation in Germany" in Derclaye (ed.), *The Copyright/Design Interface: Past, Present, and Future*, Cambridge, 2018, pp. 167 ff; *cf* Part 2 of this essay.

while Dutch law requires proof of the "author's subjective creativity,"[43] and Portugal and Italy demand that works show genuine artistic merit: "the work must have 'in and of itself' creative character and artistic value."[44] Very recently, however, the European Court of Justice reconstrued its "author's own intellectual creation" standard more in the sense of creative freedom, rather than strictly meaning the personal input that an author puts into a work as original, subjective creativity. In any case, unless a fair balancing of individual and societal interests[45] is achieved by also considering the interests of the public at large the regulatory policies of Member States will continue to be manipulated in favour of their national, protectionist interests.

Having said that, my analysis will build on two notions which underpin many laws and international conventions, albeit without providing a clear definition from the outset, those of "protectable work" and "author." Through them, I will draw attention to what is original, creative, and innovative according to a multidisciplinary approach. In Part 1, under the heading THE WORK, I will give a brief historical perspective of Design, with the aim of understanding whether the current legal framework for protecting design rights is rooted in an appropriate background by addressing the question of what industrial design is and its relationship with art, technology, markets, factories, and SMEs. In Part 2, under the heading THE AUTHOR, I will start from the legal notion of "author," dependent on the so-called originality test, and I will compare it with the designer as an author in practice, bearing in mind that "(…) *designers, unlike architects, have not operated by following a series of principles and rules that specify the purpose of their work. Rather, they have invented the contents of their profession as they went along.*"[46] In the Conclusion, after a short recap of the *sui generis* design protection regime in Europe, in comparison with the US and Chinese frameworks, and its interface with copyright protection, and after a few notes on other possible overlapping regimes such as trademark and utility

43 This was confirmed by the Dutch Supreme Court in *Kecofa v. Lancôme* (2006) and *Gavita v. Puutarhaliike Helle* (2010), although there are some more recent decisions which testify the moving of copyright's originality test towards the European test; see Part 2 of this essay.

44 "*l'opera deve avere « di per sé » carattere creativo e valore artistico*" *Trib. Milano*, 2.08.2012, *Vitra Patente AG ed altri v. High Tech s.r.l.*: "*capacità rappresentativa delle tendenze anche artistiche del dopoguerra in America che trascende la mera capacità di rendere gradevole e funzionale il prodotto seriale*", which confirms the precedents of Tribunale (hereinafter Trib.) Milano 28.11.2006, Trib. Milano 29.12.2006, and Trib. Milano, ordinance 19.07.2011 *Cassina v. High Tech*. *Cf* comments by Alvanini, *Diritto industriale* 1/2013, p. 13.

45 Davies, *Copyright and the Public Interest*, ICC Studies v. 14, Weinheim/New York, 1994.

46 Margolin, "Design History or Design Studies: Subject Matter and Methods", *Design Issues*, 1995, pp. 4–15 at 12.

model rules, contract and competition laws, I will offer my conclusive remarks. Many Member States have already set up alternative means of protection to design registration and patenting, such as unregistered design rights,[47] unregistered trademarks,[48] utility models,[49] and copyright rules. Such alternatives, however, increase the risk of overprotection and of undermining design law, raising many concerns which are essential to address.[50]

> No longer associated simply with objects and appearances, design is increasingly understood in a much wider sense as the human capacity to plan and produce desired outcomes.[51]
>
> Design – a noun referring to a specification or plan for making a particular artefact or for undertaking a particular activity. A distinction is drawn here between a design and an artifact – a design is the basis for, and precursor to, the making of an artefact. Designing – human activity leading to the production of a design.[52]

Design is definitely hard to grasp. In the following pages I will explore the concept both within the legal domain and design studies.

---

47 In the U.K., the "unregistered design right" was introduced by the CDPA 1988 as a statutory right for designs (Part III of the CDPA 1988). For its genesis see Vitoria et al. (eds.), *Laddie, Prescott, and Vitoria: The Modern Law of Copyright and Designs*, 4th ed, London, 2011. Since Regulation (EC) 6/2002, unregistered design rights have been recognized in all the 28 Member States according to the "direct effect" doctrine and the supremacy of Community (EU) Regulations over domestic law (a principle established after the judicial *querelle* between the Court of Justice of the EU on one side, and the Constitutional Courts of some Member States on the other, lasting about twenty years).

48 See Article 2598 of the Italian civil code: the user of an unregistered trademark has sole rights within the limits of the possibility of confusion. The requirements which the unregistered trademark must meet are as follows: it must be a sign, possess a distinctive capacity, be new (and therefore should not lead to confusion), and not be misleading, or contrary to public policy or good morals. See Milan Court, 9.10.2015, and also Rome Court, 31.10.2014, which protected the 3D trademark of the *Le Pliage* handbag by Longchamp under the unregistered trademark provision. See Varese, Barabino, "La tutela della forma delle creazioni di moda: problematiche e prospettiva" in Pozzo, Jacometti (eds.) *Fashion Law*, op. cit., pp. 93–107, at 103.

49 In Italy, for instance, see Articles 40 and 82 of the CPI (Industrial Property Code); *infra* in the Conclusion.

50 Schovsbo, Riis, "Design law: caught between chairs?" in Ghidini at al. (eds.), *Kritika: Essays on Intellectual Property*, Vol. 2, 2017, pp. 88–118.

51 Mau, Leonard, *Massive Change*, London/New York, 2004, p. 23.

52 Love, "Constructing a Coherent Body of Theory About Designing and Designs: Some Philosophical Issues," *Design Studies*, 2002, pp. 356–357.

Part 1: The Work

The legal notion of protectable "work" lies at the intersection between design protection and copyright protection. In addressing the notion, I will limit the discussion here to the EU, in the light of the international conventions and the legal systems of some of its Member States, with only a brief look at other, paradigmatic, legal systems around the world. A survey of those systems reveals the substantial protection our legal systems afford to design works, with the copyright/design interface revolving precisely around the protection of the outward design of objects, the visual appearance of everyday useful goods. But it also highlights how inappropriate the notion of a "work of applied art" is when talking about works of design and the design profession "after modernity."[53] It is clear that, "*In a time where everything is designed, from our carefully crafted individual looks and online identities, to the surrounding galaxies of personal devices, new materials, interfaces, networks, systems infrastructures, data* (...),"[54] the matter deserves fresh attention and debate on a new model law.[55] Ultimately, the difficulties in approaching these issues are inevitably related to the fluidity of the definition of industrial design "work" given by the broad (and largely empty) legal concept of "design work."[56] Is a work of design an "artistic work," or merely an "artefact," an "object," a "useful article," or yet still a "work of applied art"? Is it a question of "form" following "function," or is it an artefact to be perceived as a "coherent unity," as Tomás Maldonado suggested in the definition we quoted earlier? Can the external (ornamental) form of an object be so easily divorced from its mode of functioning (technical features)? Going back through history, we find antithetical viewpoints, between which there lie a wide variety of different lines of study. Even in the field of Design Studies, the answer will depend on where the focus of the analysis is placed: on the objects and artefacts themselves, on the organization of production and

53 To quote the four-monthly publication: *Design After Modernity*, DIID (Disegno Industriale Industrial Design), 64/18.

54 Colomina, Wigley, *Are we Human? Notes on an Archaeology of Design*, Zurich, 2019.

55 At the end of 2018, the WIPO General Assembly decided to continue considering the option of convening of a diplomatic conference on the Design Law Treaty (DLT), to take place at the end of the first half of 2020. See https://www.wipo.int/edocs/mdocs/sct/en/sct_41/sct_41_www_437299.pdf (accessed 3.6.2019).

56 Erdmann, "Die Relativität des Werkbegriffs", in Erdmann, Leistner, Rüffer, Schulte-Beckhausen, (Hrsg.), *Festschrift für Michael Loschelder*, Köln 2010, pp. 61 ff.

the history of the factory, or on the ideology and culture of industrial design.[57] Let's start with the insights of law.

1 The Thin Line of Artistic Speculation about Design Activity

1.1 In Law

It was XIX century law that first distinguished aesthetic art and applied art as distinct and separate spheres, on the grounds that art and manufacturing were, with a few exceptions, quite different. Such reasoning was particularly apparent in the influence of Dr. Christopher Dresser, one of the most important independent designers of modern times – certainly the first to stamp "designed by" on his creations,[58] including carpets, ceramics, furniture, glass, graphics, silver, electroplate and other metalwork, and printed and woven textiles[59] – and a pivotal figure in England's Aesthetic Movement of the late XIX century, with long-lasting international influence. At the International Exhibition in London in 1862, Dresser claimed to have designed "as much as any man,"[60] to make clear to the world Britain's role as the industrial leader of a Europe that had just scraped through two difficult decades of political and social upheaval, "*and now Britain hoped to show that technology, particularly its own, was the key to a better future.*"[61] Aestheticism was not viewed simply as a means to the material improvement of society; spiritual benefits were to be gained by those who learned how to respond to aesthetic beauty.

As Aestheticism gained ground, around the turn of the century industrialized countries began extending their copyright laws to protect the design of mass-produced goods, under the principle that "what is worth copying is worth protecting." Ironically, the principle was just the opposite of the stated purpose of the *Exposition des produits de l'industrie française* (Exhibition of Products of French Industry), the extraordinary public event organized in Paris from 1798 to 1849, "*to offer a panorama of the productions of the various branches of*

57 Riccini, "History from Things: Notes on the History of Industrial Design," *Design Issues*, 1998, pp. 43–64; Petroski, *The Evolution of Useful Things*, New York, 1993; Gregotti, *Il disegno del prodotto industriale. Italia 1860–1980*, Milan, 1982; Dorfles, *Introduzione al disegno industriale. Linguaggio e storia della produzione di serie*, Turin, 1972.

58 Vitta, *Il progetto della bellezza. Il design fra arte e tecnica dal 1851 a oggi*, Turin, 2011, p. 100.

59 Some of Dresser's metalwork designs are still in production, such as his oil and vinegar sets and toast rack designs, now manufactured by Alessi.

60 He wrote several books on design and ornamentation, including *The Art of Decorative Design* (1862), *The Development of Ornamental Art in the International Exhibition* (1862), and *Principles of Design* (1873). In 1873 he was requested by the US Government to write a report on the design of household goods.

61 Kishlansky, Geary, O'Brien, *Civilization in the West*, 7th ed., New York, 2008.

industry with a view to emulation."[62] Yet the first copyright laws had not been conceived to protect design works. During the *Ancien Régime*,[63] the relationship between "art" and "industry" was shaped in France by special laws such as the *arrêt de Saint-Jean-de-Luz* 26 May 1660,[64] a decree that declared engraving (Figure 7) a free art and required publishers to obtain a *privilege du roi* for each manuscript prior to publication:

> [...] Sa Majesté ayant été informée des mauvaises conséquences que pourrait produire l'exécution de cet arrêt à la gloire de la France dont l'avantage est de cultiver autant qu'il est possible les arts libéraux, tel qu'est celui de la gravure en taille-douce au burin et à l'eau-forte, qui dépend de l'imagination de ses auteurs et ne peut être assujetti à d'autres lois que celles de leur génie, [...] Qu'aucun [des] ouvrages [de cet art] n'étant du nombre des choses nécessaires qui servent à la subsistance de la société civile, mais seulement de celles qui servent à l'ornement, au plaisir et à la curiosité, le débit par conséquent, qui dépend du hasard et de l'inclination, en doit être entièrement libre ...[65]

Copyright was a privilege, not a right; it was a *lex privatus*, an exception from public law, conceded by royal prerogative, and granted *ad hominem*. Its personal character – and not the "artistic nature of the work" – led to the assimilation of copyright under the Enlightenment discourse on rights.[66] Even if the narrative of copyright protection has been linked to the genius of authors, it had rather less to say about art and artists. It was the grace of kings that was the source of this form of patronage, indispensable for the survival of arts in a market increasingly split in two, between Paris booksellers and the provincial *libraires*,[67] with the former defended by the *Mémoire de d'Héricourt*,[68] and the latter by

62 Courtin, *L'ancêtre des expositions universelles*, 2016, available at https://www.histoire-image.org/fr/etudes/ancetre-expositions-universelles?i=232. (accessed 9.8.2019).

63 Scott, "Art and Industry. A Contradictory Union: Authors, Right and Copyrights during the Consulat," *Journal of Design History*, 2000, pp. 1 ff.

64 See also the decree of 28 June 1714 for all members of the *Académie royale de peinture et sculpture*, a tool for controlling the reproduction of painters and sculptures' work by obtaining their consent prior to any attempt to disseminate their works.

65 De Montaiglon, *Archives de l'art français, Recueil de documents inédits*, tome XII, Paris, 1862, p. 262.

66 Scott, *Art and Industry* ..., op. cit., p. 8.

67 Izzo, *Alle origini del copyright e del diritto d'autore*, Rome, 2010, pp. 155, 159.

68 Strowel, *Droit d'auteur et copyright. Divergences et convergences*, Brussels, 1993, pp. 84 ff.; Falk, *Les privilèges de librairie sous l'Ancien régime: étude historique du conflit des droit*

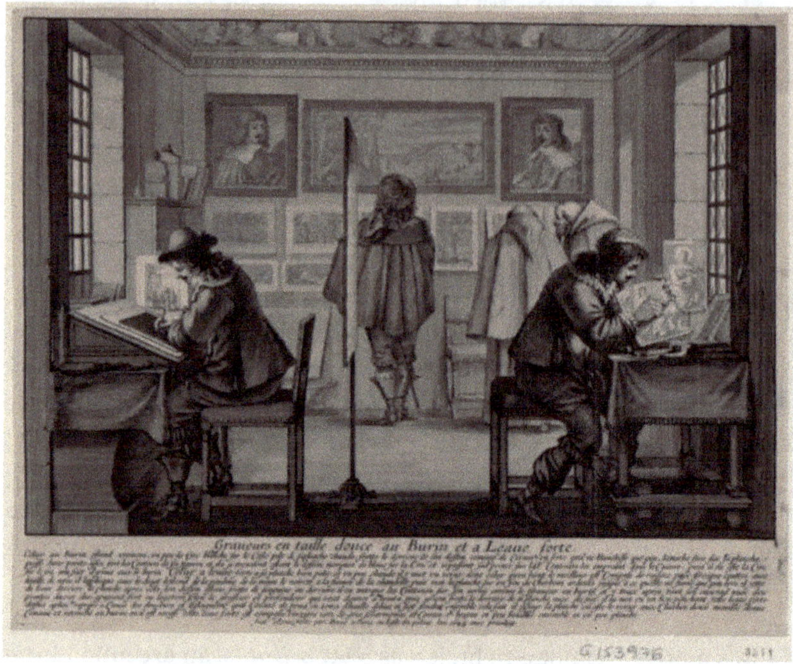

FIGURE 7 Abraham Bosse, L'atelier du graveur au burin et à l'eaue-forte (détail), 1643, BnF/Gallica.
IMAGE AVAILABLE AT GALLICA WEBSITE BIBLIOTHÈQUE NATIONALE DE FRANCE.

Condorcet in his *Fragments sur la liberté de la presse* and the *Arrêts réglementaires 30 August 1777*.[69] Copyright offered a commercial advantage to those able to pay for it. With the Revolution of 1789 and the abolition of privileges and of the corporations, the print market was left at the mercy of piracy, as the well-known dispute between a print publisher (and engraver and bookseller) and a wallpaper manufacturer in 1802 demonstrated.[70] Meanwhile, revolutionary legislators set about outlining a legal conception of "authoriality"

sous l'oeuvre litteraire, Geneva, 1970, pp. 96 ff. Laboulaye, Guiffrey, *La propriété littéraire au XVIIIe siècle*, Paris, 1859, pp. 21 ff available at https://gallica.bnf.fr/ (accessed 20.10.2019).

69 De Condorcet, "Fragments sur la liberté de la presse" in Condorcet O'Connor, Arago (eds.), *Oeuvres de Condorcet*, tome XI, Paris, 1847, pp. 255 ff; Birn, "The Profit in Ideas: privilèges en librairie", *Eighteenth-Century-Studies*, 1971, 131, pp. 156 ff.

70 *Louis Bance versus Pierre Simon*, in Scott, op. cit., pp. 9 ff. Unlike models and drawings that fell under the *Loi de brevets* (patent law) of 1791 and were deposited in sealed envelopes, wallpaper samples were available at the National Library for public inspection (and unscrupulous imitation by competing manufacturers).

that consecrated, while limiting at the same time, authors power of self-determination in the interests of public good.[71]

In the same vein, although with a different historical legal process, the *Statute of Anne* of 1709[72] (the copyright act on which US copyright law was also originally based) granted authors protection throughout Britain, upon registration of a book in Stationers Hall in London, for fourteen years from the date of first publication plus another 14-years after that deadline with "*the sole right of printing and disposing of copies,*" leaving stationers with "*the sole liberty of printing and reprinting* [*such books*]" with the author's consent. In that way, any publisher could acquire the right to print a book for a few pence, but it was the publishers and booksellers of London who benefited most from the Act, thanks to their easy access to Stationers Hall.[73] In any case, copyright helped regulate a trade in which publishers otherwise would not have published books and, therefore, would not have paid authors for their manuscripts, but in championing the cause of authors, the real target of the statute was the problem of monopolies.[74] As in France, copyright offered a commercial advantage to those able to pay for it.

> An Act for the Encouragement of Learning, by Vesting the Copies of Printed Books in the Authors or Purchasers of such Copies, during the Times therein mentioned.
>
> Whereas Printers, Booksellers, and other Persons, have of late frequently taken the Liberty of Printing, Reprinting, and Publishing, or causing to be Printed, Reprinted, and Published Books, and other Writings, without the Consent of the Authors or Proprietors of such Books and Writings, to their very great Detriment, and too often to the Ruin of them and their Families: For Preventing therefore such Practices for the future, and for the Encouragement of Learned Men to Compose and Write

71 Hesse, "Enlightenment Epistemology and the Laws of Authorship in Revolutionary France 1777–1793," *Representations*, 1990, 109, pp. 131 ff; Ginsburg, "A Tale of Two Copyright, Literary Property in Revolutionary France and America," *Tulane Law Rev.*, 1990, pp. 991–1032, pp. 1023 ff; Peeler, "From the Providence of Kings, to Copyrighted Things (and French Moral Rights)," *Indiana International & Comparative Law Review*, 1999, pp. 435 ff; Kerever, "Révolution française et droit d'auteur", *Revue internationale du droit d'auteur*, 1989, pp. 1 ff; Izzo, op. cit., pp. 177 ff.

72 1709, 8 Anne, ch. 21. See Patterson, *Copyright in Historical Perspective*, Nashville, 1968, pp. 143 ff; Davies, op. cit., pp. 4 ff.

73 McQueen, op. cit., p. 2.

74 Deazley, *On the Origin of the Right to Copy: Charting the Movement of Copyright Law in Eighteenth-century Britain (1695–1775)*, Portland, 2004, p. 46; Patterson, op. cit., p. 147.

> useful Books; May it please Your Majesty, that it may be Enacted, and be it Enacted by the Queens most Excellent Majesty [...][75]

The conception of copyright changed at the beginning of the XIX century, when the French Civil Code entered into force and the pivotal role of private property became evident. Paving the way for the change of perspective was the growing debate on the rights of the author, or *droit d'auteur*. Major philosophers such as Kant, Hegel, and Schopenhauer[76] strenuously defended the idea of every author's "right over their works against the injustice of counterfeiters."[77] The *Société des Auteurs et Compositeurs Dramatiques* established in France in 1829 insinuated the romantic conception of authorship as a moral right worthy of protection, a form of property that legislators were obliged to recognize and protect.[78] The author was seen as an independent creator of modes of expression of ideas and the author's exclusive ownership right was therefore limited to the mode of expression, whereas themes, ideas, and plots in books or plays were considered a common pool of resources from which every author could draw the basic materials of their work without restriction.[79] However, it was soon clear that the unfettered exercise of copyright was not the solution to the issue of copying, at least in design claims.[80] In the last decades of the XIX century, the romantic view of authorship, with its special aura, encountered the less romantic world of mass production, made of iron and steel, pollution and waste, and the exploitation of workers. The centrality of the object itself was soon perceived as essential by the first design protection laws, while in

75 A transcription of the Statute of Anne is available at https://www.copyrighthistory.com/anne.html (last access 22.9.2019).

76 See Veca, *Hegel e l'economia politica*, Milan, 1975, pp. 9 ff.; Hegel, *Vorlesungen über die Philosophie der Geschichte*, translated into Italian as *Lezioni sulla filosofia della storia*, 1882, vol. III, Florence, 1967, p. 22.

77 Stolfi, *La proprietà intellettuale*, Turin, 1915; Franceschelli, "Le origini e lo svolgimento del diritto industriale nei primi secoli della stampa", *Riv. dir. ind.* 1952, pp. 159 ff.

78 Bayet, *La Société des Auteurs et Compositeurs Dramatiques*, Paris, 1908, pp. 3 ff; Aide, "A More Comprehensive Soul: Romantic Conceptions of Authorship and the Copyright Doctrine of Moral Right", *University of Toronto Faculty of Law Review*, 1990, pp. 214 ff; Strömholm, *Le droit moral de l'auteur, en droit allemand, français et Scandinave, avec un aperçu de l'évolution internationale, Étude de droit comparé, t. I, L'évolution historique et le mouvement international, t. II, 1, Le droit modern*, Stockholm, 1967, pp. 4 ff.; Izzo, op. cit., pp. 143 ff.

79 Jaszi, "Toward A Theory of Copyright: The Metamorphoses of 'Authorship'," in Wilf (ed.), *Intellectual Property Law and History*, New York, 2012, pp. 62 ff.

80 McQueen, op. cit., p. 18.

copyright the attention shifted towards the "moral right" (*droit moral*) of the author, elevated above the market.[81]

With the rise of mass production, after the turn of the XX century many national laws[82] introduced specific protection for "works of applied art" that were new, or original. The protection afforded was limited, however, to matters of "visual appearance", the get-up and shape of an object, where appearance was strictly construed in the sense of sight; no other sense was relevant, meaning that music and sounds, fragrances and smells, single colours *per se*, mere words and sequences of words did not meet the definition of design. Moreover, the new design laws made no requirement of aesthetic quality, for which works did not need to be regarded as beautiful or pleasing to the eye to be eligible for protection. Yet that did not stop courts from considering aesthetic appeal as a criterion. The question is why? Early in the XX century, the exhibition of progress and modernity marked by the great international expositions and world's fairs of London, Paris, Vienna, and then New York rebuilt the bridge between works of applied art, craftsmanship, and works of fine art, with their display of iron and crystal, musical and surgical instruments, telescopes, weapons, and furniture all side by side.[83] The Arts and Crafts Movement, which began in Britain and flourished in Europe and North America between 1880 and 1920,[84] stood for traditional craftsmanship using simple forms, often recouping medieval, romantic, and folk styles of decoration. The change in style with respect to the Aesthetic Movement reflected a shift in emphasis from the new industrial art to an anti-modern desire to return to preindustrial modes of production.[85] The Arts and Crafts Movement advocated economic and social reform and was essentially anti-industrial. William Morris, in reaction to the per-

81 Loewenhelm, "Copyright in Civil and Common Law Countries. A Narrowing Gap," *AIDA* 1994, pp. 161 ff.

82 Such as the Designing and Printing Act 1794, or later the Patents, Designs and Trade Marks Act 1883 (UK), but see Ladas, *Patents, Trademarks, and Related Rights: National and International Protection*, Cambridge, 1975, p. 843, on countries without any law protecting design, such as Finland, Greece, Luxembourg, and the Netherlands (to remain in Europe). France protected designs and models under the Law of Artistic Property and its theory of the "unity of art": see Pouillet, *Traité théorique et pratique de Propriété Littéraire et Artistique et du droit de representation*, Paris, 2nd ed., 1894 and the *Traité théorique et pratique des Dessins et Modèles*, Paris, 5th ed., 1911.

83 Maldonado, op. cit., pp. 25 ff.; Lindinger, "Nähmaschine 1962," *Form*, 1962, pp. 32–43; Schaefer, *The Roots of Modem Design. Functional Tradition in the 19th Century*, London, 1970.

84 Kaplan (ed.), *The Arts & Crafts Movement in Europe & America: Design for the Modern World 1880–1920*, Los Angeles County Museum of Art, High Holborn, 2004.

85 Stankiewicz, "From the Aesthetic Movement to the Arts and Crafts Movement," *Studies in Art Education*, 1992, pp. 165–173.

ceived impoverishment of the decorative arts at the time and the conditions in which they were produced, defined the artist as a craftsman-designer working by hand,[86] while Jones declared that ornamentation "must be secondary to the thing decorated" and that "utility must have precedence over ornamentation."[87] The influence of William Morris, who was personally involved in manufacturing as well as design, and of the Arts and Crafts Movement was apparent in the UK Copyright Act 1911, which introduced the rather vague category of "works of artistic craftsmanship."[88] The Act emphasized the importance of the handicraft tradition, as practiced by individual artists/craftsmen by recognizing that "works of artistic craftsmanship" could be the subject of copyright. The UK Copyright Act 1911 had yet to envisage any form of copyright protection for artistic three-dimensional objects and it denied protection to artistic works which were "industrially applied" (defined as the application of the work to more than 50 objects). The new status of the artist-craftsman implicit in the recognition that designs were eligible for copyright was also apparent in some civil law systems, such as in Portugal, Spain, and Italy, where design works were required to show possession of characteristics usually associated with pure artworks, such as clear and independent "artistic value," once the design was industrially applied. It is no coincidence that such countries have remained reluctant to adopt fully cumulative protection under both copyright and design laws for works of applied art, unless they have an artistic value *per se*.[89] France, for its part, adopted the principle of the "*unite de l'art*" with the *Loi du 11 mars 1902 à propos des sculptures et dessins d'ornement*,[90] elevating works of applied art to the same level as all artistic works and opting for cumulative protection. The "unity of art" principle, which securely rested on the tradition of the Paris School of Fine Arts (*École des Beaux-Arts*), where the curricula of both the Academy of Painting and Sculpture and the Academy of Architecture focused on the classical arts and architecture of Ancient Greek and Roman

86 MacCarthy, "Morris, William (1834–1896), designer, author, and visionary socialist," *Oxford Dictionary of National Biography* (online ed.) 2009, doi:10.1093/ref:odnb/19322; Pevsner, *Pioneers of the Modern Movement From William Morris to Walter Gropius*, London, 1936.

87 See Jones "Grammar of Ornament (1856)" in Naylor, Gillian, *The Arts and Crafts Movement: A Study of its Sources, Ideals and Influence on Design Theory*, London, 1971.

88 As Lord Simon of Glaisdale pointed out in the House of Lords case *George Hensher Ltd v. Restawile Upholstery (Lancashire) Ltd* [1976] AC 64, 90–92. See McQueen, op. cit., p. 33.

89 See Gaubiac, "La théorie de l'unité de l'art," *Revue international du droit d'auteur*, 1982, pp. 42 ff. On Italian law see Marzano, "An Ill-Designed Protection for a Well-Designed Product: Italy and its Copyright Protection of Industrial Design," *Revue Internationale du Droit d'Auteur*, 2014, pp. 119 ff.

90 Vivant, Bruguière, *Droit d'auteur et droits voisins*, 4th ed., Paris, 2019, §256 ff.

culture, offered full legal protection. It was within that framework that Eugène Pouillet would develop his principle of *cumul de protection par le droit d'auteur et le droit de la propriété industrielle*:

> D'où vient la difficulté que l'on éprouve à déclarer clairement la nature et le caractère du dessin et du modèle de fabrique ? *Elle vient selon nous de ce que l'on s'est mis en tête de séparer deux choses faites pour s'allier et s'unir, l'art et l'industrie* [...] Mais d'abord, qu'est-ce que la beauté ? Où commence le beau ? [...] Admettez, au contraire, avec nous que la loi doit être uniforme pour toutes les œuvres qui tiennent de l'art [...] Ce vœu est aujourd'hui en grande partie réalisé grâce aux votes successifs de la loi du 11 mars 1902 et celle du 14 juillet 1909 [...] Aujourd'hui, et il faut s'en réjouir, l'idée simple et féconde de l'unité de l'art a définitivement triomphé dans notre pays (emphasis added).[91]

The complex development of copyright and design law, the bare bones of which we have only outlined here, is reflected in the oldest and most relevant international conventions in the field, namely the Paris Convention for the Protection of Industrial Property 1883[92] and the Berne Convention for the Protection of Artistic and Literary Works 1886.[93] The deliberate reticence of the fathers of the Paris and Berne Conventions to provide a legal definition of "protectable work" was probably due to the ideological conditioning of the Aesthetic Movement and the Arts and Crafts Movement, which shaped the varying conceptions developed by different countries of a "work of applied art". Thus neither of the conventions defined "protectable works," but instead illustrated all the possible instances of them, postulating, only indirectly and implicitly, a general requirement of originality. The definition of design as basically any human-created manufacture was purposefully very broad and non-exhaustive in intent. Meanwhile, the romance of iron and steel[94] had turned sour, erupting into class war. As workers mobilized for better pay and working conditions,[95] the interests and needs of the urban working class (a demographic which had dramatically increased in number) led to an economic

91 Pouillet, *Traité théorique et pratique des dessins et modèles*, op. cit., p. 91.

92 1883 (as amended, September 28, 1979).

93 828 U.N.T.S. 221 1886 (as amended, September 28, 1979).

94 Fitch, *The Steel Workers*, Pittsburgh 1910, p. 3: "There is a glamour about the making of steel."

95 See Lindinger, op. cit., on Austrian, German and English laws between 1885 and 1895.

conflict overshadowed by ideology.[96] The "shell" protecting the inner workings of tool machines became the emblem of a formal configuration in which outward form hid the technical features of function. That form/function dichotomy would soon spread beyond the world of tool machines, continuing to this day.

1.2 In Design

Striking the right balance between craft & industry, the arts & crafts, decorative art/ applied art & fine art has always been an ambition, but a hard task. Ultimately, their fates are tied. This is not the place to tackle the issue in details, but it is important to appreciate how since the turn of the XX century, the debate has pivoted on a dialectic between standardization (*Typisierung*) and ornamentation, creative freedom and technical constraints, art (*chistoviki*), crafts and folk culture (*prikladniki*), science and technology, material culture and "productivism" (*proizvodstvenniki*),[97] which has left a serious legacy in our notion of Design. What today we call "design," for Le Corbusier was "decorative art", the design of objects for ordinary use below the scale of architecture. He would ever remain faithful to the inaugural manifesto of the journal *L'esprit nouveau* (1920), where the *avion* is a *machine à voler*, the *maison* a *machine à habiter*, the *automobile* a *outil* (a tool), and where the purpose of those tools was to free humans from the unpleasantness of our more mundane tasks and leave us more time to think about more comforting things, such as art.[98] In *L'art décoratif d'aujourd'hui* (The Decorative Art of Today, 1925) in particular, he evoked the intellectual milieu of Paris with reference to near-contemporary figures auch as Adolf Loos and his absolute rejection of ornamentation, Bruno Paul and his envisaged *Typisierung* (Typenmöbel 1908), Hermann Muthesius, a founding member of the *Deutscher Werkbund*, with his *Die Bedeutung des Kunstgewerbes*, and the sociologist-economist Thorstein Veblen, who stigmatized the "leisure class" for its "conspicuous consumption" and the "conspicuous waste," where "social status" was earned and displayed by patterns of consumption.[99] Meanwhile, the fine, blurry line between decorative art and applied art was becoming more demarcated, as institutionally sanctioned by

96 Freeman, *Behemoth. A History of the Factory and the Making of the Modern World*, New York/London, 2018.

97 Harte, *Fast Forward: The Aesthetics and Ideology of Speed in Russian Avant-Garde Culture 1910–1930*, Madison Wisconsin, 2009.

98 Maldonado, *Disegno industriale. Un riesame* op. cit., p. 33; Dunnett, *The Decorative Art of Today by Le Corbusier*, London, 1987 (see the Introduction).

99 See Diggins, *The Bard of Savagery: Thorstein Veblen and Modern Social Theory*, New York, 1978, pp. 57 ff.

initiatives such as the *Salon des Arts Menagers* (Household Arts Fair) in Paris. First organized in 1923 by Jules-Louis Breton under the original name of the *Salon des Appareils Menagers*, the event was designed to "display new appliances, to encourage sales, and to facilitate an encounter between practical and elegant appliances and the masses of consumers."[100] It was an event dedicated to the collective celebration of household appliances, furniture, and architecture, where the function of the decorative arts was thought to be a kind of "purgatory" to help crystallize the tastes of large-scale production.

In those the same years, in other countries touched by industrialization and urbanization, industrial production was an issue to be tackled by the typification of objects designed for mass production. In Germany, as in France, the trend was initially to isolate the problem of the "form" of the product with respect to the production process through the debate on how decorative styles could influence the production of goods as well as tools, machines, and their technical parts. The *Bauhaus* (1919) and the *Vkhutemas* (1920), the Russian State Art and Technical School in Moscow, showed close parallels in such intents and in their organization and scope. They were the first schools to train artist-designers in a modern manner,[101] driven by a philosophy that believed the artist should had been trained to work with industry, learning design and artistic composition as much as economics and sociology.[102] Walter Gropius, the first Bauhaus director in Weimar, perfectly represented the ambiguity of using categories borrowed from expressionist aesthetics promoting the standardization and typification of goods. He sought to combine the crafts and fine arts with a view to creating the *Gesamtkunstwerk*, or total work of art, a new order in which all the arts, including architecture, would be brought together to arrive at high-end functional products with artistic merit. The turning point came when the director of the journal *De Stijl*, van Doesburg, settled in Weimar, influencing the Bauhaus, even without teaching at the school. Suddenly the morphology *Stijl* became a consistent theme and determined the

100 Catalogue officiel du Salon des appareils menagers, 1923, cited in Furlough, "Selling the American Way in Interwar France: Prix Uniques and the Salon des Arts Menagers," *Journal of Social History*, 1993, p. 503.

101 Fry, *A New Design Philosophy: An Introduction to Defuturing*, Kensington, 1999.

102 Maldonado, *Tecnica e cultura. Il dibattito tedesco fra Bismarck e Weimar*, Milan, 1979; Bassi, *Progettare gli oggetti della vita quotidiana*, Bologna, 2013, pp. 66 ff; Bassi, *Design anonimo in Italia. Oggetti comuni e progetto incognito*, Milan, 2007; Wingler, *The Bauhaus: Weimar, Dessau, Berlin, Chicago*, Cambridge MA, 1969; *Bauhaus Movement. Rethinking the world Art and Technology – A new Unity*, available at http://www.bauhaus-movement.com/en/.; *The Bauhaus, 1919–1933. The MET. The Metropolitan Museum of Art* available at https://www.metmuseum.org/toah/hd/bauh/hd_bauh.htm (accessed 10.10.2019).

shift to rationalism.[103] The second Bauhaus director, Hannes Meyer, in Dessau set out to give this new order a social content, with a decisively constructivist flavour. He described design as an organizational task with no relationship to aesthetics, emphasizing it as a technical process.[104] The third director, Ludwig Mies van der Rohe, who moved the Bahuaus to Berlin in 1932, provided little contribution to industrial design, both in theory and practice,[105] but by then the Bauhaus legend had already taken shape, identified with the Gropius era of 1923–28. When the Nazi movement denounced the Bauhaus for its "degenerate art", with the Nazi regime determined to cancel what it saw as a foreign, Jewish-influenced, cosmopolitan Modernism,[106] emigrants succeeded in spreading the concepts of the Bauhaus to other countries, including the *New Bauhaus* of Chicago when Mies van der Rohe decided to emigrate to the United States to take up the directorship of the School of Architecture at the Armour Institute (now Illinois Institute of Technology).[107] By the end of 1930s, the Hans Knoll Furniture Company registered in New York was importing not only furniture, but also Modernism from Europe to the USA.[108]

In the United States, the New Deal inaugurated what was really the first modern industrial knowledge economy. The Ford system itself had already led to a radical break with past manufacturing practices, and virtually from the start, American factories had turned to the mass manufacturing of a single standardized commodity, adopting a model of high-volume production, high wages, and strict workforce controls.[109] In declaring its economic focus, the New Deal sought to balance the competing interests of producers and consumers, and of designers and entrepreneurs who utilized their designs to create mass consumer goods for ordinary citizens. In short, new legal arrangements, which could help in the making of an informed and innovative citizenry, were needed. For the first time, the products of human skill were identified as a dynamic engine for economic growth. With the emergence of

103 See the magazine *Bauhaus* and the series of books *Bauhausbücher*. See also Gropius, "Die Entwicklung moderner Industriebaukunst," *Jahrbuch*, 1913, S. 17.

104 Meyer, "Die neue Welt," *Das Werk*, 1926, pp. 205 ff; Maldonado, *Disegno Industriale. Un riesame*, op. cit., pp. 70 ff; Dal Co, "Hannes Meyer e la venerabile scuola di Dessau," in Meyer, *Architettura o Rivoluzione Scritti 1921–1942* a cura di Francesco Dal Co, Padua, 1969, pp. 18–56.

105 Maldonado, *Disegno Industriale. Un riesame*, op. cit., pp. 52 ff; Argan, *Walter Gropius e la Bauhaus*, Turin, 1951; Woodham, *Twentieth Century Design*, Oxford, 1997.

106 Oxford Dictionary of Art and Artists, Oxford, 4th ed., 2009.

107 Spaeth, *Ludwig Mies van der Rohe*, New York, 1985; Jardi, *Paul Klee*, Hoboken, New Jersey, 1991, p. 22.

108 On Barr and his contribution see Meyer, *What was Contemporary Art?*, Cambridge MA, 2013, pp. 37 ff.

109 Freeman, *Behemoth* op. cit., pp. 118 ff.

mass production, the design for any product, from clothing to industrial goods, could be rapidly and inexpensively copied by competitors. Companies had little time to exploit the economic value of original designs, which fell outside the scope of design patent protection. Businesses sought relief from free-riding competitors in a number of ways, such as by calling for new legislation, seeking legal redress, and investing in the stylization and embellishment of products.[110] Especially intriguing was the creation of self-help mechanisms through trade associations and through New Deal-sponsored National Recovery Act Codes.[111] New Deal policies announced the birth of a "consumer republic" and a redirection of copyright policies to protect the production of mass-produced goods. Subsequently, copyright changed from a regime strictly concerned with literary property to an area of law governing industrial design (including fashion), with efforts soon extended to enforcing copyright on music broadcast over the radio through royalty collection societies.

> In New York, for example, over fifteen thousand firms produced clothing. Partly in response to a growing problem of overproduction, the fashion industry, with its focus on new designs, created a mechanism for planned obsolescence of clothing. Style creation was a costly process. It entailed the gathering of information from far away design centers such as Paris, the cost of creating multiple patterns of which only a few might become popular with the public and the additional investment required to market a novel design. Recognizing the substantial costs involved in originating designs, competitors often seized upon piracy to achieve a competitive footing. Mass-production of clothing allowed competitors to make lower priced knock-offs with the under-utilized industrial manufacturing capacity that existed in the 1930s. Designers responded to this competitive pressure by fostering product differentiation in the form of new styles. Yet information about style circulated readily, and competitors – as well as potential consumers – became aware of innovations in design almost as soon as they were released. (…) Beyond the fashion industry, the late 1930s and early 1940s was the golden age of industrial design. Major figures such as Raymond Loewy, Walter Dorwin Teague,

110 Branzi, "Design," *Enciclopedia Italiana*, 7 appendice, Rome, 2006. Since 1914, more than eighty proposals have been outlined in Congress to provide protection against the copying of fashion design products. See Scott Hempill, Suk Gersen, "The Fashion Originators' Guild of America: Self-help at the Edge of IP and Antitrust," *Columbia Public Law Research Paper*, 2013, pp. 159–179.

111 Wilf, "The Making of the Post-War Paradigm in American Intellectual Property Law," in Wilf (ed.) *Intellectual Property Law and History*, New York, 2012, pp. 361 ff.

> Norman bel Geddes, and Henry Dreyfuss combined aesthetics and mechanical engineering to transform everyday material objects[112]

Architects such as Franck Lloyd Wright dominated the scene in the United States, but industrial designers were coming to the fore, too. One was Henry Dreyfuss, known for some of the most iconic designs found in American homes and offices throughout the XX century, including the Western Electric Model 500 telephone and other iconic objects;[113] another was Raymond Loewy, renowned for the Coca Cola vending machine, the Lucky Strike cigarette pack, and the Coldspot Super Six refrigerators, and whom the press would dub *The Man Who Shaped America, The Father of Streamlining* and *The Father of Industrial Design*.[114]

As consumer mass production broke new ground around the world and the Readymade and Pop Art movements were exploiting the canonical value of art, the *artification* of design was growing in Europe, especially in what has come to be known as "Scandinavian Design". The artistic intention and quality of Scandinavian Design would become the defining principles for the internal unification and the external demarcation of the Industrial Design sector. Nordic design, and especially the Norwegian school, was intimately rooted in the applied art movement (*Brukskunstbevegelsen*). The phenomenon that brought Scandinavian Design to international repute in the 1950s was built precisely on old traditions – ideologies, movements, and organizations dating back to the late XIX and early XX centuries, restoring the design community almost exclusively to the realms of industrial art (*kunstindustri*) and applied art (*brukskunst*).[115] In particular, the strict relationship between industrial design and older craft traditions was evident in the Norwegian Group of Industrial Designers (*ID-gruppen*), established in March 1955. The members of the group were all educated at the National College of Applied Art and Craft and were also members of the Applied Art Association in Oslo and of the National Federation of Norwegian Applied Art. In 1963, the Norwegian Applied Artists association was founded as a trade union under the wing of the National Federation;[116] it welcomed designers from both industrial as well as craft

112 Ibid.

113 Available at http://collection.cooperhewitt.org/people/18041029/ (accessed 1.8.2019).

114 Available at https://www.raymondloewy.com/about/biography/#fastFacts (accessed 1.8.2019).

115 Fallan, "How an Excavator Got Aesthetic Pretensions – Negotiating Design in 1960s' Norway," *Journal of Design History*, 2007, pp. 43–59.

116 The Norwegian Applied Artists never became a formal trade organization, but remained an interest group incorporating design practitioners, theoreticians, interior architects, architects, the ID-gruppen, manufacturers, and the interested public. In 1965, it was reorganized and became an umbrella organization, coordinating the different trade unions eligible for membership. Fallan, op. cit., p. 45.

sectors, showing no discrimination on the basis of the manufacturing process involved. In 1965 the Norwegian Design Centre was founded by the Norwegian Export Council, a step towards the professionalization of Norwegian industrial design and an alignment of design with industrial organizations, governmental bodies, and export policies. In 1975, however, the members changed their name to *Norwegian Artisan Craft-workers*, defining themselves as "artists," and their activity as "art," thereby disowning any connection to the world of industry and commercial business:

> The shape of a coffee cup is also predominantly determined by its function, but at the same time we know that there are literally infinite possibilities of varying this shape without noticeably impairing the function ... [M]ost people will prefer the cup whose shape seems beautiful.... In the most superb versions, this beauty conveys something unutterable, something which it is not quite possible to grasp with words and explanations. That is when art has joined in.[117]
>
> [T]here [is] today a new type of artist, who has become familiar with the machine, and creates his works of art from the drawing-board. He virtually conducts his machine in an artistic performance.[118]

The notion of a "work of applied art" became ever more troublesome in the 1980s, when, ironically, a group of Norwegian designers and industrial design students felt the need to organize a symbolic funeral for Scandinavian Design. They carried "design" onto a boat on the quay in front of Oslo City Hall and buried it in the Oslo fjord. As Terje Meyer put it when interviewed about the funeral: "*The term [Scandinavian Design] is founded on the Nordic craft traditions and can therefore not ensure the role of industrial designers in today's society.*"[119] Lamenting that "*Scandinavian Design has become a style kept artificially alive,*" Pal Hansen stressed "*we design railroad, cars, computerized Braille printers, bloodstream meters, and ovens.*"[120]

As stormy as the relationship between industrial design, art, and manufacturing would continue to be, the movement left a lasting imprint on designers across Europe. Designers, of any conviction, were applied artists, because

117 In the words of the influential Norwegian architect, Odd Brochmann, translated by Fallen, op. cit., p. 45.

118 Jorgen Skaare went further still in his description of the industrial designer: see Fallen, op. cit., p. 47.

119 Fallan, op. cit., p. 66.

120 Hansen, director of the National Museum of Decorative Arts in Trondheim, and the director of the Norwegian Design Centre's Council, quoted in Fallan, op. cit., p. 54. See also Dormer (ed.), *The Culture of Craft*, Manchester, 1997.

their job was not only to create a standardized, functional form, but also to add art and pleasure to the project. With new incursions into domains previously dominated by engineers, seeking greater influence and acceptance in the world of business, designers sought to strike the perfect balance between form and function, beauty and efficiency. Two, opposite souls that increasingly, if somewhat tentatively, became merged by the end of XX century, as the most art-like handicrafts and the most engineering-like industrial designs both showed "artistic aspects at their core." In the words of the designer Thorbjorn Rygh, "*Even highly prosaic products, such as the Brødrene Søyland Brøyt X3 excavator, could be considered works of applied art, if they had aesthetic pretension and attitudes.*" Aesthetic expression, artistic quality, formal originality, and functionality thus all became increasingly important in the attempt to create a common ground for all types of design activities.[121]

The notion of *gute Form*, albeit with a different meaning than in the Nordic countries, was similarly the core issue in Germany after the Second World War. There, Max Bill brought together Bauhaus ideas – mainly those concerned with its aesthetic-formalistic approach, not those committed to its functionalist-productivist stance[122] – to assert that shape was tied to the quality and functionality of an object, not to the latest fashion trends, offering an alternative to the Nordic design-artist approach and to the American notion of *styling*.[123] Bill was head of the *Hochschule für Gestaltung* in Ulm, which he claimed to direct in continuity with the Bauhaus school itself. Over its brief existence from 1955 to 1968, the Ulm school became an extraordinary laboratory of design, exerting a surprising (considering its small size and location) influence all over the world, even as far afield as Latin America.[124] Conceived as a successor to the Bauhaus, the school soon abandoned that model and set out to explore the uncharted territory of design for mass production and mass consumption, becoming notable for its inclusion of semiotics as a field of study.[125] The Ulm school achieved its greatest heights working with the consumer products

121 Fallan, op. cit., pp. 51 ff: Brochmann, Skaare, Remlov, and Schjodt could accept industrial products as belonging to the field of applied art only if they were beautiful. See also Alf Boe, senior curator at the Oslo Museum of Decorative Arts, director of the National Federation of Norwegian Applied Art and also director of the Norwegian Design Centre in the 1960's.

122 Maldonado, op. cit., p. 76.

123 Bill, *Die Gute Form*, Zürich, 1949; Bill, "Form und Kunst," *Form*, Basel, 1952, pp. 6–11; Bill, *Funktion und Funktionalismus. Schriften 1945–1988*, Bern, 2008.

124 Filho, "Design and Craftsmanship: The Brazilian Experience," *Design Issues*, 2013, pp. 64–74, p. 65.

125 Lindinger (ed.), *Ulm Design: The Morality of Objects*, Cambridge MA, 1990 (translated by Britt); see also Alessi (ed.), *Oggetti e progetti. Alessi: storia e futuro di una fabbrica del design italiano*, Milan, 2011.

company Braun. In 1955, Braun recruited the young architect Dieter Rams with the aim of modernizing the interiors of its facilities along the lines of the company's new business approach. Rams, however, soon became involved in product design and finally became Braun's Chief Design Officer. Otl Aicher and Hans Gugelot, both professors at the Ulm school, adopted him as a *protégé* and worked together with him on the design of many of Braun's electronic products, the layout of Braun's exhibitions, and the construction of Braun's corporate image.[126] The SK-4 record player, designed by Dieter Rams and Hans Gugelot dubbed "Snow White's coffin" because of its transparent lid, remains an iconic design object to this day. Rams was also the author of the celebrated "Ten principles of good design."[127] Thus, the Modernist Movement and the "good design" narrative became mainstream once objects mainly developed in war-time and for public services entered the ordinary lives of common people.

The limbo of industrial design between the aesthetics of art and the world of industry, with its engineers and their design-less products, would continued well after the influence of the Ulm school, until the end of the XX century.

In 1967, one alumnus of the Ulm school, Tomas Maldonado,[128] established himself in Italy,[129] where the tension between artistic craftsmanship and industrial production was discernible from the outset. Alongside his university lecturing engagements, Maldonado also worked for the Olivetti factory and for the Milanese department store *La Rinascente*, then owned by Aldo Borletti, the businessman who in 1954 established the *Compasso d'Oro* prize (the most important Italian design award). Italian designers showed a marked craft tradition in their work,[130] based on individual creativity, on which much of the image of Italian design is still founded today.[131] They worked chiefly on consumer goods, in a peculiar ecosystem, made up of micro-businesses located mostly in the northern part of Italy, where a special figure, that of the "artisan-entrepreneur-designer" was born.[132] In an attempt to reconcile the arts, craft,

---

126 Available at https://www.ramonesteve.com/en/manufacturing-the-interior/posts/dieter-rams-and-the-ulm-school-of-design/ (accessed 2.8.2019).

127 SFMOMA *Presents Less and More: The Design Ethos of Dieter Rams*, Sfmoma.org (accessed 2.8.2019).

128 Maldonado, *Disegno e le nuove prospettive industriali*, Milan, 1958; Maldonado, Il *futuro della Modernità*, Milan, 1987; Maldonado, *Reale virtuale. Saggi*, Milan, 3rd ed., 2015.

129 Riccini, "T. Maldonado and the Impact of Hfg Ulm in Italy," in Lees-Maffei, Fallan (eds.), *Made in Italy. Rethinking a Century of Italian Design*, London/New York, 2014.

130 Riccini, *History from Things* op. cit., p. 47; De Fusco, op. cit.

131 See the classic works by Bruno Munari, such as *Fantasia, Arte come mestiere, Da cosa nasce cosa, Design e comunicazione visiva.*

132 See Chiapponi, "Design e artigianato oggi," in Tosi et al. (eds.), *Artigianato Design Innovazione. Le nuove prospettive del saper fare*, Florence, 2015, pp. 39–41; for a paradigmatic

and industry, the artisan-entrepreneur-designer worked within the specific context of what has come to be representative of what is now known as "Made in Italy" manufacturing: the small, local factory focused on the relationship between industrial design and local culture, based on traditional know-how, identity, and local heritage as a privileged means to advance and sustain the international dimension of Italian industrial design. Professional design photographers played an intense and important role, often commissioned by entrepreneurs in the furnishings sector, such as Arflex, Cassina, C & B (later B&B), De Padova, Fontanta Arte, Gavina, Kartell, Tisettanta, Tecno, and Zanotta, to produce commercial catalogues, advertisements, and publications.

The "Made in Italy" brand would never have achieved its global resonance without the "artisan-entrepreneur-designer" and the increasingly close collaboration between entrepreneurs, professional design photographers, and leading industrial designers and art directors during the 1980s and 1990s.[133] The artist-designer reached global markets thanks to the smart entrepreneurs of certain manufacturing districts, such as the furniture district in Brianza, the leatherwear district in Tuscany, and the sportsystem, leatherwear, eyewear, goldwork, and artistic glass districts in Veneto, where small craft workshops interpreted the Italian way of industrialization. In Italy, the artist-designers who dominated the market have traditionally been architects. One of them was Giovanni (Giò) Ponti, the well-known Italian architect who founded the magazine *Domus* in 1928[134] and directed it almost all his life, tracing the developments of the "Italian-style" art of living. Ponti built more than one hundred buildings and designed a considerable number of design objects as well as furniture, including door handles for Olivari, a range of bathroom fixtures for Ideal Standard, cutlery for Krupp Italiana and Christofle, lighting for Arredoluce, furniture for the Swedish department store Nordiska Kompaniet,[135] and the Leggera and Superleggera chairs for Cassina. His Distex, Round, Lotus, and Mariposa chairs are now among the classics of Italian design. Another leading name is that of Ettore Sottsass,[136] who after working as an architect with his father, then set up his own industrial design studio. In 1958, Sottsass was

---

example see the works of Paolo De Poli, an artist, craftsman, and designer, in Bassi, Cafà (eds.), *Paolo De Poli e Gio Ponti, L'artigiano-designer e l'architetto*, Venice, 2015; Bassi, "Arti applicate e design: dialogo e distinguo", in Drago (ed.), *Nuovo antico. Dalla materia all'artefatto*, exhibition catalogue, Rome, 2002, pp. 38–39.

133 See, for instance, Bassi, Masera, *Mauro Masera – Fotografo del design italiano (1957–1992)*, Venice, 2017.

134 Fiell, Irace, *Domus: 1928–1939*, Köln, 2017.

135 La Pietra, *Gio Ponti, l'arte si innamora dell'industria*, Milan, 2009; Bosoni, *Made in Cassina*, Paris, 2008.

136 Radice, *Ettore Sottsass: A Critical Biography*, London, 1993.

hired by Adriano Olivetti as a design consultant for Olivetti, where he designed electronic devices and developed the first Italian mainframe computer, the Elea 9003, for which he was awarded the *Compasso d'Oro* in 1959. With Perry King, Sottsass designed the typewriter Valentine in 1969, still considered today as a milestone of XX century design. While continuing to design for Olivetti in the 1960s, Sottsass developed a range of objects which were expressions of his personal experiences travelling in the United States, where he met the Beat poets, and in India, where he came to know its ancient culture.[137] Back in Italy, he formed the avant-garde group *Alchimia* with Branzi and Mendini. *Alchimia* was the precursor of the design collective named *Memphis*, founded in 1981[138] with Radice, De Lucchi, Zanini, Cibic, Thun, and Bedin. They drew inspiration from such movements as Art Deco and Pop Art, as well as styles such as 1950s Kitsch and futuristic themes. Provocative, eccentric, and politically engaged, they claimed to be against "good design" and all for inventing a new design vision that would reinvigorate the Radical Design Movement (Superstudio, Archizoom, Ufo, ZZIGGURAT of Branzi, Mendini, Pesce, Dalisi, and Binazzi, among others).[139] When the entrepreneur Ernesto Gismondi, founder of Artemide Group, become president of *Memphis*, the design collective lost its desecrating drive and the Radical Design Movement was reduced to a status symbol. A broader survey is not possible here of Italy's prolific and eclectic industrial designers and their contribution to shaping and defining the profession in the latter part of the XX century. Suffice it to say there is no agreement among them on a definitive, systematic conception of industrial design, beyond it being more a practice embedded in the culture of the project.

2 *Design as a Projection of the Identity of the Nation in Post-war States*

In the wake of the Second World War, design became a medium of projection of the power of the modernized state. In Europe, the reconversion of wartime industry into civil engineering was fostered by the Marshall Plan

137 *The Avantgarde: We Were Exuberant and Still Had Hope. Ettore Sottsass: works from Stockholm*, 1969, https://archive.is/20130415084647/http://www.marres.org/en/program/exhibition/we_were_exuberant_and_still_had_hope_ettore_sottsass_works_from_stockholm_1969#selection-545.0–547.81 (accessed 8.8.2019).

138 The Memphis Group, available at design-technology.org. (accessed 8.8.2019).

139 Retrospectively see Mello, *Neoavanguardie e controcultura a Firenze. Il movimento Radicale: i protagonisti di un cambiamento storico internazionale*, Florence, 2017. Mastrigli (ed.), *Superstudio, Opere 1966–1978*, Macerata, 2016. Pettena, *Radical Design. Ricerca e Progetto dagli anni '60 a oggi*, Florence, 2004. Cavart, Dalisi, De Angelis, Global Tools, Gruppo Teoria, La Pietra, Mendini, Natalini, Raggi, "L'architettura radicale è morta: viva l'architettura radicale", *Spazioarte* [10–11], 1977. Orlandoni, Vallino, *Dalla città al cucchiaio. Saggi sulle nuove avanguardie nell'architettura e nel design*, Turin, 1977. Pettena, *L'anarchitetto*, Rimini, 1973.

during the Cold War and catalyzed by the Organisation for European Economic Co-operation (OEEC), by the General Agreement on Tariffs and Trade (GATT), by the European Economic Community (EEC), and by the European Free Trade Association (EFTA), all of which opened up domestic markets as import restrictions and tariff barriers fell across national borders. World Fairs, World Expos and specialized trade exhibitions, such as the *Milan Triennale* as of the beginning of the 1950s, promoted the industrial design of domestic manufactured goods with a view to making national industries more competitive, both domestically and internationally, and to fostering an archetypal imagery for each national experience.[140] The projection of national identity through industrial design was furthered by state patronage and the process of "institutionalizing" modern design, especially in Western countries, backed largely by government-sponsored initiatives.[141] Industrial design was endorsed by states for many reasons, including the economic rationale of strengthening industries and their position on global markets, but also for the creation of a national identity rooted in a specific material culture. One of the first governmental organizations to deal specifically with industrial design was the British Institute of Industrial Design (BIIA). Established in 1918, it acted as a medium and link between modern industrial goods and the Victoria and Albert (V&A) Museum, which was the ultimate destination of objects on their road to "good taste" in Britain. Museums were particularly significant drivers of the change in attitude towards the composite nature of the phenomenon of industrial design.[142] Also overseas, New York's Museum of Modern Art (MoMA) acted as a projector of US identity and as a tool of cultural diplomacy to promote a positive image of the USA during the Cold War. To foster such an image in Europe,[143] MoMA organized a vast retrospective exhibition of a selection of twentieth-century American painting and sculpture, as might have been expected, but also of architecture, photography, printmaking, typography, film, and mass-produced industrial design items. The exhibition primarily had a French audience in mind, but after the exhibition left Paris, MoMA

140 Davies, "A Geographical Notion turned into an Artisitic Reality: Promoting Finland and Selling Finnish Design in Post-War Britain c. 1953–1065," *Journal of Design History*, 2002, pp. 101–116.

141 See also Serulus, *Design and Politics: The Public Promotion of Industrial Design in Postwar Belgium*, Leuven, 2018, pp. 132 ff.

142 Suga, "Purgatory of Taste or Projector of Industrial Britain? The British Institute of Industrial Art," *Journal of Design History*, 2003, pp. 167–185, pp. 170 ff.

143 McDonald, "Selling the American Dream: MoMA, Industrial Design and Post-War France," *Journal of Design History*, 2004, pp. 397–412.

sent a reconfigured and renamed version of it on a major tour of Europe, to Zurich, Barcelona, Frankfurt, London, The Hague, Vienna, and Belgrade, exporting American culture by doing so. The MoMA's "50 Years of American Art" exhibition was the largest and most aggressive statement to date of the vigour and originality of American visual culture ever to have been made in Europe. Another museum to have leveraged the significance of modern industrial design was the Cooper-Hewitt Museum in New York, a historic "bastion of the decorative arts" set up in 1897 to act as a repository of collections of decorative art objects dating from the sixteenth to nineteenth centuries. In 1991, it organized the exhibition "The Cooper-Hewitt Collection: A Design Resource," which drew on the 250,000 objects in its collection. The initiative marked the start of a transformation process that would lead it to become the National Museum of Design.[144] The projection of national identity through the lever of design was also marked, especially in common law countries,[145] by private initiatives for the public good, pursued by philanthropists.[146] In 1930, for instance, the publisher and philanthropist George Gough Booth founded the Cranbrook Educational Community (CEC) in Michigan, USA, and within it the Cranbrook Academy of Art, modelled after the American Academy of Art in Rome. When Eliel Saarinen (1873–1950), a well-established architect in Finland, immigrated to Chicago in 1923, bringing his vision of the Arts and Crafts Movement and a firm belief in the superiority of craftsmanship, Cranbrook would come to espouse his same ideals to achieve something of lasting value and significance. The spaces that inspired Charles and Ray Eames, Harry Bertoia, Florence Knoll, Jack Lenor Larsen, Donald Lipski, Duane Hanson, Lorraine Wild, Nick Cave, Hani Rashid, and so many others, have continued to do so year after year. The Cranbrook artists' colony that was once a grand experiment has fully cemented itself today as part of the foundation of American design.[147]

---

144 Under the new guidance of Dianne H. Pilgrim, who rejected the traditional museological structure of a museum of art and launched a series of initiatives that drew attention to the idea of design in its pluralistic sense. See Pilgrim, *Design for Life*, London, 1997.

145 Where "a more activist and explicitly Protestant tradition of direct charitable engagement during life" took hold, according to McCully, *Philanthropy Reconsidered*, Bloomington Indiana, 2008, p. 13.

146 Frazier Wall, *Andrew Carnegie*, Oxford, 1970, pp. 882–84; Ascoli, *Julius Rosenwald: The Man Who Built Sears, Roebuck and Advanced the Cause of Black Education in the American South*, Bloomington Indiana, 2006; Crocker, *Mrs. Russell Sage: Women's Activism and Philanthropy in Gilded Age and Progressive Era America*, Bloomington Indiana, 2006; Johnson, Harr, *The Rockefeller Century: Three Generations of America's Greatest Family*, New York, 1988.

147 Available at https://cranbrookart.edu/about/history/ (accessed 8.8.2019).

The most popular format to promote national industrial design, however, has been the Design Centre, conceived as a transmitter of national design culture. The British Council of Industrial Design, established in 1944, inaugurated the first International Design Conference in 1951 and opened its Design Centre in 1956. It served as a model for other promotional organizations set up in the 1960s, such as the Brussels Design Centre in Belgium, VNIITE in Russia in 1962, the Norwegian Design Centre (*Norsk Designcentrum*-NDC) in Norway in 1963, as well as centres in Greece, Japan, Sweden, Austria, and elsewhere.[148] Italy established its own version of a design centre as early as 1956 with the creation of the *Associazione per il Disegno Industriale* (ADI).[149] It typified a new alignment of design with industrial organizations, governmental bodies, and national export policy, crowned by the institution of a new Design Award for the best products of industrial design. In this regard, it is interesting to compare the products awarded at the first edition of the Norwegian Design Award (1961), with those awarded at the first edition of the Italian Design Award seven years earlier, in 1954. Of the five Norwegian products to be awarded, one was a grapnel; in Italy, the award was given to the "Lettera 22" typewriter (Figures 8–9).

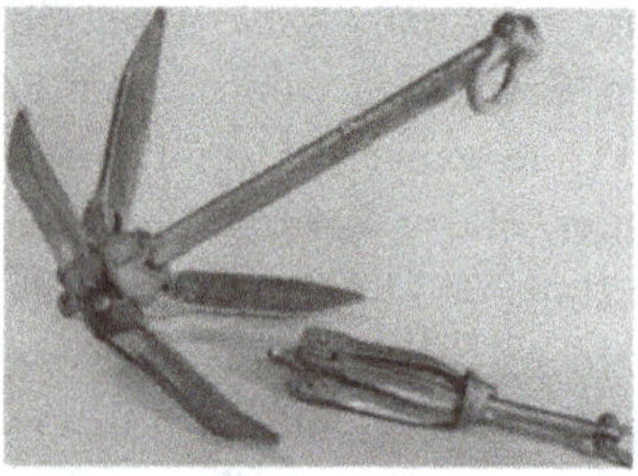

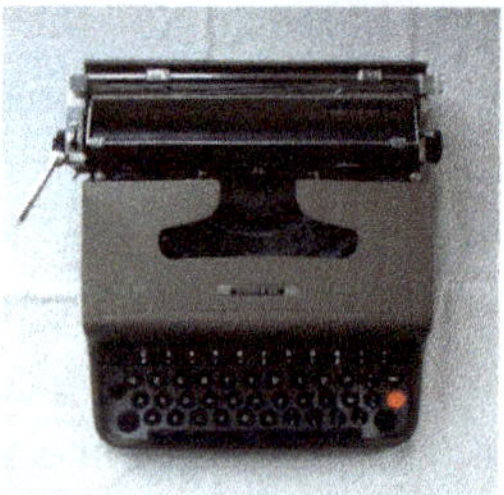

FIGURES 8–9 Grapnel SA V (malleable cast iron) Sandnes Aducerverk A/ S, 1957.
DESIGNER: KIRE ESPEDAL. (PHOTOGRAPHER: BJORN WINSNES. PHOTO COURTESY OF NORWEGIAN DESIGN COUNCIL.)
Lettera 22 Olivetti Typewriter.
DESIGNER. MARCELLO NIZZOLI, WITH GIUSEPPE BECCIO (PHOTOGRAPHER: LJL.JPEG SELF-MADE PICTURE, PUBLIC DOMAIN).

148 Fallan, op. cit., p. 46; Serulus, op. cit.

149 On the Italian experience and the humanistic education exhibited by designers in Italy, see Gregotti, op. cit.; De Fusco, op. cit.; Bosoni, op. cit.; Castelnuovo (ed.), *Storia del disegno industriale*, 3 vols. Milan, 1989–90.

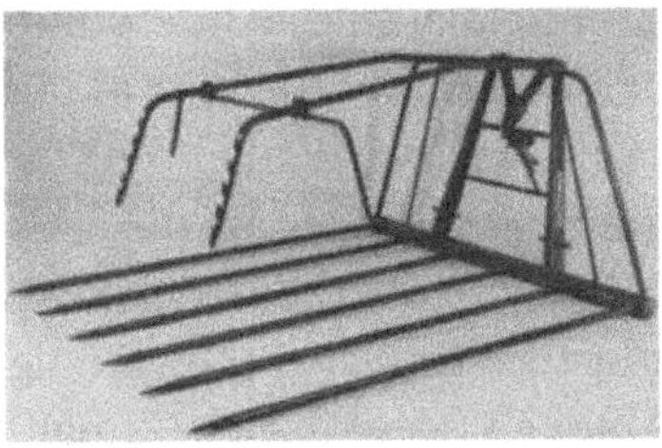

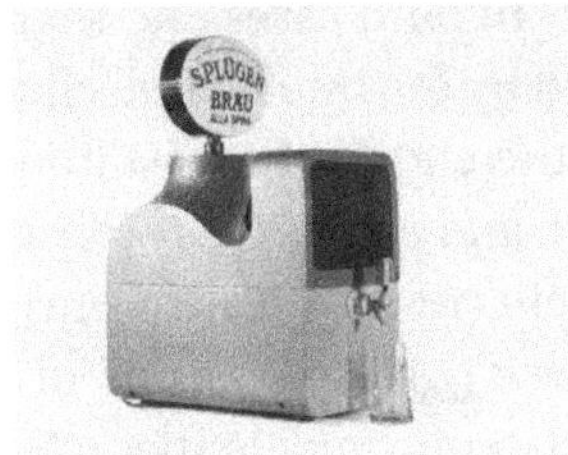

FIGURES 10–11 Hay loader (steel) Kvernelands Fabrikk A/S. DESIGNER: OLAV NJI. (PHOTOGRAPHER: BJORN WINSNES. PHOTO COURTESY OF NORWEGIAN DESIGN COUNCIL.)
Spinamatic, a beer dispensing system Poretti SpA Factory. DESIGNER: ACHILLE CASTIGLIONI AND PIER GIACOMO CASTIGLIONI. (PHOTOGRAPHER ©2018 GIORGINA CASTIGLIONI – OFFICIAL PIER GIACOMO CASTIGLIONI WEBSITE)

Moving forward to 1964, the Norwegian Design Award was given to a hay loader, while the Italian Design Award for that same year went to a beer dispensing system named "Spinamatic" (Figures 10–11).

Those award-winners epitomize how each national design association conceived the relationship between craft and industry, applied and decorative art and the fine arts, standardization and ornamentation, form and function in those years of economic recovery. As we will see, their historically and politically determined conception of "works of applied art" would be of prominent importance in the early efforts of international conventions and in subsequent European regulatory interventions.

3 *Legal Requirements for Defining Protectable Design Works*

3.1 International Legal Requirements, or the Lack Thereof: A Very Broad Definition

The Paris and Berne Conventions (see §1.1. above) adopt rather different terminology in setting out protection for design objects – a protection that was only envisaged in later revisions of the two texts. The Paris Convention only introduced protection for "industrial design" as industrial property after the Lisbon Revision of 1958, although references to "industrial designs" and "utility models" can be found in the 1925 Convention text, as revised at The Hague. The Berne Convention, on the other hand, introduced "works of applied art" and "industrial designs and models" in its list of protectable works in the 1948 revision at Brussels.[150] In both cases, the legal terminology and its interpretation was likely affected by the intellectual climate prevailing at the time of the revisions, shaped by the end of the hostilities of the Second World Word for the Berne Convention, and economic reconstruction in the 1950s for the Paris Convention. The current (revised) Paris Convention applies to industrial property in the widest sense (Article 1 "Scope of Industrial Property"), including industrial designs,[151] patents, trademarks, utility models (as well as the "small-scale patents" provided for by the laws of some countries, such as Italy), service marks, trade names (designations under which an industrial or commercial activity is carried out), geographical indications (indications of source and appellations of origin), and the repression of unfair competition. At no point, however, does the Paris Convention define "industrial design," adopting instead a legal conception shaped by the cultural environment which considers only the appearance of a product, or part of a product, as eligible for protection, meaning that the two-dimensional surface decorations and three-dimensional shapes of products have to take visible, physical form in order to be protected. Conceptions and ideas, unless and until given visible and physical form, cannot be protected. The (revised) Berne Convention instead includes "works of applied art" in its list of the literary and artistic works (Article 2(1) covered by the concept of "Protected Works",[152] where explicit reference is made to works of applied art) without requiring any further condition, in comparison to other works such as drawing, painting, sculpture, architecture or photographic works. Article 2(3) and (5) of the Berne Convention states that translations,

---

150 Whether works of applied art should have been included within the scope of the Berne Convention had been a matter of contention well before 1948, at the Berlin conference of 1908 and at Rome conference of 1928. See Ricketson, *The Paris Convention For The Protection Of Industrial Property: A Commentary*, Oxford, 2014, pp. 473 ff.; Ricketson, "The Design/Copyright overlap: is there a Resolution?" in Wilkof, Basheer, (eds.) op. cit., 2012, pp. 159–187. See also Vitoria et al., *Laddie, Prescott, and Vitoria: The Modern Law of Copyright and Designs*, op. cit., pp. 175 ff. Ricketson, Ginsburg, *International Copyright and Neighbouring Rights: The Berne Convention and Beyond*, Oxford, 2006; Reichman, "Design Protection in Domestic and Foreign Copyright Law: From the Berne Revision of 1948 to the Copyright Act of 1976," *Duke law Journal*, 1983, pp. 1143–1164.

151 The requirement of Art. 5 *quinquies* was only introduced by the Lisbon Revision of 1958. Article 5 *quinquies* states that "Industrial designs shall be protected in all the countries of the Union," while Article 11 grants temporary protection also to industrial designs "in respect of goods exhibited at official or officially recognized international exhibitions held in the territory of any of the countries of the Union."

152 Under such a broad definition, in addition to works of applied art we find (among others) "works of drawing, painting, architecture, sculpture, engraving and lithography"; "illustrations, maps, plans, sketches and three-dimensional works relative to geography, topography, architecture or science."

adaptations, arrangements of music, and other alterations of a literary or artistic work are protected as "original works," and that collections of literary or artistic works such as encyclopaedias and anthologies must constitute "intellectual creations" to be protected. Both qualifications – as "original works" and "intellectual creations" – are noteworthy and in the light of systematic interpretation, they extend to all the matters covered by Article 2.[153] Accordingly, in order to comply with Berne standards, protectable works have to possess an implicit "originality," in the sense that they have to be intellectual creations, although originality is not explicitly mentioned as a requirement in the Article as a whole or in the list provided under Article 2(1).[154] Moreover, Article 2(7) of the Berne Convention states that works of applied art and industrial designs and models are to be protected as "artistic works" if the country of origin of the works does not provide a *sui generis* protection for them. As such, it is a matter for national legislation to determine the scope of application of national laws to works of applied art, along with the conditions under which such works are protected under copyright law or under industrial design law, or both. Then there is a reservation, subject to a condition of reciprocity: Article 2(7) provides a reciprocity rule according to which works protected in the country of origin solely as designs and models are entitled in another country only to such special protection as is granted in that country to designs and models. In practice, a work which in a member country is only entitled to protection under design or model laws, would be entitled to receive in other countries of the Union only the same level of protection that the laws of those countries afford to designs and models. In the event that the laws of a member country are si-

153 Not only to Article 2(3)–(5). See Ricketson, op. cit., 2009, p. 57.

154 Originality lacks a precise statutory definition: see Margoni, "The Harmonisation of EU Copyright Law: The Originality Requirement," in Perry (ed.), *Global Governance of Intellectual Property in the 21st Century*, Berlin/Heidelberg, 2016, pp. 85 ff; Ricketson, Ginsburg, op. cit.; Bently, Sherman, *Intellectual Property Law*, New York, 2014, p. 93; Cornish et al., *Intellectual property: patents, copyright, trade marks, and allied rights*, London, 2013, p. 11; Gervais, Judge, *Intellectual Property: The Law in Canada*, Quebec, 2005, p. 16; Goldstein, Hugenholtz, *International Copyright: Principles, Law, and Practice*, New York, 2013, p. 192; Ginsburg, "No 'Sweat?': Copyright and Other Protection of Works of Information after Feist v. Rural Telephone," *Columbia Law Review*, 1992, pp. 338–388; Gervais, "Feist goes Global: A Comparative Analysis of the Notion of Originality in Copyright Law," *Journal of the Copyright Society of the U.S.A.*, 2002, pp. 949–998; Gravells, "Authorship and Originality: The Persistent Influence of Walter v. Lane," *Intellectual Property Quarterly*, 2007, pp. 267–293; Judge, Gervais, "Of Silos and Constellations: Comparing Notions of Originality in Copyright Law," *Cardozo Arts and Entertainment Law Journal* 2010, pp. 375–408; Schricker, "Farewell to the 'Level of Creativity' (Schöpfungshöhe) in German Copyright Law?," *International Review of Intellectual Property and Competition Law*, 1995, pp. 41–48.

lent as to the form of protection offered to industrial design, the latter should be protected under copyright law.

In short, in design law (the Paris Convention), the terminology referring to the "works of applied art" has been progressively abandoned to mark a distance from the "artification" of industrial design, which traditionally has been measured by different yardsticks,[155] an ambiguity which instead remains in copyright law (the Berne Convention, but also the Universal Copyright Convention 1952, made to accommodate the USA within the international copyright system[156]).

The global framework for copyright and design protection (along with other forms of IP law) was later revised, by the Agreement on Trade-Related Aspects of Intellectual Property Rights (TRIPS, 1994),[157] reached at the Uruguay Round of the GATT Agreement, setting a minimum standard for copyright law (the same already achieved across Western legal systems) for all countries wishing to participate in world trade. The TRIPS Agreement introduced the principles of national treatment and automatic and independent protection, and bound World Trade Organization (WTO) Members not party to the Berne Convention. Although it does not provide a definition of industrial design, TRIPS sets forth a series of requirements under which to be eligible for protection "independently created industrial designs" must be "new" (the requirement seems to point to patent-like protection), or "original" (potentially referring to copyright protection). Designs are considered not new or original if they do not significantly differ from known designs, or combinations of known design features. Member states *may* limit the scope of protection to exclude designs dictated essentially by technical or functional considerations (Article 25 of the TRIPS Agreement, section "Industrial Designs"). Furthermore, the TRIPS Agreement would appear to recognize an alternative between design law and copyright protection for certain products in the textile sector (Article 25.2). By comparison, The Hague System for the International Registration of Industrial Designs, as revised in 1999,[158] envisaged no substantial legal provisions on design, but introduced a key procedural improvement by offering owners of industrial designs a means of obtaining protection in several countries by filing one application in one language, with one set of fees in one currency. The single registration process is based on a simultaneous search of all current and past

155 Hasselbiatt (ed.), *Münchener Anwaltshandbuch, Gewerblicher Rechtsschutz*, 5. Aufl., Munich, 2017, §45 para. 7.

156 Geneva, September 6, 1952.

157 Marrakesh, April 15, 1994.

158 1925 (last revised Geneva Act 1999) see The Hague Registry, Brands and Designs Sector, WIPO.

international industrial designs registered under The Hague System through The Hague Express and the Global Design databases, as well as in participating national collections. Protection under The Hague System extends to a variety of products of industry and handicraft items – from packages and containers to furnishings and household goods, lighting equipment to jewellery, electronic devices to textiles – and industrial designs can also be registered in relation to graphic symbols, graphical user interfaces (GUI), and logotypes. The Hague System is complemented by the international Locarno Classification[159] system, which classifies goods for the purposes of the registration of industrial designs. Thus, the internationally-accepted notion of design is implicit, drawn essentially from instances of industrial design in practice. In having to accommodate different national approaches to industrial design, the legal definition has been left intentionally broad and non-exhaustive. Ultimately, however, it is "appearance" that is protected, as given by the features of a product, or a part of the product, such as lines, contours, colours, shape, texture, and other features, as identified on national lists, which have an effect on one single human sense, the sense of sight.[160]

3.2 European Legal Requirements: A Stricter Definition

Meanwhile, the EU Commission acknowledged its inability to harmonize national rules with regard to the eligibility of design products and artefacts for copyright protection and elaborated its own strategy. On the one hand, through the Green Paper on Copyright in the Knowledge Economy of 1988[161] and, on the other, through the Green Paper on the Legal Protection of Industrial Design of 1991,[162] where it recognized that the European legislative framework contained too many flaws to attain its main goal. Intervention in the field by

---

159 The Locarno Classification established in 1968 is an international classification used for the purposes of the registration of industrial design. The twelfth edition of the Classification (2019) comprises a list of classes and subclasses; an alphabetical list of goods which constitute industrial designs, with an indication of the classes and subclasses into which they fall and explanatory notes. Although it is "solely of an administrative character" and "does not bind the contracting countries as regards the nature and scope of the protection afforded to the design in those countries" (*cf* Locarno Agreement, Article 2), in practice it is the first document to be accessed before a design is registered.

160 Stone, *EU Design Law. A Practitioners' Guide*, Oxford, 2012; *Ibid*, 2nd ed., 2016. The author deals with the OHIM approach and highlights that "case law on what is design is sparse" (see p. 39).

161 Commission of the European Communities, Green Paper on Copyright and the Challenge of Technology, Copyright Issues requiring immediate action (Com (88) 172).

162 Green Paper on the Legal Protection of Industrial Design. Working document of the services of the Commission. III/F/5131/91-EN.

European institutions consisted of a host of directives aimed at harmonizing not only copyright law, by which specific work categories are protected (*inter alia*, software, databases, and photographs), but also design law. Directive 98/71/EC of the European Parliament and of the Council of 13 October 1998 on the legal protection of designs ("Design Directive") and Council Regulation (EC) No. 6/2002 of 12 December 2001 on Community designs ("Community Design Regulation")[163] were measures targeted specifically at providing legal protection for designs at European level. Design and model protection alone, however, was not enough, as at the time of the implementation of national design legislation in Europe industrial designs had long been on the market in most jurisdictions, and thus lacked "novelty." As a consequence, Recital 32 and Art. 96(2) of the Community Design Regulation and Recital 8 and Art. 17 of the Design Directive left Member States free to establish the extent of copyright protection and the conditions under which such protection is afforded to industrial designs.[164]

Article 17 of Directive 98/71/EC and Article 96(2) of Council Regulation (EC) No. 6/2002 deal with the interface between design and copyright protection:

> Article 17, Design Directive: A design protected by a design right registered in or in respect of a Member State in accordance with this Directive shall also be eligible for protection under the law of copyright of that State as from the date on which the design was created or fixed in any form. The extent to which, and the conditions under which, such a protection is conferred, including the level of originality required, shall be determined by each Member State.
>
> Article 96(2), Community Design Regulation: A design protected by a Community design[165] shall also be eligible for protection under the law of copyright of Member States as from the date on which the design was created or fixed in any form. The extent to which, and the conditions under which, such a protection is conferred, including the level of originality required, shall be determined by each Member State.

163 Respectively Council Regulation (EC) 6/2002 on Community Designs [2002] OJ L3/1 and Directive (EC) 71/1998 on the Legal Protection of Designs [1998] OJ L289/28.

164 See also Derclaye, Leistner, *Intellectual Property overlaps: a European perspective*, Oxford, 2011, pp. 46 ff; Quaedvlieg, "The Copyright/Design Interface in the Netherlands," in Derclaye (ed.), *The Copyright/Design Interface: Past, Present, and Future*, Cambridge, 2018, pp. 50 ff.

165 Article 1 states: "the Community design is defined as a design which complies with the conditions contained in this Regulation, which can be protected: (a) by an 'unregistered Community design', if made available to the public in the manner provided for in this Regulation; (b) by a 'registered Community design', if registered in the manner provided for in this Regulation."

The provisions contained in the Articles quoted represent an attempt to reconcile the variety of traditional national approaches to copyright protection for design objects and artefacts. If the conditions are satisfied, the same product enjoys both copyright and design protection, but the conditions are left to the discretion of Member States, as is the level of "originality" required. In particular, Article 17 of the Design Directive has proved especially controversial, despite its attempts to exclude registered designs *per se* from copyright protection, and the fact that it explicitly dictates a mandatory overlap between copyright and designs protection.[166]

Article 1 of the Design Directive and Article 3 of the Community Design Regulation both provide the same definition of design:

> (a) 'design' means the appearance of the whole or a part of a product resulting from the features of, in particular, the lines, contours, colours, shape, texture and/or materials of the product itself and/or its ornamentation; (b) 'product' means any industrial or handicraft item, including *inter alia* parts intended to be assembled into a complex product, packaging, get-up, graphic symbols and typographic typefaces, but excluding computer programs; (...).

By evoking the industrial/handicraft, art/technology dualities, the definition only revives the ongoing *querelle* concerning what a protectable work of design ought to be.

3.3 The Lack of Definition in Design Studies: What Does It Matter for the Regulatory Framework?

Design is multifaceted:[167] "*designing is an activity that is constantly changing. How then can we establish a body of knowledge about something that has no*

166 Case C-168/09, *Flos Spa v Semeraro Casa & Famiglia Spa*, [2011] E.C.R. I-00181.; Case C-219/09, Order of the President of the Court, 11.04.2011, *Vitra Patente AG v High Tech Srl*; Case C-198/10, Order of the Court (Sixth Chamber), 9.09.2011, *Cassina Spa v Alivar Srl and Galliani Host Arredamenti Srl* [2011] E.C.R. I-00124.

167 Cross, "Designerly Ways of Knowing: Design Discipline v Design Science," *Design Issues*, 2001, pp. 49–55. Design is not a discipline historically rooted in education. Except for Scotland, where it was recognized as early as 1728 by Sir John Clerk of Penicuick in the Academy of Edinburgh, established by the Board Trustees of Manufactures and where the teaching of pattern design for the linen industry was of a paramount importance. Italian design has traditionally lived in symbiosis with small and medium enterprises without a formalized educational system; it was only in the 1990s that Industrial Design started to be taught at universities. See Badalucco, Casarotto (eds.), *Continuità e mutamenti nella didattica per il design*, Padua, 2017.

fixed identity? From a 19th century point of view, this is a troubling question. (...)".[168] The fundamental role of design is to create and shape the world around us, now and in the future. Its critical role in creating a world that is environmentally sustainable, economically viable, socially equitable, and culturally diverse is widely acknowledged, as is the value of its approach in working in a collaborative, holistic, and integrated way, to foster a common benefit:

> DESIGN IS the application of intent: the process through which we create the material, spatial, visual and experiential environments in a world made ever more malleable by advances in technology and materials, and increasingly vulnerable to the effects of unleashed global development.[169]

The *Montreal Design Declaration* avoids the use of words such as "objects," "products," "artefacts," and "features," precisely because their boundaries are uncertain, as underscored by historical research into design, which has focused more on the relationship between the history of the factory,[170] technology,[171] and industrial design,[172] drawing on anthropology and archaeology. But uncertain boundaries do in fact matter, also in the legal domain.

3.3.1 *Categories of Goods: Objects, Artefacts, and Useful Articles*

The attitudes of scholars towards the "object" and its image is known to stand in stark contrast with their attitude to the written document. With objects, they constantly have to tackle the problematics of representation (sketches, plans, and drawings) and description (reports and photographs) to fully grasp their significance and value – a value that derives from the multiplicity of meanings that accumulate around objects, and from the different types of information

168 Margolin, "Design History or Design Studies: Subject Matter and Methods," *Design Issues*, 1995, pp. 4–15.

169 See *Montreal Design Declaration*, signed on 24 October 2017 by the representatives of the international community of designers, architects, planners, and landscape architects. Available at http://www.designdeclaration.org/declaration/ (accessed 10.10.2019).

170 The *History of the Factory* is a recent discipline, one which is seeking to create its own identity, in part through engagement with other fields of study: see Riccini, *History from Things*, op. cit.

171 Petroski studied the evolution of some of the simplest and most common artefacts that we use today, bringing small utilitarian objects such as pencils and paper-clips to the core of an important discussion aimed at drawing the creative process of invention and design out of the realms of the unknowable; Basalla in the "Evolution of Technology" claims that "any new object that appears in the world of artifacts is based on some object that already existed". The *History of Technology*, as Gillo Dorfles pointed out, is a complex field of study: the risk is to overestimate the evolutionary approach. See Riccini, *History from Things* op. cit., pp. 49 ff.

172 The *History of Industrial Design* represents an opportunity for understanding artefacts as both subjects and documents of research. See Riccini, op. cit., pp. 49 ff.

that can be obtained from them. Such information is stratified and shows strict correlations between manufacturer, technological enterprise, and economic developments. As a result, the "artefact" would come to be preferred. In everyday language, the word "artefact" often stands in contrast to "natural," evoking the negative connotations associated with the term "artificial", whose semantic range comprises the sense of being contrived or affected.[173] In anthropology, by contrast, the notion of artefact has became a systematic part of human culture: "*Culture comprises the artifacts, goods, technical processes, ideas, habits, and values that are transmitted socially.*"[174] Artefacts have acquired a decisive importance in understanding the functioning and organization of a society and in identifying patterns of behaviour and the distribution of roles among its members; in other words, in defining culture.[175] In that sense, the role of the *Centre de Recherche sur la Culture Technique* in the 1970s is of particular significance to the history of industrial design, especially through the articles published in *Culture technique*, where the study of the typology of objects and machines, such as television sets and washing machines, was developed by investigating "*the technical culture of the consumer.*"[176] On the other hand, the communicative elements of artefacts and their connection with art were highlighted in research carried out in the 1960s and 1970s by Abraham Moles and Jean Baudrillard, whose study of mass society helped restore the reputation of certain types of artefacts – not just paintings and sculptures, but also objects of the "minor arts." Until the XX century, in fact, artefacts as "mere objects," were largely ignored in representation.[177] Another category often found in Anglo-American design literature is that of "useful articles" of the ordinary kind, meaning anything from toys to kitchenware, objects that bear witness the lives of the young, the old, the poor, and women – in other words, of those members of society traditionally represented as the indistinct masses.[178]

---

173 Anceschi, *Monogrammi e figure. Teoria e storie della progettazione di artefatti comunicativi*, Florence/Milan, 1981, p. 13; Prown, "The Truth of Material Culture: History or Fiction?" in Lubar, Kingery (eds.), *History from Things, Essays on Material Culture*, Washington, 1995, pp. 2 ff.

174 Bronislaw Malinowski, op. cit. in Eches, "L'anthropologie cognitive hier et demain. Vers une anthropologie industrielle?" *Encyclopedie de la Pleiade, Histoire des Moeurs, vol. II, Modes et Modeles,* Paris, 1991, pp. 1403–1418.

175 Riccini, *History from Things*, op. cit., p. 51.

176 Eches, op. cit., pp. 1403 ff.

177 The artistic boycott of objects has been analyzed on several occasions in the context of the general attitude of contempt for technical matters shown by ancient and medieval Western culture; see Riccini, *History from Things*, op. cit., p. 52.

178 They constitute the most authentic of all historical sources, rather than written documents. See Giedion, *Mechanization Takes Command: A Contribution to Anonymous Design*, New York, 1948.

According to some commentators, useful articles are particular types of manufactured objects of common use, whose genesis is largely anonymous[179] as to the technical and social circumstances of their design, their production process, and their use. In the words of Paola Antonelli, senior curator of the Department of Architecture and Design, MoMA:

> most everyday objects, like paper clips or bubble wrap, speak of the timeless role of craftsmanship, the timelessness of innovation and the continuous guidance that material culture can provide. They are anonymous designs in that we often do not know the name of the person who drew them up. They are frequently identified by a brand (…). Remarkable traits … are useful, so useful that they have become necessary.… are affordable … are ingenious and innovative in the way they propose a new solution or altogether new typology of objects … all these characteristics make them beautiful.[180]

The "uncommon beauty of common things," to borrow Eames words, has only recently attracted much attention,[181] – i.e., things which embody a "beauty that works", a beauty which is a completely natural consequence of a correct process in which the "logical form necessary produces a product of high aesthetic quality":[182]

> without redundancy or waste, the anonymous or unknown design of everyday objects, [which] are indispensible, work, and show aspects of physical or formal agreeableness …[183]
>
> even these phenomena should be part of the Italian design panorama; otherwise it is unclear what Italy is, or what design is …[184]

179 Herbert Read's old and classic work *Art and Industry* and Lindinger's extensive essay on *Designgeschichte*, which both stress the relevance of anonymous objects.

180 Antonelli, *Humble Masterpieces: 100 Everyday Marvels of Design*, London, reprinted, 2006, pp. 2–3.

181 See, for example, Lichtenstein, *Unbekannt – Vertraut. Anonymes Design im Schweizer Gebrauchsgerät seit 1920* Katalog zur Ausstellung im Museum für Gestaltung, Zürich, 1987.

182 Bassi, *Design anonimo* op. cit.,: for example Bialetti La Moka express by Alfonso Bialetti; see also Anonymous, "Gli anonimi che hanno cambiato la nostra vita," *DOMUS*, 811, 1999, p. 82.

183 "senza ridondanze né sprechi, il design anonimo o incognito degli oggetti di uso comune, sono indispensabili, funzionano, esibiscono caratteri di piacevolezza fisica o formale …": see Polano, *Achille Castiglioni tutte le opere 1938–2000*, Milan, 2001, p. 10.

184 "anche questi fenomeni debbono far parte di un panorama del design italiano, altrimenti non si capisce né cosa sia l'Italia, né cosa sia il design": Eco, *Italian Re Evolution. Design*

> [what is] anonymous is not banal (…) [but] susceptible to bad taste, precisely because it has no great artistic pretensions, exhibits no stylistic acrobatics, and makes no compromise with styling and marketing; its sole aim is to fulfil its function.[185]

Lawmakers and judges could learn from these suggestions. The prominence placed on the creative and individual aspects of design showed little interest in the past in machinery and anonymous objects. The Modernist Movement,[186] in particular, with its masters Le Corbusier, Mies van der Rohe, Lloyd Wright, Gropius, and Aalto (see §1.2 above), ended up placing more emphasis on designers than on products and the processes for their production. Contemporary design, by contrast, places the emphasis on the representative value of all these objects and artefacts as a means of accessing the intelligibility of the world, its coherence, and stability.[187] Fundamentally, it shares the same key assumption on which ethnography is based, which is that all material goods are endowed with social significance, without which it would not be possible to go beyond a mere "descriptive archaeology."[188]

3.3.2 *Features Solely Dictated by Technical Function*

As the *Montreal Design Declaration* testifies (see §3.3 above), design encompasses a very broad ecosystem. Legal definitions of industrial design are similarly broad in their wording and non-exhaustive in intent. Ultimately, the cornerstone of design protection laws around the world is "appearance", as given by the "features" of a product or its parts, both "aesthetic" and "technical."

---

in Italian Society in the Eighties, catalogue La Jolla Museum of Contemporary Art, 1982, at p. 128; Frateili, *Il disegno industriale italiano: 1928–1981 (Quasi una storia ideologica): lezioni tenute nel corso di disegno industriale presso la facoltà di Architettura del Politecnico di Torino a.a. 1981–1982*, Turin, 1983. See also Heskett, *Toothpicks & Logos. Design in everyday Life*, Oxford, 2002, pp. 12 ff.

185 "l'anonimo non è banale (…) intaccabile dal cattivo gusto proprio perché senza grandi pretese artistiche, senza l'esibizione di acrobazie stilistiche, senza compromessi con lo styling e il marketing, ma con l'unica meta di corrispondere alla propria funzione," Dorfles, "L'anonimo non è banale," *Architettura arte design moda*, 2003, p. 92.

186 For more in-depth discussions of the legacy of Modernism in twentieth century design theory and practice, see Fuller, "The Search for a Postmodern Aesthetic," in Thackara (ed.), *Design after Modernism: Beyond the Object*, London, 1988; Burkhardt, "Design and Avant-Postmodernism," in *Ibid.*

187 Douglas, Isherwood, *The World of Things: Objects, Values, Consumption*, New York, 1979.

188 According to Eches, op. cit., the ethnology of industrialized societies has flourished in English-speaking countries and France.

The distinction between aesthetic and technical features in design studies alludes to the difference between technical products that require the intervention of a designer to enable the final user to interact with the object, and products which establish a direct functional relationship (sitting, eating, wearing) with the end-user, which is, at the same time, perceptual, aesthetic, symbolic, and communicative. The design of machinery is an example of the former; the design of consumer goods such as furniture, knick-knacks, clothing, fashion accessories, and textiles an example of the latter.[189] With the advent of the Internet of Things and AI-driven design, however, such a distinction will soon be a thing of the past. Whereas the distinction grounded the relationship between the technical features of products and their form, today the relevant relationship is between analogue and digital mechanisms and their containers. The visual appeal of a design work purposefully combines form and function, becoming a marketing tool which affects the purchasing decisions of consumers, and has a strong impact on the competitiveness and commercial success of a product. Appealing designs thus shape the reputation of a company. In this context, "appearance" as "form" is the determining factor for the "identity" of an object at two levels: in terms of the typology to which the object belongs, and in terms of the individuality of the single product belonging to that typological family.[190] Thus both the quality and functionality of products are essential characteristics of certain typologies of design works as much as of the individual product's overall appearance.

In law, features dictated solely by technical function are excluded from design protection.[191] The test for determining whether or not a feature of the appearance of a product is solely dictated by technical function remains an issue of debate.[192] Three different possible tests have been developed and are offered in different jurisdictions: 1) the multiplicity of forms test (mainly applied

189 Newell, "Archeologia industriale e scienze umane," in Castellano (ed.), *La macchina arrugginita. Materiali per un'archeologia dell'industria*, Milan, 1982, p. 18.

190 Chiapponi, "Le forme degli oggetti," *Il Verri*, 2005, p. 17.

191 As well as features which must fit another product, and which are contrary to public policy or to accepted principles of morality (at least in the EU). See Article 8, Regulation (EU) 6/2002, and Article 7(1), Directive 98/71/EC, op. cit.

192 Stone, op. cit., p. 74; Musker, *The Overlap between Patent and Design Protection* op. cit., pp. 45, 51: "Functional appearance itself may for some users be no more than a fashion statement." See Di Roma, "La complessità tra funzione ed esperienza d'uso del prodotto," DIID (*Disegno Industriale Industrial Design*), 64/2018, pp. 142–148; Langella, "Design e scienza: tracce di una nuova modernità," DIID (*Disegno Industriale Industrial Design*), 64/2018, pp. 156–163.

in the OHIM[193] invalidity decision, and by German, French, Spanish, and English courts), where "if the designer can opt at least for another configuration then the design feature is not solely dictated by technical function"; 2) the aesthetic consideration test (applied by the Board of Appeal and courts in the Netherlands), where "if the feature achieves an aesthetic effect which does not necessarily help to solve a technical problem, then the design is not solely dictated by technical function"; and 3) the designer freedom test (applied by the OHIM invalidity division), where "if the designer has some freedom in the development of the feature appearance, then the feature is not solely dictated by technical function." In all three tests, however, what a "technical function" is remains uncertain. On a plain reading of the legal texts, the decision appears to turn on a binary distinction between technical and non-technical functions, whereby a feature is either solely dictated by technical function, or it is not.[194] The reality, however, is more complex. A contemporary design artefact is always made up of an internal functioning part – a mechanical, analogue, electronic, or digital intestine – and an external aesthetic part. The role of the designer is to resolve the dualism in a synthetic manner, to design an object perceived as a coherent unity. Also a piece of furniture, on the other hand, is a unitary product: "*Here, too, the non-separation of function and ornament has, in my view, led to very interesting results, even though the product is aimed at an elite market* (…)."[195] Thus, the binary choice between technical/non-technical functionality for industrial design protection is problematic, and any proposal to determine the percentage of "functional choices" and of "aesthetic elements" in every object,[196] when setting the scope of protection, will be very difficult to achieve.

193 The Office for Harmonisation of the Internal Market (trademark and designs), since 2016 has been renamed the European Union Intellectual Property Office (EUIPO). Its remit extends beyond registration to cover the harmonisation of registration practices for trademarks and designs. The OHIM invalidity decision on registered Community design helped to clarify the meaning of wording "features of appearance of a product which are solely dictated by its technical function," where what counts is the designer's motivation for the purpose of enhancing the product's visual appearance, no matter if there are alternative features available: see OHIM, decision of the 3rd Board of Appeal, 22.10.2009, in Case R 690/2007-3, Lindner v Franssons (confirmed in the decision of the Invalidity Division of 12.06.2013, in Case ICD 8538 Samsung v Apple).

194 Stone, op. cit., p. 75.

195 Bellini, "II designer e l'industria," in Camera del lavoro territoriale di Milano-CGIL, *Per chi lavora il designer. Il progetto, il prodotto, l'immagine e il mercato*, proceedings of the congress in Milan, January 20–21, Rome, 1983, pp. 21–26, p. 25.

196 Ritscher, Landolt, "Shift of Paradigm for Copyright Protection of the Design of Products," *GRUR* 2/2019, pp. 125–135, at p. 134.

"Technology" is an issue that deserves more careful attention in Design Studies, as historians and ethnologists who study technology have often stressed. Too many scholars treat technology like a "black box,"[197] as little more than a schematic abstraction of the functional parts of a product. As Mark Brutton has suggested, mechanical engineering has become a great manufacturer of stereotypes – so if we want to understand technology, perhaps it is better to ask historians and ethnologists, and not just technologists.[198] From their broader point of view, technology can be seen as a means of production, in the shape of inventors, innovators, and entrepreneurs, as well as in archetypal machines (the mechanical loom, the steam engine, the locomotive). Among the eminent historians who have turned their attention to the history of technology, Hervin Schaefer suggested that in the XIX century, functional form characterized both scientific and technical artefacts (means of transportation, sports equipment, musical instruments, machine tools, etc.) as well as anonymous, common objects. Clive Dilnot stresses the contributions made by Walter Dexel[199] and Herbert Lindinger[200] in underscoring how functionality is the point of equilibrium between technology and creativity.[201] As technology permeates the whole of human activity, the analysis of objects and artefacts has made it possible to treat the system as a "circular chain" joining design, manufacturing, distribution, and consumption, built on use, perception, social organization, and interaction with other artefacts and objects of design.

Technology brings with it the idea of artefacts and objects as "interfaces" between an internal environment (the materials of which they are made and the processes to make them) and an external environment (the conditions in which they operate).[202] Technology and related industrial processes contribute to fixing a product within a typology of objects, which remain crystallized in a precise form until the next challenge comes along, determined by "contingent circumstances" such as economic conditions, intellectual movements, politics, and lobbying, as well as the "interpretation" of other objects and artefacts.[203] One example of an object which did not change for a hundred years is the

197 Riccini, *History from Things* op. cit., p. 50.

198 Beckman, Marx, d'Espinas, Reuleaux, Mumford and Gill, Usher and Bloch, Mauss and Leroi-Gourhan: Riccini, *History from Things* op. cit.

199 Art historian and graphic designer linked to the Bauhaus, see Dexel, *Deutsches Handwerksgut, eine Kultur-und-Formgeschichte des Hausgerats*, Berlin, 1939.

200 Professor of Design at HfG Ulm from 1962 to 1968. See a series of articles published in *Form* 1963–64.

201 See Kouwenhoven, *Made in America*, New York, 1948, which investigates the contribution made by popular creativity in contrast to the cultured tradition in the United States.

202 Simon, *The Sciences of the Artificial*, Cambridge MA, 1981.

203 Giedion, *Evolution of Useful Things* op. cit., p. 9.

sewing machine, which provides an excellent illustration of what can also be explained by the path dependence theory. A technological object which has struggled to find its formal and functional balance will, once that equilibrium has been achieved, put up greater resistance to change, even in the face of further technological innovations.

> By the time Barthelemy Thimmonier patented his sewing machine on April 13, 1830, attempts to achieve the goal of mechanical sewing had been under way for many years. Tackled by British and German inventors ever since the middle of the eighteenth century, no satisfactory solution to the problem had been achieved due to an error of approach that was as banal as it has been common in the history of technological inventions. Thimmonier's predecessors had not been able to divorce the idea of mechanical sewing from that of sewing by hand, whose methods and techniques they strove to reproduce. Thimmonier, the son of a tailor, had managed to overcome this impasse by resorting to another analogy, basing his insight on analysis of the chain stitch produced in crochet work, which made it possible, among other things, to use a continuous thread. Around the same time, a series of partial inventions and even brilliant attempts followed one another in both America and Europe, though without overcoming the stumbling blocks of continuous operation and industrial applicability on a large scale. It is customary to identify the period between 1830 and 1845 as the one in which a series of results were achieved in the field of mechanical sewing (…) Ever since its birth, the sewing machine had had to cope with the problem of the transmission of movement to the needle. As early as 1852, Singer had introduced the pedal and belt drive which, with respect to the previous hand- wheel, offered the enormous advantage of leaving both of the operator's hands free. A second factor was the tension of the thread, and the precision and regularity of the stitches. As can easily be imagined, the introduction of electricity brought considerable advantages to both of these key elements of the mechanism. The first electric sewing machine was the 15K model brought out by Singer in 1889. Notwithstanding the application of electricity, the older machine made of black cast-iron resisted any change up until the 1940s, when the introduction of materials such as light alloys and plastics and of new functions …[204]

---

204 Riccini, *History from Things* op. cit., p. 63.

In the second half of the XX century, the so-called miniaturization of objects brought about by electronic technology in the development of household artefacts and, finally, by research and experimentation into large-scale industrial machinery changed industrial processes and modes of productions. A series of goods entered the household realm, such as the refrigerator (which was first developed for the transportation of perishable foodstuffs and only later, and very slowly, applied to the domestic sphere), the air conditioner (developed by an American doctor who, in 1844, invented a device for cooling air in the hospital where he worked), and the mechanical washing machine (initially designed for hospitals, firms, and restaurants).[205] Today, robots and artificial intelligence have expanded beyond the factory floor to enter the domestic hearth. The consumer goods market has undoubtedly been the lever steering mass production – with respect to design, it has been the driving factor for bridging industry and business. But now a new world of artefacts is on our doorsteps, as the big data market becomes the lever steering computational design and open design, as the projects *What3Words* and *Zipline*, winners of the INDEX: Design to Improve Life Award 2017[206] show.[207]

3.3.3 *"Appearance": Canons and Styles*

In Design Studies, the "morphological overview" was an approach used to classify objects and artefacts on the basis of predetermined stylistic features, where the set of features that characterizes a "style" is treated as an element representative of a "canon." The approach was championed by Modernists, such as Siegfried Giedion.[208] However, the elusive character of style has long fuelled considerable debate among art historians. Designers similarly have felt compelled to avoid the inherent ambiguity of style in theory and practice.[209] Such a view of style reflected the Modernist division between form and function in

205 Anderson, *Refrigeration in America. A History of New Technology and its impacts*, Princeton, 1953; Cooper, *The Invention of the Sewing Machine*, Washington, 1968; Hounshell, *From the American System to Mass Production 1800–1930*, Baltimore and London, 1984; Lupton, *Mechanical Brides. Women and Machines from Home to Office*, New York, 1993. Bosoni, "La macchina per cucire," in Gregotti, *Il disegno del prodotto industriale*, op. cit., pp. 306–7.

206 Available at http://www.challenge.designtoimprovelife.dk/ (accessed 20.8.2019).

207 Kadushin, *Open Design Manifesto*, available at https://www.ronen-kadushin.com/open-design-manifesto (accessed 8.8.2019); van Abel at al., *Open Design now: Why Design Cannot Remain Exclusive*, Amsterdam, 2011; Lessig, *Free Culture*, New York, 2014; Brown, *Change by Design. How Design Thinking Transforms Organizations and inspires Innovation*, New York, 2009; Papanek, *Design for a real world: Human Ecology and Social Change*, New York, 1971.

208 Baudrillard, *Le systeme des objets*, Paris, 1972, p. 6.

209 Lorenz, *The Design Dimension: The New Competitive Weapon for Product Strategy & Global Marketing*, Oxford, 1990.

XX century design. When reflecting on the cursory treatment of style in product design, in particular, it should be acknowledged that Design Studies and practices have sought to avoid being reduced to "*the wrapping of products in nice shapes and pretty colours*," as one cynical designer describes the traditional role of designers as stylists in companies.[210] Given the Modernist ideal that there can be only one rational (and optimal) solution to any design problem, decisions regarding decorative elements were seen as redundant,[211] and this typically positioned the concept of style outside the scope of design,[212] with stylistic decisions apparent from the lavish decoration of a product's technical or utilitarian function. But the so-called "style" of product design was quickly recognized as an important subject, especially in the USA and in relation to the market's reception of new consumer goods.[213] Consumer psychology literature recognized that abstract stylistic attributes were seen as a way of comparing products that share few concrete attributes, such as products from different product categories.[214] Indeed, consumers associate the style of a product with a designer, and the latter is associated with a company brand. Eliot Noyes's typewriter designs have become associated with the style of IBM, and Jacob Jensen's stereo equipment with that of Bang & Olufsen. Even the Ulm school, still considered the most important European school of design since the Bauhaus, has an "Ulm style" embodied in the familiar Krups and Braun product lines – pearl grey with matte finish, adjustable legs, the reduction of ornamentation to a fundamental and pure geometry of form[215] – which defines the look of contemporary electronic instruments, tools, and transportation and communication systems. Ernesto Gismondi established Artemide in 1960 with

210 A reductionist view is still deep-rooted in Italian management literature: see the traditional view against new instances discussed in Sabbadin, *L'innovazione tra marketing e arte*, Turin, 2018, pp. 3 ff.

211 True functional solutions were identical with true formal solutions: each and every function was meant to have one and only one solution proper to it, and, consequently, only one proper form. Michl, "Form Follows What? The Modernist Notion of Function as a Carte Blanche," *Magazine of the Faculty of Architecture & Town Planning*, 1995, pp. 25 ff. An edited electronic version is available at http://janmichl.com/eng.fff.hai.html (accessed 10.7.2009).

212 Pulos, *American Design Ethic: A History of Industrial Design to 1940*, Cambridge MA, 1986, pp. 402–403.

213 Holme, *Industrial Design and the Future*, London, 1934, pp. 18–21; Lippincott, *Design for Business*, Chicago, 1947, pp. 51–58; van Dyren, *Industrial Design: A Practical Guide to Product Design and Development*, 2nd ed., New York, 1954, pp. 15–16; Earl, *The Look of Things*, Detroit, 1955.

214 Johnson, "Consumer Choice Strategies for Comparing Non Comparable Alternatives," *Journal of Consumer Research*, 1984, pp. 741–753.

215 Lindinger, Britt, *Ulm Design: The Morality of Objects*, Cambridge MA, 1991.

its own design canon; Kartell, established in 1949 by Giulio Castelli, Michele Pistorio, and Eros Rastelli (Castelli being a pupil of the 1963 Nobel-prize laureate Giulio Natta, who invented polypropylene) produced its first product, a ski carrier, in 1950 with Pirelli, and continues to design stylish household objects with the contribution of leading designers such as Marco Zanuso, Richard Sapper, Joe Colombo, and Philippe Starck. Designers create brand recognition by replicating design attributes in new products.

All in all, the current discourse on brand styles is confronted with the problem of where and how to search for tangible evidence of styles in products. The skills associated with producing a style for a brand have long been recognized in the management literature as a key contribution of design,[216] even if that same literature has traditionally reduced design to a mere "marketing tool." For many years, industrial design was viewed as serving a mere cosmetic function and scholars of the history of industrial design (apart from a few emblematic cases) devoted too little attention to economic and industrial factors. That attitude changed when the model of organization based on mass production processes and its efficiency gave way to a business model that concentrates more on goods & services and digital markets.[217] Likewise, in the management literature, brand style has been recognized in more recent times as an important sign for identifying and attributing allusive meanings to a brand, including symbolic (or brand iconic) meanings.[218] Nowadays, the concept of style is connected to market differentiation through recurrent design features in products, set within a larger goal of positioning a brand in the global market.[219] Such studies have had the merit of highlighting the contribution of enterprises to the development of the design profession.[220] The traditional reluctance of business to see the overall identity of its products as a decisive part of its own "brand identity" has ceased. Many enterprises identify their products, right from the start, as a resource even in terms of memory, which is indissolubly bound up with the way that the business has developed. Looking

---

216 Nash, "Product Development," *Journal of Marketing*, 1937, pp. 257 ff; Menge, "Style Change Costs as a Market Weapon," *Quarterly Journal of Economics*, 1962, pp. 632 ff; Kotier, Rath, "Design A Powerful but Neglected Strategic Tool," *Journal of Business Strategy*, 1984, pp. 18 ff.

217 See Freeman, *Behemoth* op. cit., for an insightful account of how Modernist ideas spread from Lancashire to Detroit, from Wolsfsburg to Nova Huta and to Shenzen through the history of the so-called Behemoth, the giant factory and the people whose lives it shaped.

218 Holt, *How Brands Become Icons: The Principles of Cultural Branding*, Boston, 2004, pp. 155–87.

219 See, among others, Kotler, *Marketing Management*, London, 2000, p. 312.

220 Riccini, *History from Things* op. cit., p. 45; cf Bassi, *Progettare gli oggetti* op. cit.

back in time, Wedgwood for porcelain, or Richard-Ginori for pottery and tableware, showed their foresight in grasping that the manufacturing of objects was part of a broader system, encompassing the phases of research, design, prototyping, production, marketing, and sales. Bahlsen and Siemens also provide good examples of the inclusion of designers in their business; other examples are certainly the well-known case of Peter Behrens for AEG, Philippe Stark for Alessi, or Ford and General Motors in the American automobile industry.[221] In addition to these illustrious precursors, numerous other companies have made industrial design a central element in their approach to product planning and to branding. Just to stay in Italy, one of the most widely studied and celebrated cases even at the international level[222] is Olivetti (in Piedmont), working in collaboration with BBPR, Marcello Nizzoli, Ettore Sottsass, Mario Bellini, and Michele De Lucchi; another is Piaggio (Tuscany), working in collaboration with Corradino D'Ascanio. Other leading examples include Cassina (in Lombardy) for furniture, Flos (in Tirol Alto Adige) for lighting design, Alessi (in Piedmont) for homewares and kitchen utensils, with many fruitful design collaborations to its credit; FILA (Fabbrica Italiana Lapis e Affini), which created the "tratto pen", a pen with a synthetic tip and an ergonomic cap, in collaboration with Design Group Italia,[223] and even smaller companies such as Brionvega (in Milan), which produced iconic sound and television equipment.[224] Brand styles can help identify a product's origin and make sense of its place in the world.[225] In such sense-making, the attribution of a product to a brand style is based on perceived similarities and differences between products within the brand and between different brands.[226] Also in this respect, the regulatory framework needs to be updated and developed to reflect new insights provided by Design Studies.

---

221 Gartman, "Harley Earl and the Art and Color Section: The Birth of Styling at General Motors," *Design Issues*, 1994, pp. 3–26.

222 See Settis, *Fordismi. Storia politica della produzione di massa*, Bologna, 2016; Silmo, *M.D.C. Macchine da calcolo meccaniche, Olivetti e non solo. Natale Capellaro, Il genio della meccanica*, Ivrea, 2008.

223 Sabbadin, op. cit., p. 11.

224 See Bellini, op. cit., pp. 25–26.

225 Holt, *How Brands Become Icons: The Principles of Cultural Branding*, Cambridge MA, 2004, pp. 155–88. The relevance of such misconceptions by design experts and consumers in attaching meaning to products has been discussed by Richardson, "The Death of the Designer," *Design Issues* 1993, pp. 34–43; Lloyd, Snelders, "What Was Philippe Starck Thinking Of?" *Design Studies*, 2003, pp. 237–253.

226 This is similar to style attribution in art; see Gombrich, *Gombrich on the Renaissance*, 4th ed., vol. 1, New York, 1985, p. 9.

4 *Parameters to Define Protectable Works*

4.1 The Courts Parameter: "Original Work" as "Author's Own Intellectual Creation"

In *Flos v. Semeraro*, 2011,[227] the European Court of Justice was asked to determine whether the Italian moratorium on copyright protection for industrial design was compatible with Articles 17 and 19 of Directive 98/71/EC of 13 October 1998 on the legal protection of designs. In ruling against such compatibility, the Court also hinted at another aspect concerning the originality requirement, an allusion which attracted growing attention, possibly more than what it might have deserved.[228]

At paragraph 34, the Court stated:

> (34) However, it is conceivable that copyright protection for works which may be unregistered designs could arise under other directives concerning copyright, in particular Directive 2001/29, if the conditions for that directive's application are met, a matter which falls to be determined by the national court.[229]

According to some commentators, there are two possible interpretations of paragraph 34 of *Flos*: either it applies only to unregistered designs other than unregistered Community designs, or it overturns the explicit allocation of powers to Member States set forth in Article 96(2) of the Community Design Regulation. Both conclusions, however, are troublesome.[230] Given that within the internal market, any unregistered design is virtually always also an unregistered Community design, it should be concluded that *Flos*'s harmonizing effects apply to the Community Design Regulation even though the latter is not mentioned anywhere in the *Flos* decision, nor in the nationally referred questions. More importantly, the second proposed interpretation disregards what seems to be the plainer meaning of the Community Design Regulation, which reserves specific powers to Member States. It also seems to contradict the plain meaning of both the Design Directive and the Community Design Regulation, since

227 C-168/09, *Flos Spa v. Semeraro Casa e Famiglia Spa* [2011] E.C.R. I-00181.

228 See Margoni, *The Harmonisation* op. cit.; Derclaye, "The Court of Justice Copyright Case Law: Quo Vadis?" *European Intellectual Property Review* 2014, pp. 716–723; Koenraad, "Dutch Supreme Court Tripp Trapp Children's Chair Cases," *Journal of Intellectual Property Law and Practice*, 2013, pp. 909–912; see also Griffiths, "Dematerialization, pragmatism and the European Copyright Revolution," *Oxford Journal of Legal Studies* 2013, pp. 769–790.

229 C-168/09 *Flos* cit.

230 According to Bently, op. cit., *Flos* was wrongly decided because it ignored the legislative history of the Community Design Regulation and the Information Society Directive. See Ritscher, Landolt, op. cit., at 131; and Margoni, *The Harmonisation* op. cit.

they were drafted on the basis of very similar considerations and definitions.[231] Accordingly, to avoid such conflict, it is reasonable to assume that the cited paragraph of the *Flos* decision has the effect (almost certainly intended) of harmonizing "originality" in any design (registered or not) and mandating a "perfect cumulation" between design and copyright protection; furthermore, if unregistered design works are protected under the so called *Infosoc Directive* (Directive 2001/29), which has come to require the fully harmonized standard of the "author's own intellectual creation,"[232] it follows that there is no room for a different originality threshold for unregistered designs. A different conclusion cannot be accepted even if the Design Directive applies only to registered designs (and not to unregistered ones). It would be very problematic if courts in the European Union were to apply different standards of "originality" to registered and unregistered design objects and artefacts.[233] For instance, if an object of design were not initially registered as a design work, but registered later on, would its protected status vary over time as a result of the 12-months grace period for the unregistered Community design right? The answer in countries implementing "partial cumulation" would be that a non-registered design can be protected by copyright if it satisfies the European legal standard of "originality" (the author's own intellectual creation); after registration, the same design would most likely not qualify for copyright protection any longer, since the usually higher national standard (such as "artistic value") needs to be met.[234] The partial cumulation between design protection and copyright in countries requiring a different, usually higher, level of originality for industrial design is, indeed, no more acceptable.[235]

The matters referred by the Italian court in *Flos v. Semeraro*, however, did not ask for the standard of originality in design rights to be addressed; they concerned the moratorium on the protection of industrial design that the Italian government insistently tried to maintain, in order to avoid the cumulation of design and copyright protection. Italian law, in fact, had introduced

231 Margoni, "Not for Designers: On the Inadequacies of EU Design Law and How to Fix It", *JIPITEC*, 2013, pp. 225 ff; cf also Bently, op. cit., 2012; Griffiths, op. cit., 2013; Koenraad, op. cit., 2013; Derclaye, op. cit., 2014.

232 C-5/08, *Infopaq International A/S v. Danske Dagblades Forening* [2009] E.C.R. I-06569. In *Infopaq*, the Court had to decide whether the storing and subsequent printing out of a 11-word text extract from an article in a daily newspaper could be regarded as an act of reproduction in the meaning of Article 2 of the InfoSoc Directive.

233 Opinion of the European Copyright Society in relation to the case *Cofemel v G-Star*, C-683/17, available at https://europeancopyrightsocietydotorg.files.wordpress.com/2018/11/ecs-opinion-cofemel_final_signed.pdf (accessed 7.8.2019).

234 The paradoxical interpretative results of *Flos* decision can be a "message" of the Court of Justice to those Member States that are still taking advantage of the possibility offered by article 17 Design Directive and article 96 Community Design Regulation.

235 Margoni, *The Harmonisation* op. cit.

questionable transitional measures oscillating between a ten-year moratorium, up to the last solution introduced by Law 14/2012 of 24 February 2012, which extended the deadline for the moratorium to thirteen years, extending the non-availability of copyright to those who manufactured and sold industrial design until 19 April 2014;[236] if it had not, all those Italian enterprises that had been legitimately manufacturing design classics for years, would have fallen foul of anti-counterfeiting law.[237] It was an issue of balancing the opposing interests of big corporations, that claimed exclusive rights to iconic design works, and those of smaller manufacturers and medium-sized companies, that had been producing and marketing copies of those classics for years, with the aim of safeguarding those companies which (before amendments to Italian law resulting from the transposition of the Design Directive) had invested significant human and financial capital in the production and marketing of design works by then in the public domain, and whose activity would have become unlawful. In view of such considerations, another possible interpretation of the *Flos* decision is that only registered designs that had entered the public domain, and not those in the public domain because they were never registered, should be afforded copyright protection. While it could be argued that this latter interpretation sounds reasonable, there is yet another aspect that may cause discomfort, concerning a question of policy that ought to be determined by EU lawmakers and which involves important considerations regarding the goals of the registered and unregistered design system (in defining property rights and giving notice) and the impact of those goals on automatic, lengthy, copyright protection.[238] At the time the EU design legislation was discussed, it was recognized that different Member States treated the copyright/design (registered, but in some countries such as the UK, for instance, also unregistered) interface very differently, ranging from those which accepted full cumulation to those which sought to keep the application of the two regimes firmly separate. European lawmakers chose to deal with this issue by deciding that the registration of a utilitarian object as a design should not *ipso facto* render a work ineligible for copyright. The EU lawmakers specifically left other matters, such as the threshold of protection, up to Member States,[239] which, in the end, turned to the European Court of Justice for instruction on how to deal with the issue. Now that the "originality" test for copyright protection has been harmonized at the EU level, it is time for the issue to be settled (see Part 2).

---

236 Art. 239 *Codice della proprietà industriale* (Italian Industrial Property Code).

237 C-168/09, Flos s.p.a. c. Semeraro Casa e Famiglia s.p.a., *Diritto industriale* 3/2011, p. 252, commentary by Fittante.

238 European Copyright Society, op. cit.

239 European Copyright Society, op. cit.

Ultimately, the opportunity to develop an autonomous concept of protectable work was left to Directive 2001/29/EC of the European Parliament and of the Council of 22 May 2001 on the harmonization of certain aspects of copyright and related rights in the information society, otherwise known as the InfoSoc Directive.[240]

Article 2 (a) and Article 9 of the InfoSoc Directive provides what potentially could be the statutory basis for a general EU-wide concept of a "work":

> Article 2 Reproduction right. Member States shall provide for the exclusive right to authorise or prohibit direct or indirect, temporary or permanent reproduction by any means and in any form, in whole or in part:
>
> (a) for authors, of their works; [...]
>
> Article 9 Continued application of other legal provisions. This Directive shall be without prejudice to provisions concerning in particular patent rights, trade marks, design rights, utility models, topographies of semi-conductor products, type faces, conditional access, access to cable of broadcasting services, protection of national treasures, legal deposit requirements, laws on restrictive practices and unfair competition, trade secrets, security, confidentiality, data protection and privacy, access to public documents, the law of contract.

The European Court of Justice addressed the matter in the *Levola* case[241] of 2018. It referred to the interpretation provided by the InfoSoc Directive with regard to the question of copyright protection for the taste of a cheese.

> (33) In that regard Articles 2 to 4 of Directive 2001/29 state that the Member States are to provide for a set of exclusive rights relating, in the case of authors, to their 'works', while Article 5 sets out a series of exceptions and limitations to those rights. The directive makes no express reference to the laws of the Member States for the purpose of determining the meaning and scope of the concept of a 'work'. Accordingly, in view of the need for a uniform application of EU law and the principle of equality, that concept must normally be given an autonomous and uniform interpretation throughout the European Union.[242]

240 OJ 2001 L 167, p. 10.

241 C-210/17, *Levola Hengelo BV/Smilde Foods BV* [2018], EU:C:2018:899.

242 C-210/17, *Levola*, op. cit., paragraph 33.

In the *Levola* decision, the Court explicitly stated that in view of the need for a uniform application of EU law and the principle of equality, the concept of "work" must be given an autonomous and uniform interpretation throughout the European Union. However, since the existence of a work was ultimately denied with regard to the taste of a cheese because of its unidentifiable nature,[243] the Court of Justice did not rule on the qualitative requirements for copyright protection in that case (the taste of a food), passing up the opportunity to further strengthen its interpretation of the InfoSoc Directive as a statutory basis for a general EU-wide concept of protectable work.[244]

In its most recent judgment in *Sociedade de Vestuário (Cofemel) SA v G-Star Raw CV*, better known as the *Cofemel* case of 2019,[245] the Court of Justice returned to the matter of protectable work. In its request for a preliminary ruling, the Supreme Court of Portugal referred to the European Court of Justice the question of whether the InfoSoc Directive precludes the strict criteria which, under Portuguese Copyright Law, affords copyright protection only to "*original works of applied art and works of industrial designs which, in addition to their utilitarian purpose, create their own visual and distinctive effect from an aesthetic point of view, in the light of a particularly rigorous assessment of their artistic character,*" taking into account the dominant views in cultural and institutional circles. In other words, the question was whether Portuguese law could grant copyright protection to designs subject to requirements other than originality, e.g. to "artistic creations" imbued with a high level of artistic value (Article 2(3) and (5) of the Berne Convention comes to mind, see §§ 1.1 and 3.1 above).[246] Thus the essence of the question was which criteria a "work" must generally satisfy in order to enjoy cumulative (design and copyright) protection. The answer apparently depends on the notion of "work," but in substance it depends on the notion of "author," because the work must be the author's personal intellectual creation and must be expressed in a manner

243 According to Schulze, the European Court of Justice should have left it open to national law to decide how the individuality of a taste is to be determined; see Schulze, ZUM 2/ 2019, 65.

244 See the Opinion of Advocate General Maciej Szpunar of 2 May 2019 in the preliminary ruling C-683/17, *Sociedade de Vestuário SA v G-Star Raw CV*, [2019], ECLI:EU:C:2019:363.

245 C-683/17, *Cofemel Sociedade de Vestuário SA v G-Star Raw CV* [2019] ECLI:EU:C:2019:721.

246 The Portuguese Copyright Code contains a provision which affords copyright protection to works of applied art, industrial designs, and works of design in the light of a particularly rigorous assessment of their "artistic character." According to the dominant views in cultural and institutional circles, a work of applied art may qualify as an "artistic creation" (see Article 2(1)(i) *Código de Direitos de Autor e Direitos Conexos*), which is in sharp contrast with Article 2(a) of Directive 2001/29.

which makes it identifiable with sufficient precision and objectivity, in order to be protected (see Part 2 of this essay).

Indeed, according to the *Cofemel* decision, the notion of "work" in Article 2(a) of the InfoSoc Directive presupposes the fulfilment of two cumulative requirements (§§ 29, 30, 31, 32 of the judgment): a) the existence of an original object, in the sense that the object is the "intellectual creation of its author"; b) the subject matter must be expressed in a manner which makes it identifiable with sufficient precision and objectivity, even though that "expression by its author is not necessarily in permanent form". Thus, it is an autonomous, European, notion which requires uniform interpretation across the EU. The Court of Justice went on to declare that, in line with the Berne Convention which does not preclude cumulative protection, different objects might fall equally under the InfoSoc Directive, the Design Directive, and the Community Design Regulation, which pursue fundamentally different goals. In the wake of the *Cofemel* decision, then, Member States cannot maintain their traditional standards: perfect harmonization and full cumulation between design and copyright protections is required, at the expense of Member State discretion, for the sake of an efficient EU market. As far as designs are concerned, the judgment brings to its natural consequences the evolutionary reading signalled by earlier case law: copyright protection simply arises upon

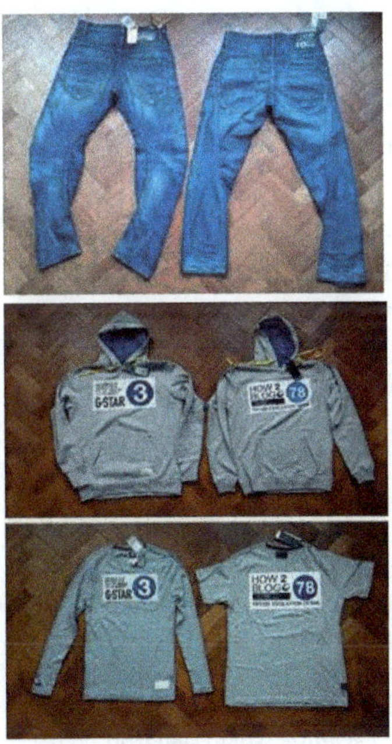

FIGURES 12–13
Cofemel and G-Star jeans. Images available at https://www.lexology.com/library/detail.aspx?g=3f654254-3b75-4a2d-a81d-e263aba1e701
"high fashion garments are both works of art and clothes, if not even more works of art than clothes" (…) "It is therefore not justified to exclude the objects of the applied arts from the protection offered by copyright for the sole reason that they have (even) functional character. Furthermore, other categories of works for which copyright protection is not in doubt may also have utilitarian functions, while remaining original intellectual creations. This is the case of some literary, photographic or even musical works."
SEE THE OPINION OF ADVOCATE GENERAL MACIEJ SZPUNAR OF 2 MAY 2019 AVAILABLE ONLINE

fulfilment of the "originality" test, understood as "the authors' own intellective creation" standard. Nothing further is required. However, according to the European Court of Justice, a design is protectable by copyright only when it is an own intellectual creation based on "free and creative choices" by the designer, and when it can be "identified with precision and objectivity" and the "purpose" of protection justifies the extended duration of protection. In this respect, the fact that jeans and T-shirt designs generate an "aesthetic effect," as G-Star highlighted, makes it impossible to determine whether the design is an intellectual creation that reflects the freedom of choice and the personality of its author. Thus, according to the originality test a design needs to satisfy in order to be qualify for copyright protection was not fulfilled in the *Cofemel* case.

4.2 The Parameters Available from Design Practice: "Original Work" as "Designer's Provenance of the Project"

As outlined above, designers combine artistic ability and problem-solving skills. Such richness is synonymous with the complexity that designers are required to manage during the design process, from the visualization of an idea to prototype development, through to the production of the final good.[247] At the same time, their works deserve a protection which cannot hamper fair competition, encouraging innovation rather than imitation. Designers' works[248] are inseparable from processes and are nowadays products of new technology.[249] Their projects, that is, are an elaboration prior to execution, and so are always part of a process. Process standardization is actually what lies at the foundations of any work of design, as represented in the following "project roadmap" (Figure 14).

The elaboration of a work into a multilayered process is significant for every designer, in particular within new fields of design, from circular design (Figure 15) to design for ageing and design for sustainability.[250]

247 Lutters et al., "Tools and Techniques for Product Design," *CIRP Annals – Manufacturing Technology*, 2014, pp. 607–630.

248 Having in mind product design mainly. The notion of "Product Design" has been discussed and debated for a long time. It seems to have an overlapping meaning, especially with Engineering Design, which underlines the variability of interpretation and the cross-disciplinary inclination of the process. Many definitions of "Product Design" have been proffered, but its unclear shape will probably remain, due to the users of the open-ended concept and the nature of design as an open discipline. Cross, op. cit.

249 Ex multis, Maldonado, op. cit.; see also Riccini, "Le cose che ci fanno intelligenti," in Riccini (ed.), *Imparare dalle cose. La cultura materiale nei musei*, Milan, 2003, pp. 26 ff.

250 See Badalucco, Casarotto, Costa, *Packaging Design*, Milan, 2017.

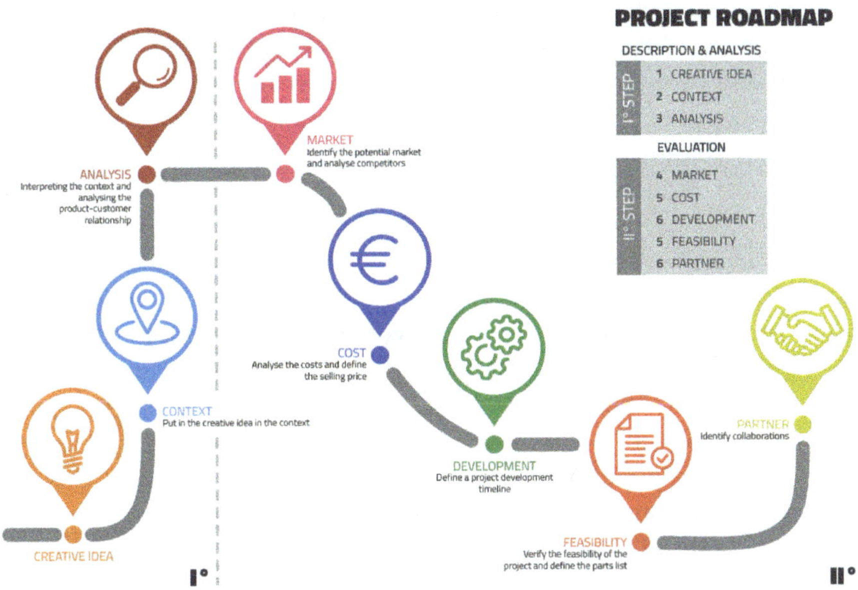

FIGURE 14 Project roadmap by Martina Frausin, Ph.D. Student in Design Sciences at Università Iuav di Venezia.
TUTOR: BARBARA PASA

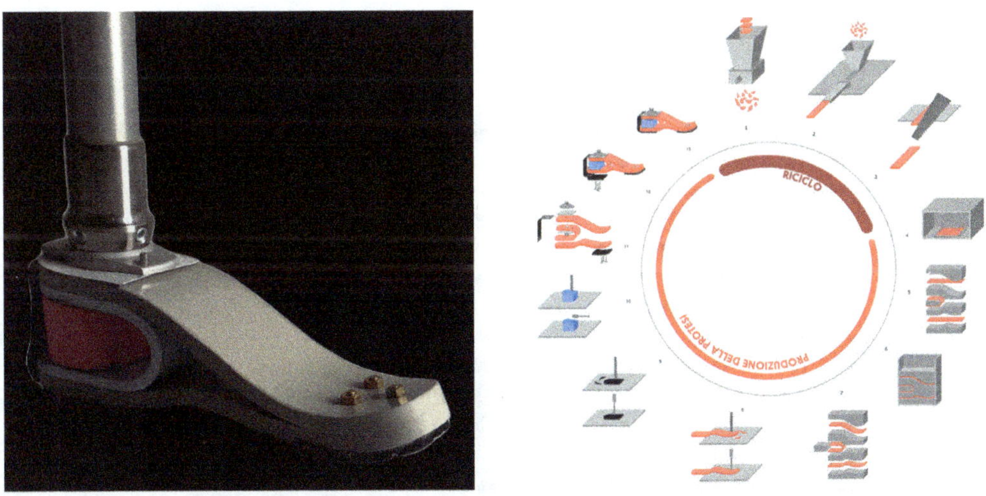

FIGURE 15 PROTIUM, by Allegra Corrente Fornoni, Alice Forestan, Laura Sguotti (Università Iuav di Venezia) Prosthetic foot for children by a circular design process.

The expectations of any design intervention are that, on the one hand, it generates a financial return (economic sustainability); on the other, that it raises production levels without adverse impacts on the environment (environmental sustainability), so that the welfare of the community (social sustainability) is assured.[251] To satisfy those expectations throughout the standardization of processes is of the utmost relevance for industrial design.[252]

5 *Protecting Works of Design Today: A Wide Variety of Legal Tools*

The fact that design can be protected alternatively as well as cumulatively under various forms of IP law and under competition law, at least in Europe, simply reflects the hybrid nature of industrial design. Design combines functional and aesthetic elements into a coherent whole, but, as seen above (§§1.2 and 3.3), its boundaries with respect to artistic craftsmanship, on the one hand, and to science and engineering, on the other are weak – "fragile" when it comes to expressing a sort of trans-temporal collective project; "very fragile" when it comes to creating complex artefacts to make up for what our ageing bodies can no longer do, such as, for example, innovative prostheses with sensors connected to apps, or the application of biomarkers and biosensors for personalized medicine, or geolocalisation systems and smart textiles for safe sports training,[253] or Algorithm-Aided Designs and parametrics applied to new technological goods,[254] also in fashion design.[255] As explained earlier

251 Filho, *Designer as an instrument of social change among the group being influenced*, op. cit., p. 73. See also Manzini, *Il tramonto dell'era meccanica, Storia del disegno industriale*, III, Milan, 1991.

252 Product graphics, fluent in the language of standards, serve to help users make the right connections: see for instance the Web Open Font Format developed by three typeface designers in 2009. Available at https://www.w3.org/2009/08/WebFonts/charter.html (accessed 9.8.2019). *Cf*, for instance, the webfont Kit 'Titillium', born inside the Accademia di Belle Arti di Urbino, as a didactic project in the Course of Type design taught by Luciano Perondi. The aim of the project was the creation of a collective fonts released under Open Font License (available at http://nta.accademiadiurbino.it/titillium.html accessed 12.11.2019).

253 Maldonado, *Critica della ragione informatica*, Milan, 1997, p. 140; Chiapponi (ed.), *Smart Sport. Innovazioni di prodotto per gli sport invernali*, Treviso, 2008.

254 Maldonado, op. cit., p. 141; Chiapponi, Ciotti, "Design medicale e Internet of Things," *MD Journal*, 2016, pp. 24–31; Chiapponi, "Design, oggetti e mondi fantastici," in Riccini (ed.), *Design e immaginario. Oggetti, immagini e visioni fra rappresentazione e progetto*, Padua, 2016, pp. 37–49; Chiapponi, "Design medicale," DIID (*Disegno Industriale Industrial Design*), 2007, pp. 12–19; Chiapponi, "Health Care Technologies: The Contribution of Industrial Design," in Fortunati, Katz, Riccini (eds.), *Mediating the Human Body: Technology, Communication, and Fashion*, New Jersey, 2003.

255 Ciammaichella, "Immagini e immaginari di moda. Il disegno della divisa perfetta", in UID per il disegno, *Riflessioni: l'arte del disegno/il disegno dell'arte. Reflections: the art of*

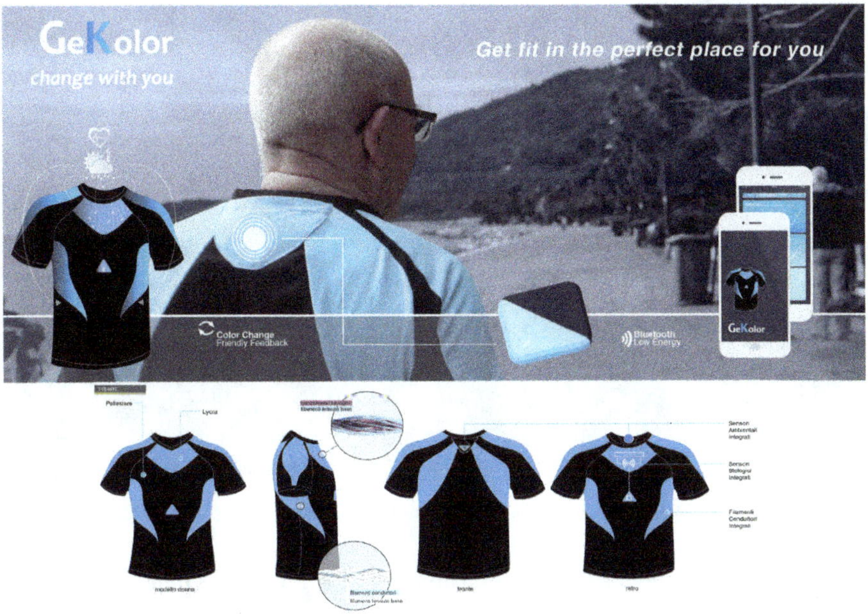

FIGURE 16 GEKOLOR by Martina Frausin (Università Iuav di Venezia)

(§ 3.3.2,), the three tests developed in different jurisdictions to exclude those "features solely dictated by technical function" from design protection can help, but what a "technical function" is *per se* remains uncertain. Designers are not artists; they follow a "project roadmap" (see Figure 14 above), analyzing final users, market segments, costs, materials, processes, and the feasibility of partnerships and collaborations, and so the designed features are always (if not solely) dictated by technical function and alternative arrangements are always possible. Take for example, GEKOLOR (Figure 16), a smart T-shirt for outdoor training that can simultaneously monitor and combine physiological and environmental parameters with a network of nanosensors built into the

drawing/the drawing of art, convegno n. 41, Rome, 2019, pp. 1139–1146; Kim, Seong, Her, et al., "A study of the development and improvement of fashion products using a FDM type 3D printer", *Fashion and Textiles*, 2019, pp. 1–24; Frisa, *Le forme della moda*, Bologna, 2015; Tedeschi, *AAD_ Alghorithms-Aided Design. Parametric strategies using Grasshopper*, Brienza, 2014; Koerner, *Digitally Crafted Couture*, in *Architectural Design*, 2017, pp. 40–47; Rocamora, "Mediatization and Digital Media in the Field of Fashion," *Fashion Theory*, 2016, pp. 505–522.

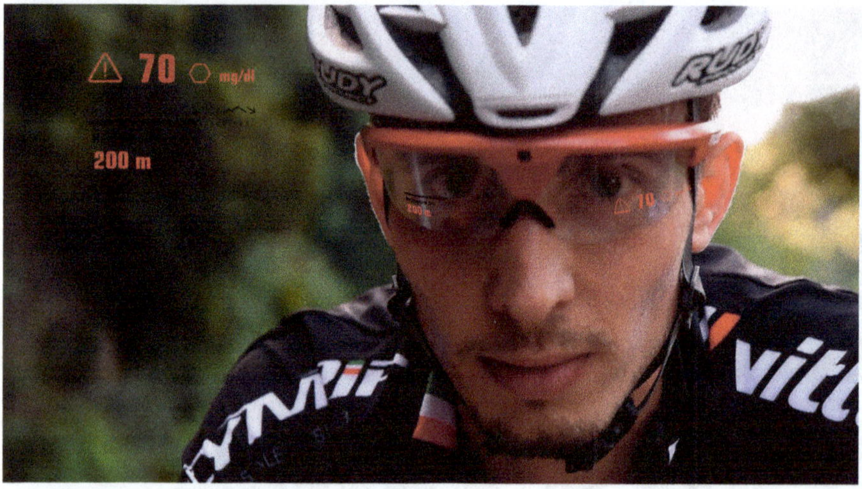

FIGURE 17 PULSE by Giada Michiante (Università Iuav di Venezia)

fabric fibres and a device located on the back of the T-shirt. Once the training session is completed, the user can view the related data through a smartphone application. The features of the T-shirt are dictated by the technical function of the product, *and* alternative arrangements for the T-shirt, as well as the smartphone app, are clearly possible.

Another example is PULSE (Figure 17), a kit of devices designed to improve performance in cycling. The intelligent tank monitors loss of fluids, the change in blood glucose levels, and the accumulation of lactic acid. Augmented reality glasses display physiological and performance data in real time. Also in this case, the design of the integrated kit is dictated by the technical function of the "ecosystem of products" *and* alternative features are possible.

Another example again is KLETO (Figure 18), an ankle brace with bending and load textile sensors that allows the degree of mobility of the patient's ankle to be monitored during the phases of recovery from an ankle injury. Thanks to the real time programming of rehabilitation exercises by the physiotherapist, it reduces recovery time and anticipates the return to activity. Both the ankle brace with its sensors and the app could have been designed differently.

A final example is SWAFE (Figure 19), a monitoring system for professional swimmers. It consists of a device to be applied to the athlete's swimsuit, and a smartphone application. The kit is designed to adapt to the needs of the coach and the athlete, facilitating the planning of a balanced training session.

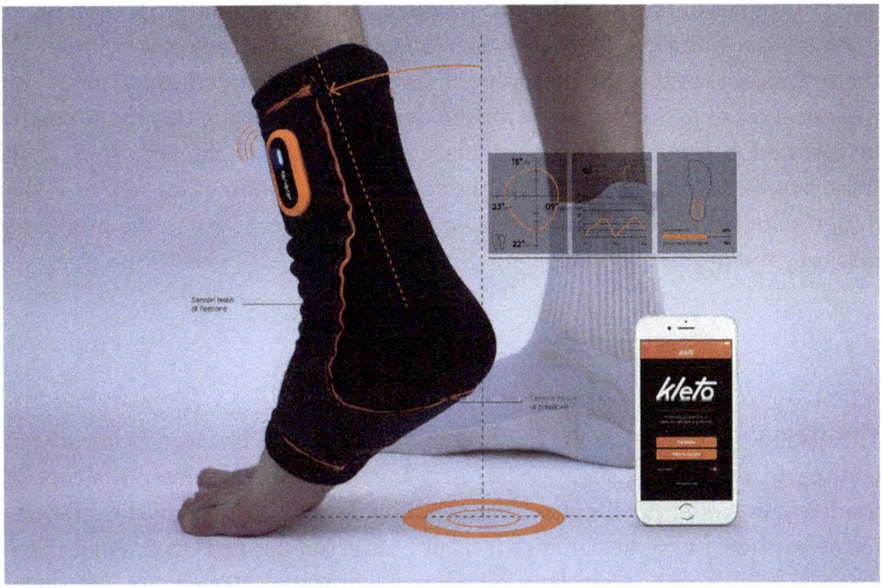

FIGURE 18 KLETO by Stefano Paglia (Università Iuav di Venezia)

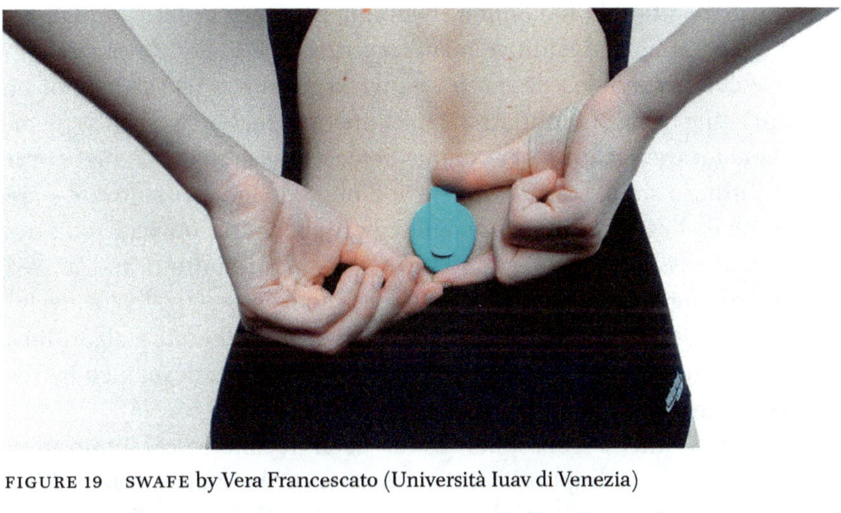

FIGURE 19 SWAFE by Vera Francescato (Università Iuav di Venezia)

As the European Court of Justice stated in the *Doceram* case,[256] a design is dictated solely by its technical function if *every* feature of that design was selected

256 Case C-395/16, *DOCERAM Gmbh V Ceramtec Gmbh* [2018] ECLI:EU:C:2018:172 on the interpretation of Article 8(1) Regulation 6/2002 "designs dictated by their technical function and designs of interconnections."

merely because of *the need to fulfil* a product's technical function. It went on to rule that it is *indecisive whether or not the features are the only means* by which the technical function can be achieved. Therefore, the perception of an objective observer or an informed user is not decisive in assessing this requirement for protection (unlike in the assessment of individual character). Thus, if all these small ecosystems fall within the scope of the notion of design, then the design/copyright interface provides only a minimal response to the problems raised by the protection of design rights.

Part 2: The Author

The notion of "author" in EU law and in Member State laws tends to vary according to the type of creative industry involved. Nevertheless, in all those frameworks, under no circumstances can the designer be deprived of the status of "author" as the designer's art "is not pure, but applied" in the mass production of objects and artefacts which serve a utilitarian purpose. However, it is true that with the growth of the digital market, the notion of "author" has become more complicated: digital technologies which facilitate interactions and collaboration in the online environment – such as transformations driven by 3D printing and additive manufacturing where models can be created with a computer-aided design (CAD) package with a 3D scanner, or by using 4D printing using appropriate 4D softwares and materials, such as memory polymers for the creation of dynamic objects whose shape changes over time, or by using a simple digital camera and photogrammetry software – are favouring the co-design, co-creation, and co-production of objects and artefacts, raising the issue of whether and how the work of multiple and "mixed authors" (computer-human interaction design) can be protected "collectively." A good example is given by parametric modelling with generative algorithms in fashion design, as in the case of the "*Voltage*" prototype, developed by Iris van Herpen for his Haute Couture Spring 2013 collection (Figure 20).

Exploring the aesthetic consequences of such technological innovation in design practice is as important as an analysis of the matter from a legal perspective. The "computational designer" enters a set of parameters (the desired result – a chair, a floor plan or a coat – along with parameters such as materials, manufacturing methods, and cost constraints) and then chooses the best outcome generated by the software. Some parameters are set in advance, others are not, then the computer builds all the possible solutions for the user to choose from, learning their preferences as it does so. As it is up to the designer to choose from the many options of designs and models generated by the computer, the author is both the designer and the computer scientists who

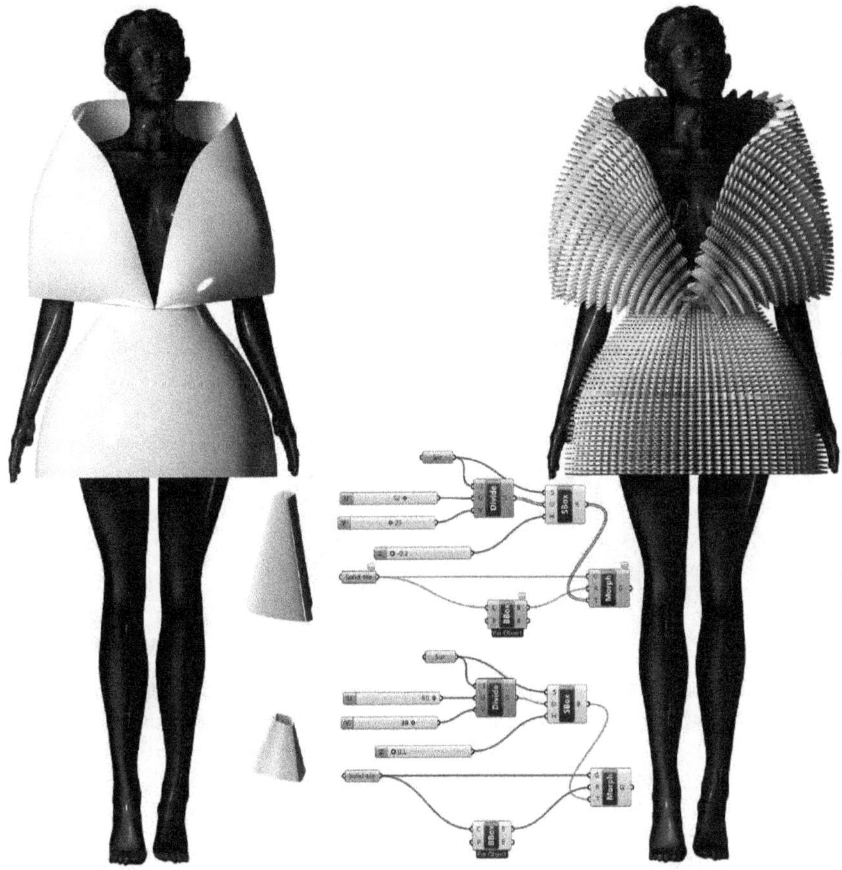

FIGURE 20 Massimiliano Ciammaichella, *Immagini e immaginari di moda. Il disegno della divisa perfetta*, op. cit. Rendering 2019.

programmed the software. The situation becomes trickier, however, when machine learning comes into the picture, namely the use of data-driven Artificial Intelligence to teach computers the ability to perform tasks based on examples without explicit human programming, directly generating solutions for the user to choose from. Here it is clear that the classical meaning of "author" falls apart.

6 *Who Is Protected*

6.1 The "Author" According to Law in the Design/Copyright Interface

A legal definition of "author" is lacking at both the supranational and the national levels.

When the European Court of Justice interprets "intellectual creation," it alludes to a strict conceptualization of "author" as the person who expresses her creativity in an autonomous and original manner through her "personal

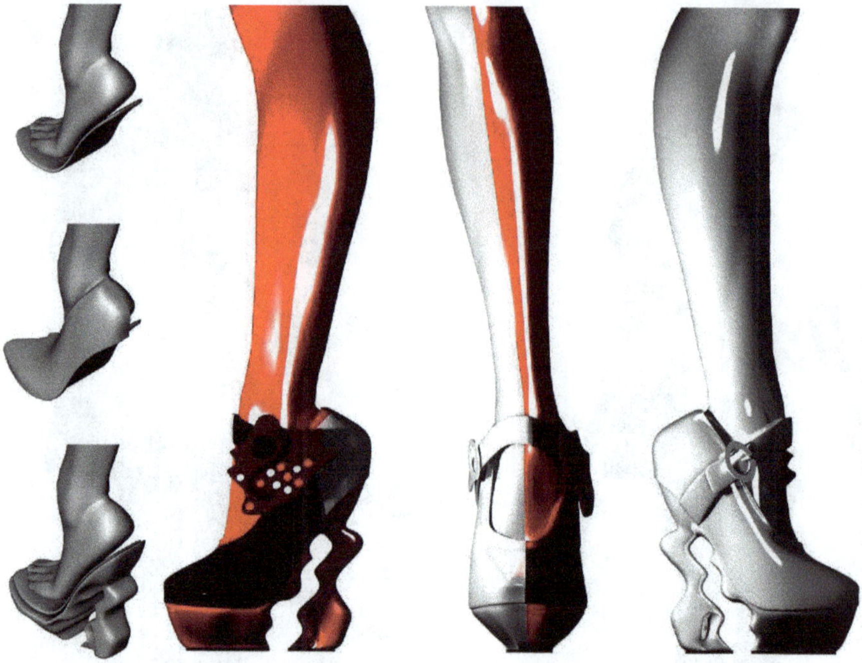

FIGURE 21 Massimiliano Ciammaichella, *Immagini e immaginari di moda. Il disegno della divisa perfetta*, op. cit. 3D modelling – prototype shoes by John Galliano, Maison Martin Margiela, "*Artisanal*" Haute Couture Collection Spring 2015. Rendering 2019.

touch."[257] What the author's personal touch entails and what the limits are to her autonomy and expression of personality in creative processes affects the practical application of the European Court of Justice's "originality test." At national level, the notion of author, as well as co-author, varies between strict and broad approaches.[258] National requirements and attempts by judicial authorities to outline predictable tests to determine who the author is ultimately remain faithful to different protectionist national policies. It is doubtful whether national conceptualizations of the originality threshold in the design/copyright interface are all compatible with the European legal framework, and in particular with the independent European definition of originality, as shaped over the last decade by the Court of Justice. Where there is conflict, Member

257 See below in this §.

258 Priora, "Copyright Law and the Promotion of Scientific Networks: Some Reflections on the Rules on Co-authorship in the EU," *Queen Mary Journal of Intellectual Property*, 2019, pp. 217–232.

State courts should apply the European standard of "the author's own intellectual creation."[259]

Another issue related to the notion of author concerns the subjective element in the "intention to co-create," and the objective element usually required at national level of the "distinguishability of contributions", which together constitute the requirements for determining "co-authorship" also in the design sector (Figure 21).

A statutory definition of the "author" of intellectual creations is also lacking at international level, although the position of the "copyright owner" has been strengthened by the international structure of copyright law. Under the Berne Convention of 1886, a Member State can contemplate protection of a work in other Member States only when there is evidence of a personal connection of an author with the work. As we saw earlier (§3.1), however,[260] the Convention refers to works of applied art as a broad concept, which would appear to encompass industrial designs and models in general, then it refers to "intellectual creations" and "original works," but it only gives its Members freedom to determine the scope of application of their copyright laws to such works and to decide the term of protection (minimum 25 years) from the making of the work. It provides only one rule concerning "co-authorship," whereby the duration of copyright protection for a co-created work is to be measured starting from the death of the last surviving co-author.[261] The TRIPS and WIPO treaties make no mention of co-authorship in any their provisions.[262] The determination of the precise meaning of authorship in relation to "intellectual creations" is thus left to their Members' national laws. In the European Union, that means that the determination of the precise meaning of authorship is left to the Court of Justice of the European Union, which intervenes under Article 267 TFEU

259 European Copyright Society, op. cit.

260 The international copyright landscape has been sketched out to show that notions such as "intellectual creation" and "originality" ultimately have always been a matter of national law: Peukert, "Individual, Multiple and Collective Ownership of Intellectual Property Rights – Which Impact on Exclusivity?" in Kur, Mizaras (eds.), *The Structure of Intellectual Property Law: Can One Size Fit All?*, Cheltenham 2011, p. 196; Ginsburg, "The Concept of Authorship in Comparative Copyright Law," *DePaul Law Review*, 2002, pp. 1067 ff. For an historical perspective see Waldenberger, *Die Miturheberschaft Im Rechtsvergleich. Zugleich Ein Beitrag Zur Lehre von Der Miturheberschaft Nach Deutschem Recht*, Munich, 1991.

261 Article 7 bis, Berne Convention for the Protection of Literary and Artistic Works (as amended in 1979), op. cit.

262 WTO Agreement on Trade-Related Aspects of Intellectual Property Rights 1994; WIPO Copyright Treaty and WIPO Performances and Phonograms Treaty 1996.

when, in a case before a national court, a question of interpretation (which is new and of general interest for the uniform application of EU law) is raised, or where the existing case law does not appear to give the necessary guidance to deal with a new legal situation.

The notion of author is therefore strictly dependent on the concept of intellectual creativity. As such, let us now look more closely at who the author is by retracing the European Court of Justice's interpretation of "the author's own intellectual creation", which is how the Court has construed the "originality threshold" in design/copyright interface case law. The notion itself is quite remarkable, but given that copyright regulates such a wide variety of cultural production and potentially impacts the use of the most routine creations, such as ordinary objects that surround us in everyday life, it can only be presumed that it should be interpreted uniformly across the European Union.

6.1.1 *EU "Author's Own Intellectual Creation"*

According to some commentators,[263] the development of the "author's own intellectual creation" standard as the "originality threshold" has witnessed at least three historical phases of harmonization: a first phase, which saw the harmonization of EU law on specific subject matters and, consequently, of the originality thresohold only in relation to those subject matters (vertical harmonization);[264] a second phase, where the Court of Justice construed the EU legislative framework in such a way as to expand the originality test to all subject matters covered by EU copyright law (horizontal harmonization); and a third phase, where the Court of Justice had a direct impact on copyright harmonization and, in particular, on the understanding of "originality."[265] Arguably, the *Cofemel* decision (§4.1 above) marks the start of a fourth phase.

In brief, in the interpretation of the European Court of Justice, an "author's own intellectual creation" (originality) means:

263 Margoni , *The Harmonisation,* op. cit.

264 Legislative interventions have regulated specific subject matters: software (Directive 2009/24/EC of 23 April 2009 on the legal protection of computer programs, Article 1(3)), databases (Directive 96/9 of 11 March 1996 on the legal protection of databases, Article 3(1)), and photographs (Directive 2006/116/EC of 12 December 2006 on the term of protection of copyright and certain related rights, Article 6).

265 *Cf* Roder, *Die Methodik des EuGH im Urheberrecht: die autonome Auslegung des Gerichtshofs der Europäischen Union im Spannungsverhältnis zum nationalen Recht,* Tübingen, 2016, p. 420, who states that the European Court of Justice did not fully harmonise the level of originality and that Member States may continue to determine the threshold at national level, since originality is only one aspect of the concept of work.

1. that an author's work will only be protected where there is scope for "creative freedom" in its production (*Infopaq*,[266] *Football Association Premier League*,[267] *Funke Medien*,[268] and *Cofemel*[269]);
2. the autonomous expression of personality in creative processes – the so-called "personal touch" of the author – must be identifiable (*Eva-Maria Painer*)[270] and paired with autonomous and creative choices in the production of the work (*Football Dataco*);[271]
3. the intellectual creative work must be identifiable with precision and objectivity (*Levola*[272] and *Cofemel*[273]);
4. it cannot be creative if the achievement of the work is dictated solely by technical functions, where the idea and the expression of the work are indissociable (*Football Dataco*[274] and *BSA*[275]);
5. the application of a "labour and skill test," without the exercise of creative freedom, in the making of a utilitarian article is insufficient to demonstrate the originality required for copyright protection (*Football Dataco*[276]).

---

266 C-5/08, *Infopaq International A/S v. Danske Dagblades Forening*, op. cit. In §§46–47, the Court held that the expression of the author's intellectual creation can be reflected in isolated sentences, or even parts of sentences, of a work such as a newspaper article.

267 C-403/08 and C-429/08, *Football Association Premier League and Others v. QC Leisure and Others* and *Karen Murphy v. Media Protection Services* [2011] E.C.R. I-09083.

268 C-469/17, *Funke Medien NRW GmbH v Bundesrepublik Deutschland* [2019] ECLI:EU:C:2019:623.

269 C-683/17, *Sociedade de Vestuário SA v G-Star Raw CV*, know as "Cofemel," op. cit.

270 C-145/10, *Eva-Maria Painer v. Standard VerlagsGmbH and Others* [2011] E.C.R. I-12533: in §§88–89: "if the author was able to express his creative abilities in the production of the work by making free and creative choices."

271 C-604/10, *Football Dataco v. Yahoo! UK and Others* [2012] EU:C:2012:115. In §38: "the personal touch is the authors' creative ability of making free and creative choices during its production." It is somewhat surprising that the Court applied the "originality/creative freedom" test to football matches, because by doing so it seems to imply that sports events are in principle eligible subject-matter. That in turn raises the question of authorship: who qualifies as the author of a football matche? The players, captain, technical staff, the coach, one team, both teams, or all of the above? See van Gompel, "Creativity, Autonomy and Personal Touch. A Critical Appraisal of the CJEU's Originality Test for Copyright," in van Eechoud (ed.), *The Work of Authorship*, Amsterdam, 2014, pp. 95–143.

272 C-210/17, *Levola*, op. cit.

273 C-683/17, *Sociedade de Vestuário*, op. cit.

274 C-604/10, *Football Dataco*, op. cit.

275 C-393/09, *Bezpečnostni softwarova asociace v. Ministerstvo kultury* [2010] E.C.R. I-13971.

276 C-604/10, *Football Dataco*, op. cit.

The "author's own intellectual creation," which indeed corresponds to the copyright law's originality threshold, is not a particularly high standard to attain.[277] Copyright protection could not be excluded in the case of an 11-word extract (*Infopaq*), a portrait photograph (*Eva-Maria Painer*), and a graphic user interface (*BSA*). Instead, football fixture lists (*Football Dataco*) and sports games (*Football Association Premier League*) were excluded from protection due to the lack of free and creative choices; the taste of cheese (*Levola*) was excluded because of its unidentifiable nature; and T-shirts and jeans were excluded because their design generates an aesthetic perception which made it impossible to determine whether the design was an intellectual creation that reflected the freedom of choice and the personality of the designer (*Cofemel*).

At this point, the European Court of Justice needs to ensure that the principles stated in its case law (the idea/expression dichotomy, merger doctrine, technical constraint aspects linked to the requirement of free and creative choices, and personal touch) are clearly applied to design objects or artefacts by each Member State at national level.[278] The low threshold captured by the expression "the author's own intellectual creation" favours industries which usually rely on the prior state of art and produce through incremental design improvements, as well as industries which need to test their products in the market at an early stage of market-testing without fear of forfeiting protection. The design of ordinary household items should therefore be eligible for copyright protection just as much as creations of pure art, with anonymous, even trivial objects manufactured on either a small or massive scale treated legally as equivalent to artistic works when they are recognized as "intellectual creations" that reflect the freedom of choice and the personality of the designer.[279]

277 C-145/10, *Eva-Maria Painer*, op. cit.: this case involved a simple school portrait photograph, one of those school portraits that are impossible to tell apart, except for the images of the people they portray.

278 European Copyright Society, op. cit.

279 The exhibition "Castiglioni's Design. Research \ Experimentation \ Method," promoted by Unindustria Pordenone in collaboration with the Achille Castiglioni Foundation and the City of Pordenone (Pordenone \ Galleria Harry Bertoia \ 25.01.2019 > 17.03.2019) for the 100th anniversary of the birth of Achille Castiglioni, celebrated the importance of anonymous objects of the past and present, bearing witness to a passion and interest in "anonymous" design. The Achille Castiglioni Foundation's permanent exhibition in Milan shows four rooms of the architect's studio, testifying to the importance of everyday objects. The first two rooms are furnished with prototypes and models; the third with drafting machines; while the fourth room displays a seriesof anonymous objects collected by Castiglioni during his lifetime for use as examples in his lectures at the Polytechnic Universities of Turin and Milan.

Nevertheless, some difficulties persist in identifying when the supposed originality of a work goes no further than its technical, i.e., functional, features (also called "non-original features"), that is to say, when the space for authors to express their creativity in a personal manner is too narrow to create a work that constitutes an intellectual creation of their own (see Part 1, § 3.3.2. above and Part 2, §6.2 below).[280] Ultimately, however, there are always constraints on an author's autonomy and such constraints ought to be accommodated for in copyright law's originality test. The point here is that tradition, conventions, and constraints affect creative processes. As other commentators have remarked,[281] there are substantial limits and constraints to creative processes, both internal – voluntary and involuntary psychological barriers in the choice of audience and topic, the choice of medium, format, method, and materials, the specific genre in which authors create their works, mood, habits, and preferences – and external – such as fixed deadlines and limited budgets,[282] trends and audience expectations, language restrictions, and so on. Such restrictions are precisely an integral and essential part of creativity and originality, where sometimes those limits simply need to be overcome, sometimes lines have to be redrawn to stay within them. An essential aspect of avant-garde works, for instance, is the pushing back of the boundaries of existing norms or genres, allowing artistic conventions to evolve and change over time, but to be understood and accepted, authors usually cannot deviate from the conventions too much.[283] For Igor Stravinsky, the musical compositor: "*My freedom thus consists in my moving about within the narrow frame that I have assigned myself for each of my undertakings. I shall go even further: my freedom will be so much the greater and more meaningful the more narrowly I limit my field of action and the more I surround myself with obstacles.*"[284] Turning to more contemporary examples, the Internet is a huge source of digital constraints, requiring authors

280 C-393/09, *Bezpečnostni softwarova asociace*, op. cit., §§49–50.

281 Budd, *Values of Art*, London, 1995, p. 11: "that the role of the artist, properly understood, requires the artist, in the creation of her work, to adopt or bear in mind the role of the spectator." See Goncalo, Vincent, Audia, "Early Creativity as a Constraint on Future Achievement," in Cropley et al. (eds.), *The Dark Side of Creativity*, New York, 2010, pp. 114–133.

282 There is a correlation between available budget and what the author can achieve, but as Alfred Hitchcock's thriller *Psycho* illustrates on low-budget films, it is not a strict correlation: see Barnwell, *Production Design: Architects of the Screen*, London, 2004, p. 48.

283 "A play cannot usually sustain the audience's attention for more than a couple of hours; a movie's duration depends on the eye's tolerance to strain"; see Pavel, *Fictional World*, Cambridge MA, 1986, p. 98.

284 Stravinsky, *Poetics of Music in the Form of Six Lessons* (translated from the French by Knodel and Dahl, preface by Seferis) Cambridge MA, 1970, pp. 64–65.

to communicate their works as clearly and effectively as possible. Usability studies show that, on average, it takes only a few seconds to grab the attention of website visitors. If a webpage loads too slowly,[285] or visitors do not promptly find something of interest to them,[286] then the website is likely to be abandoned. Terms and conditions of use further restrict autonomy. Thus the production of digital works pivots on a fair trade-off between creative expression and constraints: "[*t*]*he choice of whether to program or to use a software application can be critical to how much the artist has control over the character of the constraints to be specified.*"[287] Every creative choice, even if imposed by entirely idiosyncratic constraints, entails subsequent restrictions that may have an effect on the creative room for manoeuvre available to authors.[288] It would be reasonable to expect, therefore, that in assessing the original character of a work (or the lack of it), courts should give ample consideration to the impact of limits and constraints, with the originality test passed as long as authors have made free and subjective choices within the minimal or symbolic creative space that is available to them.

The question at this point would appear to revolve closely around the notion of "personal touch," which very much recalls the "aura" of artworks.[289] But how can we measure whether the author's personality is sufficiently reflected in her works (and in jointly created works in particular)? In evaluating the "personal touch" parameter, judges usually pose the theoretical question of whether it is conceivable that two or more authors, independently of each other, could create exactly the same work.[290] If they consider that to be nearly

285 Krishnan, Sitaraman, "Video Stream Quality Impacts Viewer Behavior: Inferring Causality Using Quasi-Experimental Designs," *IMC '12: Proceedings of the 2012 ACM conference on Internet measurement conference*, New York, 2012, pp. 211–224.

286 Nielsen, Pernice, *Eyetracking Web Usability*, Berkeley, 2010.

287 Candy, "Constraints and Creativity in the Digital Arts", *Leonardo*, 2007, pp. 366–367, p. 366.

288 Elster suggests in his book *Ulysses Unbound: Studies in Rationality, Precommitment, and Constraints*, Cambridge MA, 2000, p. 176, that artistic creation must be envisaged as a two-step process, i.e., as a "*choice of constraints* followed by *choice within constraints*."

For a different approach see Moeran, "Perspectives in Business Anthropology: Cultural Production, Creativity and Constraints", *International Journal of Business Anthropology*, 2011, pp. 16–30, at 16: according to him, cultural productions differentiate because of material, temporal, spatial, social, representational, and economic restrictions.

289 Aura is a quality integral to an artwork that cannot be communicated through mechanical reproduction techniques. The term was used by Walter Benjamin in his influential 1936 essay *The Work of Art in the Age of Mechanical Reproduction*.

290 According to van Gompel, op. cit., the courts' reliance on a hypothetical situation, whereby a comparison is made with fictitious creators, seems to be based on a doctrine developed in scholarly literature. One of the leading treatises on copyright law in the Netherlands suggests that, in practice, the courts can apply such a pragmatic comparison as a rule

impossible, they will typically assume that the work satisfies the originality test;[291] otherwise, they will rule that the work lacks originality and deny protection.[292] After the formulation of "multiple theory,"[293] however, we should assume that two or more authors, independently of each other, can indeed create the same thing at the same time – the theory holds that when a brilliant creation or invention occurs to somebody somewhere in the world, the author will go public with the remarkable finding only to discover that at least three other minds have already come up with the same idea independently elsewhere in those same years. Thus the "personal touch" test, which reflects author's personality, can only be required to show that the work must be the author's own individual expression, i.e., that it "originates from" the author in the sense of "not being copied."

To sum up, "authorship," in the European arena at least, remains strictly related to the notion of the originality of a work, which for the European Court of Justice means applying the "author's own intellectual creation" test to the work itself. As noted earlier, the European Court of Justice has confirmed on several occasions that copyright protection extends to any subject-matter that is "original" in the sense that it is "the author's own intellectual creation," for which the only threshold that a work must satisfy to be eligible for copyright protection is that its expression is sufficiently "original" in the legal sense of the term (the "author's own intellectual creation"). In the *Cofemel* case of 2019,[294] the European Court of Justice declared that any requirement by national law of some sort of "aesthetic" or "artistic" value for a design to be eligible for copyright protection would contradict the objectivity requirement mandated under EU law. So, for now, the "author's own intellectual creation" standard, as construed by the European Court of Justice, is mandatory for all national courts.

As concerns "co-authorship," EU lawmakers have enacted only a few provisions, setting the duration of copyright protection for jointly-created works at 70 years from the death of the last surviving author, and imposing it on music

of thumb to determine whether a work meets the originality standard. See Spoor et al. (eds.), *Auteursrecht: auteursrecht, naburige rechten en databankenrecht* 3rd ed., Deventer 2005 (last ed. 2019), p. 66.

291 *Eek BV v. Esfera*, 2007, cited in van Gompel, op. cit., p. 128.

292 *Social Deal v. Wowdeal*, 2012, cited in van Gompel, op. cit., p. 128.

293 Johnson, *Where Good Ideas Come From?*, New York, 2010, p. 34; according to Johnson, goods idea are built out of a collection of existing parts, both conceptual (definitions, way of solving problems) and physical (mechanical or technological). See Ogburn and Thomas, who found 148 instances of independent innovations, most of them occurring within the same decade, in "Are Inventions Inevitable? A Note on Social Evolution," *Political Science Quarterly*, 1992, pp. 83–98.

294 See § 4.1 above.

composers, lyricists, and the co-creators of databases and software.[295] In practice, national courts seemingly tend to overlook the "actual author" in assessing whether a work is the "author's own intellectual creation." Such a tendency is highly relevant to the digital environment, where works are increasingly produced in the context of online creative communities,[296] or with the help of crowd participation.[297] Online communities often share a set of norms and ethics, guided by principles of etiquette on how to work with others in the community and by requirements on attribution, modification, and exploitation of the output. User-generated productions that involve the public in creating a movie, book, song, or other type of work, such as a design work, also rely on self-governance within creative communities.

For the purposes of establishing whose "personal touch" is reflected in a work (e.g., whether the requirements for copyright protection are met), one approach is to identify one or more creative leaders, with creativity assessed at the "community-level." But if no creative leader can be identified, that does not mean that works produced by large-scale creative communities lack originality in a copyright sense. Since copyright must not punish group creation, when it comes to ascertaining the existence of creative space, the originality test should focus on community-level creativity, rather than on individual creative choices.[298] Another option available to creative communities is to relinquish legal protection, as in the case of Open Design projects (CAD information published online under a Creative Commons license to be downloaded, produced, copied, and modified). In Open Design, designers have access to an unprecedented flood of freely available creative content. Through the Open Source method, and the revolutionary Arduino stance in the software and hardware industries, for instance, different mass production processes are available, combining the Internet's disruptive nature with easy access to CNC

---

295 Article 1(2) of Directive 2006/116/EC of the European Parliament and of the Council of 12 December 2006 on the term of protection of copyright and certain related rights [2006] OJ L 372/12. See also the amendments thereto introduced by Directive 2011/77/EU of the European Parliament and of the Council of 27 September 2011 amending Directive 2006/116/EC on the term of protection of copyright and certain related rights [2011] OJ L 265/1. See Stamatoudi, Torremans, *EU Copyright Law: A Commentary*, Cheltenham, 2014, p. 16.

296 Kelty, *Two Bits: The Cultural Significance of Free Software*, Durham 2008; Ciuccarelli, *Design Open Source. Dalla partecipazione alla progettazione in rete*, Bologna, 2008; Reagle, *Good Faith Collaboration: The Culture of Wikipedia*, Cambridge MA, 2010.

297 Vines et al., "Configuring Participation: On How We Involve People In Design," *CHI* 2013, April 27–May 2, 2013, http://www.johnvines.eu/wp-content/uploads/2013/01/ConfigPart_ACMArchiveCameraOptimised.pdf (accessed 8.8.2019).

298 van Gompel, op. cit., p. 138.

machines.[299] More often than not, however, designers willingly welcome legal protection, although it is not easy to set up in works which are created within (online or offline) creative communities, or with the help of crowd participation. In such cases, authors whose contributions are used are not immediately entitled to copyright protection in the joint work. Whether they are depends on legal rules on co-authorship, which can vary between different jurisdictions;[300] where the requirements to qualify legally as co-authors are met, the contributors enter a regime of "legal community," with similar practical effects, in spite of the wide spectrum of national rules.[301] The legal community regime significantly lowers the risk of fragmenting rights, but it does not always convince businesses, which face difficulties in negotiating with three or four designers as joint co-owners, for example, unless the joint exercise of economic rights is counterbalanced by the possibility of specific contractual agreements in which co-authors can independently decide upon the economic exercise of their rights.

299 See https://www.ronen-kadushin.com/ (accessed 5.6.2019).

300 Ginsburg, *The Concept of Authorship* op.cit., pp. 1063 ff; Van Eechoud et al., *Harmonizing European Copyright Law: The Challenges of Better Lawmaking*, Alphen aan den Rijn, 2009, pp. 236–243; Margoni, Perry, "Ownership in Complex Authorship: A Comparative Study of Joint Works," *European Intellectual Property Review*, 2012, pp. 22–32. Some authors (Stamatoudi, Torremans, *EU Copyright Law*, op. cit., pp. 255 ff) in particular highlight the different approach by Germany and France: the so called 'strict approach' adopted by German law, where two requirements are to be met in order to qualify as a co-author – a subjective one (the intention to co-create) and an objective one (the impossibility to distinguish each single contribution in the original work), §8(1) of the German Copyright Act – and the so called "broad approach" embraced by French law, similar to the USA, where the vast category of "works of collaboration," interpreted as a community of inspiration by the *Cour de Cassation, Chambre Civil* 1, 11 Mai 2017, 16–13.427, is jointly owned by all its co-authors, and runs on the common accord of the co-authors involved, Art. L 113-3 French Intellectual Property Code. See Schack, *Urheber- Und Urhebervertragsrecht*, Heidelberg, 2017, pp. 160–161; Daverat, *Droit de la propriété littéraire et artistique*, Rosny-sous-Bois, 2011.

301 The dualistic nature of the copyright paradigm, which distinguishes between moral and economic rights in the French style, can also be found in German law; thus the exercise of the economic rights, in both cases, must be a joint exercise in the sense that use by third parties requires the unanimous consent by all co-authors, unless otherwise agreed (with the exception of the *bona fide* third party in Germany, and with the exception of the abuse of rights doctrine in cases where a co-author vetos the exploitation of a work without providing any motive). In France, moreover, the co-authors can separately exploit their own personal contributions where the contribution of each of them is of a different kind and without prejudicing the exploitation of the common work in France. Moral rights remain enforceable by each co-author.

Another difficulty posed by co-creation is the identification of the "personal touch" of each individual contributor in all parts of a co-production.[302] Joint creation is about the collective selection of materials and data, and joint decision-making processes concerning research and design, from project briefs to design concepts, to the final integrated product-service system. If copyright protection were to depend on how the personality of individual co-creators is reflected in a collaborative work, that could have the unintended outcome that no protection may be granted at all, where due to the large number of contributors, or due to the contribution of Artificial Intelligence, the work does not express the personal touch of each and every co-contributor. For collaborative productions, then, it is better to focus on the creativity of the entire group when it comes to ascertaining both the existence of creative space and how it is used.[303] In practice, therefore, the weaker the connection between a work and the author who created it, the more difficult it becomes to apply the "author's own intellectual creation" (originality) standard, as it is currently defined by the European Court of Justice.

6.1.2 *National Variances: The "Author" According to Different Courts*

Copyright law needs an author. It is always about a work in search of an author, a story in search of its reputation, but the author is no longer the romantic recluse of the past. Today, there are pools of authors who create collaboratively. Co-production and peer-production are increasing the number of co-created works, not only in design,[304] but across scientific sectors in which practical skills and intellectual efforts are shared among peers in order to achieve better results, better quality standards, and more competitive products. In copyright law, the notions of authorship and co-authorship are not treated as comparative concepts, but rather as independent, normative concepts linked to "originality." The originality test is primarily an author-oriented test, which does not require any comparison of works with prior art. Copyright law's originality test "is primarily concerned with the relationship between the creator and its work,"[305] not with how novel or meritorious a work is, compared with earlier works. Originality is examined solely on the basis of the author and his or her work. Reference to pre-existing authors and works is only made if there is

302 See van Gompel, op. cit., p. 135.

303 The growing body of literature on group creativity cited in van Gompel, op. cit., can perhaps provide helpful guidance in this respect.

304 On the uncertain success of the notion of "discipline" in Design Studies see Cross, op. cit. See also La Pietra, *Argomenti per un dizionario del design*, Macerata, 2019: "Design does not exist as a discipline" ("il design non esiste come disciplina").

305 Bently, Sherman, op. cit., p. 93.

doubt about whether a work is truly "the author's own intellectual creation," for example, if there are indications that the author copied parts of earlier works, or drew on unprotected elements of style, or materials that are not in the public domain.[306]

"Distinguishability" is a second author-oriented test, likewise essentially concerned with intentional collaboration based on creative efforts for the joint realization of an original, copyrightable work. The general principle is that the degree to which co-contributions merge is decisive, meaning that co-authorship will be acknowledged and remunerated when it is impossible to perceive the different contributions as separate, or singularly exploitable. The reason for that is largely historical (see Part 1, §1.1 above). In the XIX century, the justification for copyright was found to exist in the imperative of protecting the labour and expenses invested by an author in creating a work,[307] and hence the author's personality as manifested in the work. The possibility of having multiple authors was admitted with respect to works "originally composed and made" by more than one person.[308] Since copyright extends only to the author's individual expression, and not to facts and ideas, an "originality criterion" that focuses on the author's own intellectual endeavours in creating the work has been considered a sufficient threshold.[309] Common law systems have traditionally phrased the requirement in the sense that the work must originate with the author, i.e., it must not be copied, and it must be the result of "skill, judgement and/or labour."[310] Outside Europe, the United States and Canada developed their own standards.[311] The United States, for instance, requires a "modicum of creativity"[312] that implies a higher degree of originality than the traditional "skill, judgement and labour" criterion. On the other hand, civil law countries have shown a tendency to stress the "personal relationship" or "personal input that the author puts into the work."[313] This difference between

306 Van Gompel, Lavik, "Quality, Merit, Aesthetics and Purpose: An inquiry into EU Copyright Law's Eschewal of Other Criteria than Originality," *RIDA*, 236/2013, pp. 100–295, p. 217.

307 See Buydens, *La propriété intellectuelle: Evolution historique et philosophique*, Brussels, 2012, pp. 258–309, 315–340.

308 Bently, Kretschmer (eds.), *Primary sources on Copyright (1450–1900)* available online: they mention the Bill for the Further Encouragement of Learning in the United Kingdom of Great Britain and Ireland of 1801, Paper No. 112, I.381–8, paragraph 7; the US Copyright Act of 1831, Chapter XVI, Section 2; and the Austrian Copyright Law of 1846, §8.

309 Van Gompel, Lavik, op. cit., p. 215; van Gompel, op. cit., p. 103.

310 Margoni, *The Harmonization* op. cit.; Bently, Sherman, op. cit., p. 96; Cornish et al., op. cit., p. 11.

311 Judge, Gervais, op. cit., p. 378.

312 *Feist Publications v. Rural Telephone Service* 499 U.S. 340 (1991), 346.

313 Goldstein, Hugenholtz, op. cit., pp. 192–193.

common law and civil law countries, however, should not be misinterpreted and is often more declamatory than material. Historically, the level of originality required by civil law countries has not always been very high at all, especially in relation to certain subject matters, such as catalogues and technical manuals.[314]

Such high levels of variance in what is considered "protectable" in different historical periods, however, can be found not only across different legal traditions, but even within the same legal system.[315] As anticipated in the Introduction, case law demonstrates[316] how industrial design works (or registered designs, at least) traditionally did not always benefit from copyright protection, as the same product can be protected by copyright in one country (say Germany) but not in another country (say Italy), causing clear friction in transnational negotiation and trade. As concerns, in particular, the implementation of the "author's own intellectual creation" standard by national courts, it is plausible that national courts will soon recognize the European originality test, as construed by the European Court of Justice, but it is likely that they will continue to interpret it in a way that reflects their own traditional standards. Some national courts are indeed already showing more indulgence towards the eligibility of product designs for copyright protection; others continue to maintain a hard line. Below, I offer a bird's eye view of current national case law offering copyright protection to industrial design. For as declamatory as the formal legal rules may be, the issue ultimately will be resolved at the more practical, interpretative level.

6.1.3 *Low Threshold: German, Swiss, Dutch and Belgian Laws*

The personal intellectual creation criterion laid down in §2(2) of the German Copyright Act[317] is essential for copyright protection. Any work of art, including products of applied art and industrial design, enjoy copyright protection if they fulfil the criterion. Works are protected as long as they are a "personal intellectual creation of an author," which essentially replicates the EU's "author's own intellectual creation" standard. It is interesting to note how German

---

314 See the *kleine Münze* doctrine in Germany: Goldstein, Hugenholtz, op. cit., pp. 192–193; Lucas et al., op. cit., p. 121.

315 See Gordon, "A Property Right in Self-expression: Equality and Individualism in the Natural Law of Intellectual Property," *Yale Law Journal*, 1993, pp. 1533–1609; Merges, "Locke for the Masses: Property Rights and the Products of Collective Creativity," *Hofstra Law Review* 2007, pp. 1179–1191.

316 C-5/11, *Criminal proceedings against Titus Alexander Jochen Donner* [2012] ECLI:EU:C:2012:370; See Margoni, *The Harmonization* op. cit.

317 *Gesetz über Urheberrecht und verwandte Schutzrechte* vom 9. September 1965 (BGBl. I S. 1273) (German Copyright Act, as amended).

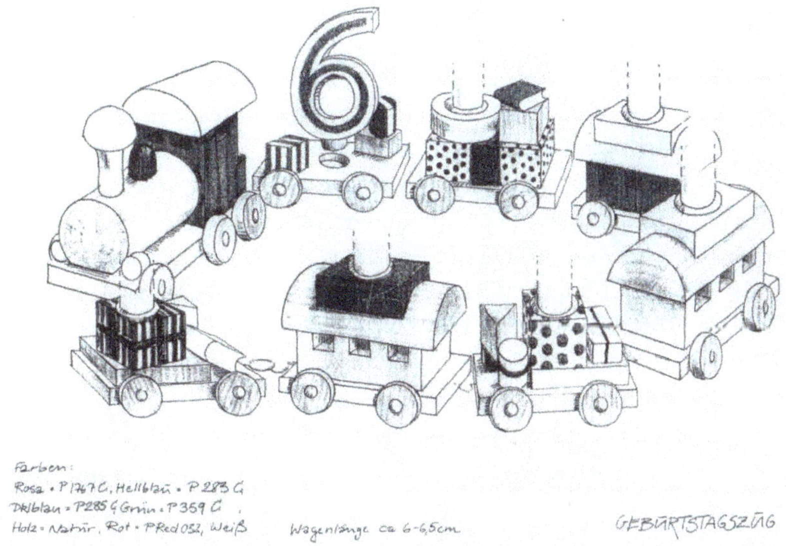

FIGURE 22 *Geburtstagszug*/Birthday train
IMAGE AVAILABLE AT HTTPS://CDN.OPENJUR.NET/ANLAGEN//7/4/1/7/5/6/1.JPG

courts appear to have spontaneously anticipated the Court of Justice's interpretation of the originality parameter.[318] However, even the *Geburtstagszug* decision (Figure 22)[319] still contains the "artistic achievement" criterion,[320] a parameter that marked previous case law concerning design classics from the Bauhaus, which were eligible for copyright protection only for their artistic-historical fame.[321]

---

318 According to Ohly, the departure of the BGH from its previous case law was not mandated by EU law but rather a "home-made solution": see Ohly, "The Case for Partial Cumulation in Germany," in Derclaye (ed.), *The Copyright/Design Interface: Past, Present, and Future*, op. cit., pp. 128–170, p. 167.

319 Decision of the Federal Supreme Court (Bundesgerichtshof BGH) 13.11.2013, Case No. I ZR 143/12, BGH, *GRUR* 2014, 175 (177) – *Geburtstagszug*. See Ritscher, Landolt, op. cit., p. 128.

320 Loewenheim, *Werke der bildenden Künste*, in Schricker, Loewenheim, *Urheberrecht – Kommentar*, III ed., Munich, 2006, p. 117.

321 BGH, *GRUR* 1987, 903 (905) – *Le Corbusier-Möbel*; BGH, *GRUR* 1974, 740 (742) – *Sessel*; BGH, *GRUR* 1961, 635 (638) – *Stahlrohrstuhl I*. According to some authors (Ritscher, Landolt, op. cit., p. 128), there are various explanations for the "legal bigotry" shown with regard to the application of copyright to works of applied art/industrial design: one is certainly to be found in the prevalent conceptual differentiation of *applied* art with utilitarian purposes

In the past, the stringency with regard to works of applied art was justified by the fact that such works already benefited from special protection under the Copyright in Designs and Models Act[322] if they stood out from purely craftsman-like and average, everyday designs. In the former Copyright in Designs and Models Act, the "above-average achievements" covered were located below the scope of the "small coin/*kleine Münze*, or *petite monnaie*" doctrine, which turned on the distinction between minor copyright protection for designs and models with a low protection threshold, and major copyright for works of pure art, and was abandoned with the implementation of the EU Design Directive. That was followed by the so called "step theory" for product designs developed by the BGH (Federal Supreme Court),[323] which required a particularly high level of creativity (an aesthetic surplus) for obtaining copyright protection. The German Registered Designs Act (*Geschmacksmustergesetz*) based on the Community design legal framework entered into force on 1 June 2004, but it took several years for the BGH to harmonize the requirements for copyright protection across all categories of works. That would finally happen with the BGH's landmark decision *Geburtstagszug*.[324] Accordingly, there is no justification now for a higher protection threshold for works of applied art than for other categories of works. Thus, it is no longer required that an object or artefact of design exceeds an average level of creativity.[325] Nevertheless, it still remains to be seen how the precedent set by the BGH will be reflected in lower and upper court cases in the longer term,[326] although after the *Cofemel* decision, the issue seems to have been resolved by the European Court of Justice. While

from *pure* art; BGH, *GRUR* 2014, 175, para. 16 – *Geburtstagszug*; see Obergfell, "Abschied von der "Silberdistel": Zum urheberrechtlichen Schutz von Werken der angewandten Kunst", *GRUR* 2014, 621.

322 On the former Act on Copyright in Designs – *Gesetz betreffend das Urheberrecht an Mustern und Modellen*, see Kriesel, *Einheitlicher europäischer Werkbegriff und Herabsenkung der Anforderungen an die Gestaltungshöhe bei Werken der angewandten Kunst*, Frankfurt a.M., 2014, pp. 33 ff; Zentek, "Designspezifische Absenkungen der urheberrechtlichen Gestaltungshöhe Keine Angst vorm BGH", *WRP* 1/2010, 74; Obergfell, op. cit., p. 622.

323 BGH, *GRUR* 1995, 581 (582) – *Silberdistel*; *GRUR* 1998, 830 (832) – *Les-Paul-Gitarren*; BGH, *GRUR* 2004, 941–942 – *Metallbett*.

324 BGH, *GRUR* 2014, 175 – *Geburtstagszug*. See Obergfell, op. cit., p. 621; Klawitter, *GRUR-Prax* 2014, 30.

325 Against this decision, understood as a step backwards rather than a lowering of protection requirements, see Liebenau, "Star Athletics v Varsity Brands – German Comparative Perspectives and European Harmonization of Copyright for Applied Art," *GRUR*-Part II, 2017, 922. See also the critical commentary by Klawitter, op. cit., p. 31.

326 For an overview of German case law following the *Geburtstagszug* decision see Hartmann, "Geburtstagszug in voller Fahrt?," *WRP* 11/2016, 1327. See also Mezger, *Die Schutzschwelle für Werke der angewandten Kunst nach deutschem und europäischem Recht*, Göttingen, 2017.

the Higher Regional Court of Schleswig Holstein ultimately denied copyright protection to the locomotive toy, which was the subject of BGH's landmark *Geburtstagszug* ruling,[327] the Higher Regional Court of Cologne affirmed copyright protection for many table models by referring to the *Geburtstagszug* doctrine.[328] Following the same reasoning, the Higher Regional Court of Nürnberg ruled that a well-known and popular *Bundesliga* table by Kicker magazine qualifies for copyright protection,[329] and the Regional Court of Hamburg held that the product design of the *5,0 Original* beer is protected by copyright.[330]

The sparse and partly outdated case law of the Swiss courts indicates a similarly high threshold for design copyright,[331] as was the case in Germany until its paradigm shift.[332] The Swiss Federal Supreme Court adopts a principle according to which works of applied art are, in case of doubt, to be regarded as purely handcrafted products (*"Nachdem im Zweifelsfall von einem rein handwerklichen Erzeugnis auszugehen sei ..."*).[333] Such a "rule of doubt," as it has been defined,[334] is certainly questionable, as the Court itself has conceded, and it does not satisfy the needs of contemporary design. The Swiss Federal Supreme Court, in its judgment of 12 July 2017 (First Civil Law Division), granted protection for a bar stool designed by the famous Swiss artist Max Bill (Figure 23), but the reasoning was odd and based exclusively on design law (and trademark law), not on federal copyright law (respectively: Federal Act on the Protection of Designs

327 Judgement of OLG Schleswig, 11.09.2014, 6 U 74/10.

328 Judgement of OLG Cologne of 22.03.2018, 140 24/18.

329 Judgement of OLG Nürnberg 20.05.2014, Az. 3 U 1874/13.

330 Judgement of OLG Hamburg, 7.07.2016, 310 o 212/14.

331 *Bundesgesetz über das Urheberrecht und verwandte Schutzrechte* (*Urheberrechtsgesetz, URG*) vom 9. Oktober 1992 on line at https://www.admin.ch/opc/de/classified-compilation/19920251/201701010000/231.1.pdf.

332 Ritscher, *Hält der Geburtstagszug auch in der Schweiz? – Gedanken zur urheberrechtlichen Schutzschwelle und zum Schutzumfang von Produktgestaltungen in Deutschland und in der Schweiz*, in Dreier, Pfeifer, Specht (eds.), *Anwalt des Urheberrechts, Festschrift für Gernot Schulze zum 70. Geburtstag*, 2017, pp. 31 ff.

333 BGE 68 II 55; BGE 113 II 190, pp. 196 ff; BGE of 2 May 2011 (4A_78/2011) § 2.4. – *Le Corbusier*: "Die bis dahin ergangene Rechtsprechung wurde demnach mit dem neuen Urheberrechtsgesetz nicht einfach überholt, sondern es kann grundsätzlich darauf zurückgegriffen werden. Die Rechtsprechung zum neuen Urheberrechtsgesetz hat sich insofern weiterentwickelt, als nicht mehr auf die Urheber-Individualität, sondern allein auf die Werk-Individualität abgestellt wird (vgl. die Angaben in Erwägung 2.1). Dabei werden bei der Werkkategorie der Werke der angewandten Kunst vergleichsweise hohe Anforderungen an den individuellen Charakter gestellt" available on line at http://relevancy.bger.ch/php/aza/http/index.php?lang=de&type=simple_query. See Tissot, *La protection de designs en droit Suisse: bilan de la LDes et perspectives*, in de Werra (ed.), *Le droit du design/Design law*, Genève /Zurich, 2015, pp. 61–80.

334 BGE 143 III 373 of 12 July 2017 – *Max Bill*.

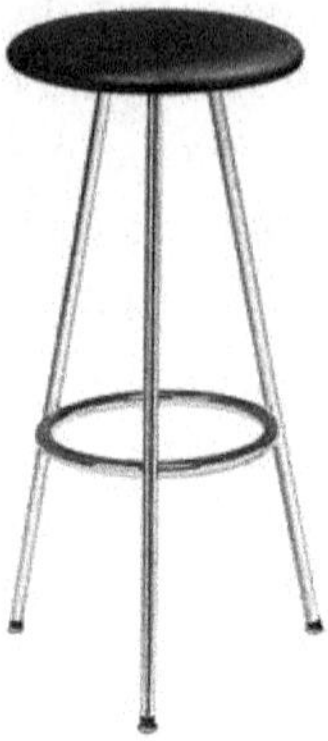

FIGURE 23
Barhocker 12–073 designer: Max Bill 1951, for Hochschule für Gestaltung (HfG) Ulm
PHOTOS AVAILABLE AT: HTTP://WWW.DESIGNKLASSIKER.COM/UPLOADS/_DK_OBJEKTE_O_BILD1_4E9EAE442AECD/DK-OBJEKT_BILL-MAX_STUEHLE_KREUZZARGENSTUHL-S-5-50_OB_1.JPG

and Federal Act on Copyright and Related Rights).[335] The Swiss Design Act protects "unique" designs. For a design to be unique, according to the court and commentators quoted in the judgment, persons who are immediately interested in buying such a product must believe that the design stands out substantially from previously known products. The decisive factor, therefore, is that the artistic design within the context of the purpose must be so clearly different that it appears to be unique. It was on those grounds that the Swiss Federal Supreme Court granted *de facto* protection for the personal uniqueness of Bill's authorship and consequently his bar stool.

According to the Dutch Copyright Act,[336] works of applied art and industrial design, such as furniture, upholstery, utensils, and fashion accessories, are eligible for copyright protection. Copyright has similarly been granted to passport photographs, striped wallpaper, designs of simple games like "four in a row," and designs of basic holiday homes,[337] but not, for instance, to caravan awnings because of their lack of "originality."[338] As elsewhere, the overlap

335 BGE 143 III 373, 384, § 2.8.5. The decision is available in English at https://www.mll-legal.com/fileadmin/redaktion/PDF-Artikel_etc/Max_Bill_Decision_12July2017.pdf (accessed 10.10.2019).

336 Article 10(1) number 11, of the Dutch Copyright Law available at https://www.vevam.org/wp-content/uploads/2016/09/Dutch-Copyright-Act-2015.pdf (accessed 12.10.2019).

337 Hugenholtz et al. (eds.), *A Century of Dutch Copyright law*, Amsterdam, 2012.

338 In *Doréma v. Isabella* 1996, the Arnhem Court of Appeal declined copyright protection because the different elements of the awnings, including the austere lines and simplicity of the design, the combination of colours, the dimensions, the circular canopy, and the layout of panes that creates a special light effect, were either technically or functionally determined, or elements of style, or existing features of known awnings produced by third parties, or clearly designed to fit in with current trends in the awning industry. The awnings followed patterns and trends in the caravan awning market that were too common to constitute personal intellectual creations eligible for copyright protection.

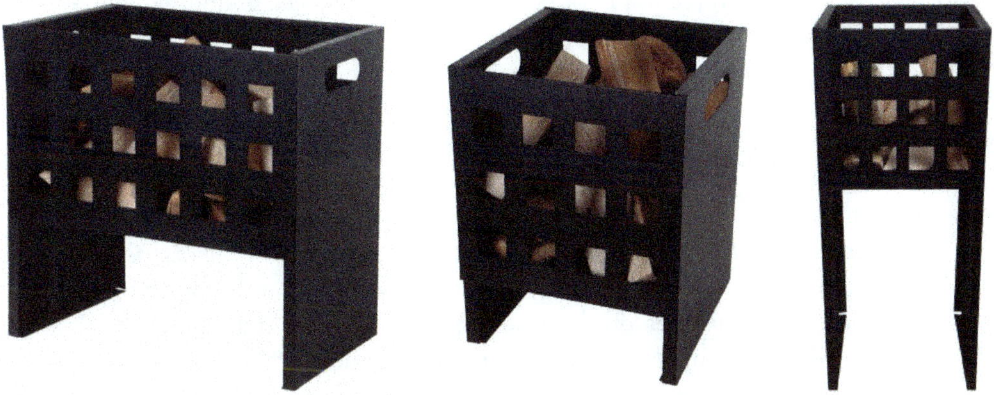

FIGURE 24 Esschert designs: "Fancy Flames" product line, encompassing a fire basket available in three different sizes: FF87, FF88 and FF89
PHOTOS AVAILABLE AT ESSCHERT DESIGN WEBSITE

of copyright and design protection in the Netherlands gives rise to delicate questions concerning the accumulation of the two IP regimes, the threshold and scope of protection, and the duration of the exclusive rights. Nevertheless, Dutch courts appear to have accepted the "author's intellectual creation" test of the European Court of Justice, and have extended it to protect industrial design.[339] The Supreme Court of the Netherlands, for example, granted copyright protection to a rather simple fire stove by referring to *Flos*.[340] In that well-known case – *S&S Import en Export v. Esschert Design* of 2013[341] – which confirmed the Court of Appeal decision, the Dutch Supreme Court came to the conclusion that the fire pit, the packaging, and the wrapper of Esschert (Figure 24) could, each and separately, be considered as works within the meaning of the Copyright Act, but the legal arguments used by the Court were

339 van Gompel, op. cit., p. 119.

340 Judgement of the Supreme Court of the Netherlands of 25.10.2013, *S&S Import en Export v. Esschert Design*, available at https://uitspraken.rechtspraak.nl/inziendocument?id=ECLI:NL:HR:2013:1036 (accessed 10.10.2019).

341 See Ritscher, Landolt, op. cit.; Quaedvlieg, op. cit., p. 51; Bently op. cit., p. 661; von Lewinski, "Introduction: The Notion of Work under EU Law," *GRUR Int.* 2014, p. 1097; Schulze, "Schleichende Harmonisierung des urheberrechtlichen Werkbegriffs? Anmerkung zu EuGH 'Infopaq/DDF'," *GRUR* 2009, pp. 1019 ff. See Judgement of the Supreme Court of the Netherlands of 25.10.2013 – *S&S Import en Export v. Esschert Design cit. supra*; Judgements of the Court of Appeal of Arnhem of 16.03.1999, *Vredestein v. Ring* and that of the Court of Appeal of The Hague of 03.02.2000 *Slagboons Electric v Koz Products*.

centred on the "overall impression" test derived from designs and models law, not from copyright law.[342]

Decisions have been deeply ambivalent, however. In the *Melano v. Quiges Fashion Jewels* case of 2013, the Court of Appeal of 's-Hertogenbosch dismissed a claim for copyright protection on pieces of jewellery with interchangeable coloured elements on the grounds that the plaintiff insufficiently substantiated the authorship of the jewellery and his "personal touch." That stands in contrast to the *SEVV v. AY Illuminate* case of 2010, where the District Court of Amsterdam held that the plaintiffs, of which it was sufficiently convinced that they were the actual creators, had made creative choices in designing decorative lamps with comparable, interchangeable elements.[343] It is hard to draw a clear line between works that possess just enough creativity and those that are too obvious or trivial to enjoy copyright, as the case *Zonen Endstra v. Nieuw Amsterdam* of 2013 demonstrated.[344]

As in other EU Member States, Dutch case law has ruled that the technical features of a work – aspects of form that are solely determined by functional demands – cannot be protected by copyright, as they fail to reflect the author's creativity. However, copyright protection may extend to design features dictated by their technical function if the author had sufficient room to make creative choices. The cases *Hauck v. Stokke, Stokke v. Fikszo*, and *Stokke v. H3 Products* of 2013[345] are remarkable on this point, even if, from a doctrinal

342 § 3.2.3 of the judgment *S&S Import en Export v. Esschert Design*, op. cit.

343 Cases reported in van Gompel, op. cit., pp. 130 ff.

344 Judgement of the Supreme Court of the Netherlands, 30.05.2008, *44* IIC 103 (2013). Case reported and commented in van Gompel, op. cit., p. 100. The case dealt with the question of whether copyright subsists in (transcripts of taped) conversations; the conversations took place during a series of secret meetings between police officers and Endstra, a real estate broker who was later murdered. The tapes were transcribed into official police reports, a copy of which found its way to crime reporters who published a book of the transcripts, with minor edits. The sons of the murdered businessman sought to stop publication by claiming copyright on the conversations. The Court of Appeal of The Hague in 2013, ruled that Endstra's conversations with the police were not original works, because Endstra had expressed himself in a nigh-endless sequence of incomplete, badly versed phrases that involved insufficient creative labour. Copyright protection was denied because Endstra had construed his speech in a form too ordinary or trivial. Many authors have strongly criticized the court decision, based on allegedly "aesthetic quality." See §5.13 of the judgment available at https://www.ivir.nl/publicaties/download/Annotatie_AMI_2013_6_7.pdf (accessed 10.10.2019).

345 See the judgement of the Dutch Supreme Court (Hoge Raad) of 22.02.2013 – *Stokke v. H3 Products*, and of 12.04.2013 – *Stokke v. Fikszo* in Köklü, Nérisson, "How Public Is the Public Domain? The Perpetual Protection of Inventions, Designs and Works by Trademarks," in

viewpoint, they are not necessarily satisfactory. In practice, what happened in the three *Stokke* cases is that the defendants unpacked various elements of form in the *Tripp Trapp* chair to show that they could not qualify as "original." The Dutch Supreme Court, however, clearly instructed the Court of Appeal to look at the chair's "overall impression" and to repack all the elements together in order to determine whether the collection of elements constituted an intellectual creation by the author. Moreover, the Dutch Supreme Court assumed that works of applied art are subject to the same European "author's own intellectual creation" test as all other creations are. Likewise, the Dutch Supreme Court held that the EU test is in line with the standard commonly employed by courts in the Netherlands: Dutch courts use copyright protection even for technically functional product designs, if the party can prove a minimum level of creative autonomy of the designer in creating the work. Ultimately, copyright protection would only be extended to the specific combination of unprotected elements.[346] In other words, that means that competitors can create similar products using a different combination or a different set of elements, but the overall impression of the product must differ from that of the original work. Once again, Dutch case law illustrates a dissonant combination of assessments: the "originality" test from copyright law and the "overall impression" test derived from designs and models law. Thus, only trivial or banal designs without any creative features fall outside of the scope of the Dutch interface between design and copyright protection,[347] an "indulgent practice" which has attracted some criticism.[348]

In a similar way, the Supreme Court of Belgium in 2013 confirmed that in light of European Court of Justice precedent, in particular *Eva-Maria Painer v. Standard Verlags GmbH*, a work – specifically a fireplace design – is original if it is the intellectual creation of the author, bearing the author's personal touch.[349] The ruling reversed a previous decision by the same court holding that the "personal touch" element was not required under Belgian law.[350] As early as 1987, with the *Screeno prints* judgement, the Benelux Court of Justice

Ullrich et al. (eds.), *TRIPS plus 20: From Trade Rules to Market Principles*, Heidelberg, 2016, pp. 561–580, p. 567. *Cf* van Gompel, op. cit., p. 121.

346 Van Gompel, op. cit., p. 121.

347 *Endestra* case, op. cit.

348 Quaedvlieg, "The Tripod of Originality and the Concept of Work in Dutch and European Copyright," *GRUR Int.* 2014, pp. 1105 ff, p. 1109.

349 *M-Design Benelux SPRL v. Geoffrey Bontemps SPRL* [2013] S.C.C.12.0263.N/1.

350 *Artessuto v. B&T Textilia* [2012] S.C.C.11.0108.N.

laid down that the originality criterion also applies to designs.[351] The principle was that of cumulative protection under copyright and design laws, but it does not apply to necessary, merely technical features dictated solely by their function. The relationship between copyright and design law in the Benelux was established at an earlier stage than in other countries, with the Uniform Benelux Law on Designs and Models (UBLDM) 1975.[352] That law still states that, in order to be eligible for copyright protection, models and designs must be of "a clearly artistic character."

6.1.4 *France's Equal Treatment of All Intellectual Creative Endeavours*

French copyright law and design legislation share the same scope of protection and are of cumulative application (*cumul absolu*).[353] As in others EU Member States, technical features solely dictated by functional goals fall outside the "*cumul*" of the copyright/design interface, as they are protected by patent law. The French Supreme Court has specifically excluded cumulative protection where aesthetic elements are "inseparable" from technical and functional elements.[354] In particular, works of applied art are cumulatively protected by copyright law if they are *oeuvres de l'esprit* (intellectual works), as the law underscores personal elements and, implicitly, that authorship is an entirely human endeavour. In practice, authors of copyrightable works must be human, a condition which seems needlessly cumbersome in today's world of Algorithm-Aided Design (AAD) (see Part 1, §5 and Part 2, §§6 and 6.1 above). "*Les dispositions du présent Code protègent les droits des auteurs sur toutes les oeuvres de l'esprit, quels qu'en soient le genre, la forme d'expression, le mérite ou la destination.*"[355] French law does not impose any other conditions,[356] although

---

351 Judgement of the Benelux Court of Justice of 22 May 1987, § 23 – *Screeno prints v. Citroen.*

352 When Benelux adopted UBLDM, copyright acts were already in force in The Netherlands (the Act dates back to 1912) and in Luxembourg (Copyright Act 1972); Belgium adopted its Copyright and Neighboring Rights Act in 1994.

353 See Article L. 511–1 *Code de la propriété intellectuelle* créé par Loi n. 92–597 du 1 juillet 1992 relative au code de la propriété intellectuelle (French Intellectual Property Code) available at https://www.legifrance.gouv.fr. See Zech, *Der Schutz von Werken der angewandten Kunst im Urheberrecht Frankreichs und Deutschlands*, Munich, 1999, p. 29.

354 See Mandel, Bootherstone, Massot, op. cit., pp. 28 ff and the case law they quote (*Cass* 29 juin 2010 for example).

355 Article L. 112–1 *Code de la propriété intellectuelle.*

356 Article L 111–1 and L 111–2 *Code de la propriété intellectuelle.*

the form of expression in practice must be "manifest and objectified"[357] (a requirement which resembles fixation in common law and recalls the Court of Justice's *Cofemel* judgment), and "original,"[358] a standard which coincides with the European Court of Justice's "author's own intellectual creation" standard, and in particular with its personalist vision of copyright law. In the non-exhaustive list of protectable works, a broad definition of design can be outlined, encompassing communication design – graphic and typographic works, logotypes,[359] maps, architectural plans, and website architecture;[360] product design within the category "*oeuvres des arts appliqués*";[361] and fashion design, explicitly mentioned as "*créations des industries saisonnières de l'habillement et de la parurein.*"[362] As said, French judges apply the principle of the unity of art (*unité de l'art*), which implies the equal treatment of all intellectual works (*oeuvres de l'esprit*) without requiring any special level of artistry for deciding whether a design object or artefact is protectable. At the same time, however, the principle is only apparently detached from any level of originality: *l'originalité portant la marque de la personalité de son auteur*, equivalent to "*l'esprit qui porte l'empreinte personelle de ses auteurs*," comes into consideration every time the question of the scope of protection is at issue, for instance in infringement proceedings.[363] The following are a few examples of things which have been granted copyright protection because they reflect "the personality of the author": the famous *cafetière Bodum* (Figure 25),[364] the Chaise LC4 by Le Corbousier with Perriand and Jeanneret (Figure 26),[365] and the stainless steel nail clipper by Vitry Frères Paris (Figure 27).[366]

357 Pignatari, *Le support en droit d'auteur*, Brussels, 2013, pp. 121 ff.

358 Article L 112–4 *Code de la propriété intellectuelle* "Le titre d'une oeuvre de l'esprit, dès lors qu'il présente un caractère original, est protégé comme l'oeuvre elle-même."

359 CA Lyon, 19.02.2010 *Logo Société Renault*, design: Yvaral and Vasarely.

360 *Cass civ 1re*, 12.05.2011, pourvoi n. 10–17852, availabale at https://www.legifrance.gouv.fr. CA Versailles, 2.07.2013 *Vente-privée.com/Club privé*: "au motif que la combinaison de ses différents éléments selon une certaine presentation procède d'une recherce esthétique, nullement impose par un impératif fonctionell, qui confère au site une physionomie particulière et révèle un effort créatif qui caractérise l'originalité de ce site."

361 Article L 112–2, point 10, *Code de la propriété intellectuelle*.

362 Article L 112–2, point 14, *Code de la propriété intellectuelle*.

363 Mandel, Bootherstone, Massot, op. cit., pp. 22 ff.; König, *Der Werkbegriff in Europa – Eine rechtsvergleichende Unter suchung des britischen, französischen und deutschen Urheberrechts*, Tübingen 2015, p. 190.

364 CA Paris, 8.3.2000.

365 CA Paris, 7.10.1993.

366 TGI Paris, 11.02.2011.

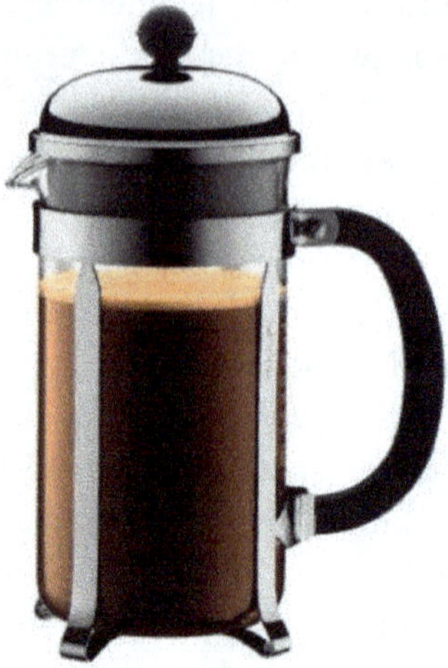

FIGURE 25
Cafetière à piston Chambord de la société Bodum France
IMAGE AVAILABLE AT HTTPS://WWW.MAXICOFFEE.COM/IMAGES/PRODUCTS/LARGE/CAFETIERE-PISTON-CHAMBORD-1L.JPG

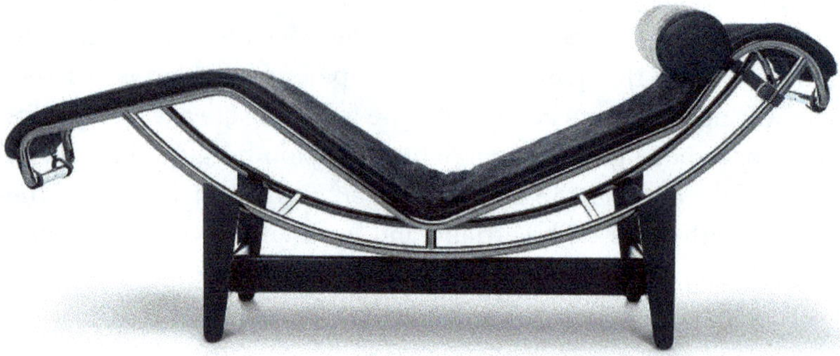

FIGURE 26 Chaise LC4 Le Corbousier with Perriand and Jeanneret.
LOUNGE CHAIR & OTTOMAN BY CHARLES AND RAY EAMES

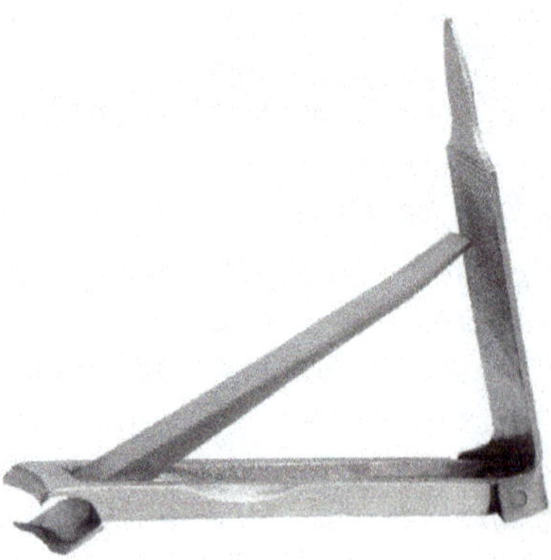

FIGURE 27
Nail clipper in stainless steel Vitry Frères Paris
IMAGE AVAILABLE AT HTTPS://WWW.VITRY.COM/1841-THICKBOX_DEFAULT/COUPE-ONGLES-MANUCURE-EXTRA-PLAT.JPG

6.1.5 *The High Thresholds of Italian and Portuguese Laws*

Both Italy and Portugal set a high threshold for copyright protection for works of applied art, otherwise cumulative protection does not apply. In addition to the common requirement that all works must be an "intellectual creation of its author" (*opera dell'ingegno di carattere creativo/particolare espressione del lavoro intellettuale/obras as criações intelectuais/desde que seja original*),[367] Italian and Portuguese laws require the work have "inherent artistic value,"[368] in contrast to other civil law countries such as France or Spain,[369] which only require originality,[370] and admit a perfect cumulation of remedies.[371]

Focusing on the copyright/design interface in the Italian legal system, before European harmonization, Italian law imposed a "separability test" (*scindibilità*) on the premise that "applied art" did not mean "industrial design" in general, but rather artworks (e.g. drawings, paintings, and sculpture) "applied" to a "useful article." That provision[372] tended to exclude from copyright protection three-dimensional works of industrial design, while admitting two-dimensional works of very modest value, reflecting the strong influence of the philosophy of art of Benedetto Croce, for which copyright should protect only

---

367 Articles 1 and 6 of Italian Royal Decree of 21 April 1941, n. 633, as amended, available at https://www.normattiva.it/uri-res/N2Ls?urn:nir:stato:legge:1941-04-22;633!vig=. Articles 1 and 4 Portuguese Copyright and Neighbouring Rights Protection Code, availabale at https://www.spautores.pt/assets_live/165/codigododireitodeautorcdadclei16 2008.pdf.

368 Article 2(10) *Regio decreto sulla protezione del diritto d'autore e di altri diritti connessi al suo esercizio* and Article 2(1)(i)) *Código de Direitos de Autor e Direitos Conexos.*

369 *Real Decreto Legislativo 1/1996, de 12 de abril, por el que se aprueba el texto refundido de la Ley de Propiedad Intelectual, regularizando, aclarando y armonizando las disposiciones legales vigentes sobre la materia* (*texto consolidado*). Article 1: "La propiedad intelectual de una obra literaria, artística o científica corresponde al autor por el solo hecho de su creación", Article 10(1): "Son objeto de propiedad intelectual todas las creaciones originales literarias, artísticas o científicas expresadas por cualquier medio o soporte, tangible o intangible, actualmente conocido o que se invente en el futuro, comprendiéndose entre ellas: (….) e) Las esculturas y las obras de pintura, dibujo, grabado, litografía y las historietas gráficas, tebeos o comics, así como sus ensayos o bocetos y las demás obras plásticas, sean o no aplicadas. f) Los proyectos, planos, maquetas y diseños de obras arquitectónicas y de ingeniería. g) Los gráficos, mapas y diseños relativos a la topografía, la geografía y, en general, a la ciencia. (…)". Available at https://www.boe.es/.

370 In France, *l'esprit qui porte l'empreinte personelle de ses auteurs*, while in Spain *un cierto grado de creatividad y originalidad de nivel artístico, la altura creativa.*

371 Article 3, Legislative Decree 1/1996, op. cit. See Vivas Tesón, "La tutela del diseño industrial por el derecho de autor. A propósito de la STS de 27 de septiembre de 2012 (RJ 2012, 9707)," *Revista Aranzadi de Derecho Patrimonial*, 2013, pp. 407–426.

372 Article 2(4) of Royal Decree No. 633 of 21 April 1941, op. cit.

intellectual creations belonging to the pure arts[373] – for which, for example, copyright protection for Le Corbusier's *chaise-longue* was at first refused.[374] So Italian courts have traditionally drawn a sharp distinction between copyright protection (for unique works of art) and design protection (for industrially manufactured utilitarian products), by using the criterion of separability.[375] It meant that only those designs that could be separated from their intended use could be protected by copyright. That criterion defined the differentiation between the artistic value and the usefulness of a product itself, by requiring that the artistic value of an object had to be "separable" from the mere function of the object. Such a requirement has been the subject of much debate, with some commentators insisting that the divisibility between art and functional use had to be material and achieved in practice, while others instead believed it need only be potential. One interpretation that has been widely applauded was proposed by Vanzetti and Di Cataldo,[376] who defined as "*scindibile*" any work that could be aesthetically appreciated regardless of the usefulness of the product and could, therefore, be applied to functionally different products.

The design/copyright interface in Italian law finds its source in Italian Royal Decree No. 1411 of 25 August 1940 (the first Italian law on Utility and Ornamental Models)[377] and Royal Decree No. 633 of 21 April 1941, (Protection of Copyright

---

373 See "Relazione di accompagnamento alla proposta di legge dell'On. Minervini, Modificazioni alla legge 22 aprile 1941, n. 633 ed al codice civile per la protezione del diritto d'autore sulle opere del disegno industriale," *Dir. aut.*, 1984, pp. 242 ff.

374 *Cass. Civ. sez I*, 10516/1994, *Foro It.*, 1995, I, 810; *AIDA*, 1995, 3014; *Dir. Ind.*, 1995, 113, commentary by Floridia; *Dir. Autore*, 1996, 410 commentary by Fabiani; *Giust. Civ.*, 1995, 2169 commentary by Schermi. See also *Cass.* 6664/1996, *GADI*, 1996, 71; *Cass.* 7077/1990, *Riv. dir. ind.*, 1991, II, 24, commentary by Sena: "*il diritto d'autore protegge* [...] *la forma che abbia un valore estetico in sé, in assoluto*". See Sarti, *La tutela estetica del prodotto industriale*, Milan, 1990, p. 12; Sena, "I diritti sulle invenzioni e sui modelli industriali," in *Tratt. Dir. Civ. e Comm. Cicu – Messineo*, Milan, 1990, p. 572. On Le Corbusier's *chaise-longue* see Trib. Monza, 23.04.2002 (ord.), *Dir. Autore*, 2002, p. 433, commentary by Fittante; Trib. Monza, 16.07.2002, *Dir. Ind.*, 2003, p. 55, commentary by Fittante; and Trib. Bologna, 02.08.2004 (ord.), *Dir. Ind.*, 2005, p. 577. Scuffi, Franzosi, *Diritto industriale italiano*, Padua, 2014.

375 Sarti, *La tutela estetica del prodotto industriale*, op. cit., pp. 12 ff; Bergomi, "Industrial design," *Contr. e impr.*, 1987, pp. 966 ff; Floridia, in AA.VV (eds.)., *Diritto industriale proprietà intellettuale e concorrenza*, 4th ed., Turin, 2012, pp. 322 ff; Cresti, "La protezione dell'industrial design tra tutela brevettuale e diritto d'autore", *Contr. e impr. Europa*, 2005, pp. 176 ff.; Roder, op. cit., 2016, p. 380.

376 Vanzetti, Di Cataldo, *Manuale di diritto industriale*, 7th ed., Milan, 2012, p. 479.

377 Article 5(2) of the Royal Decree No. 1411 of 25 August, 1940 identified ornamental designs and models as industrial products made valuable by their specific shape, or colours, or other elements conceived by the author. However, the only protection contemplated was

and Neighbouring Rights),[378] both of which required the application of the "separability" criterion until the legislation was amended by Legislative Decree No. 95 of 2 February 2001 implementing Directive 98/71/EC on the legal protection of designs and models (see Part 1, §3.2 above).[379]

Still today, notwithstanding the abandonment of the separability criterion with the adoption of Directive 98/71/EC, many Italian judges continue to use it tacitly. At present, Article 2(10) of Royal Decree No. 633 of 21 April 1941 (as amended) limits the scope of protection to industrial design works showing "creative character" and "artistic value" ("*le opere del disegno industriale che presentino di per sé carattere creativo e valore artistico*"[380]). Thus two conditions are required for a design work to be granted copyright protection: creative character, where the author's personal contribution, even if very modest, is sufficient;[381] and artistic value, a rather vague notion, the aim of which is to exclude industrially designed objects of common use from copyright protection, by requiring a special artistic assessment of design products and artefacts. In Italy, a key epicentre of the international design community, the

---

patent protection. It was not easy to draw a line to distinguish which forms could benefit from patent or utility model protection (Article 2), and which from copyright protection; therefore, the Italian lawmakers relied on the so-called "*criterio di scindibilità*" (see below in the text). Sanna, "Introduzione al Titolo III R.d. 25 agosto 1940, n. 1411, Brevetto per modelli e disegni ornamentali," in Ubertazzi (ed.), *Commentario breve al diritto industriale*, Padua, 2004, pp. 1063, 1069; Del Gallo Rossoni, "Modello ornamentale nel diritto Italiano," in *Disegno industriale e protezione europea* (International Conference, Treviso, 12–13 October 1988), Milan, 1989, pp. 284 ff.

378 Article 2(4) of the Royal Decree No. 633 of 21 April 1941, op. cit.

379 It also amended Articles 31–44 of Section III, Chapter II of the Italian Industrial Property Code, which set forth the requirements needed for protection, the definition of design and models, and the duration and rights deriving from registration. See Marzano, op. cit.; Vanzetti, *Codice della proprietà industriale*, Milan, 2013; Di Cataldo, "Dai vecchi "modelli ornamentali" ai nuovi "disegni e modelli". I requisiti di proteggibilità secondo il nuovo regime," *Europa e diritto privato*, 2002, pp. 67 ff.; Vanzetti, Di Cataldo, *Manuale di diritto industriale*, op. cit.; Galli, "L'attuazione della direttiva comunitaria sulla protezione di disegni e modelli," *Leggi civ. comm.*, 2001, pp. 883 ff, p. 893; Giudici, "La protezione giuridica dei disegni e dei modelli," *Riv. Dir. Ind.*, 2001, III, pp. 60 ff, p. 63.

380 Article 2(10) of Royal Decree No. 633 of 21 April 1941, op. cit.

381 "(…) *il concetto giuridico di creatività – come osservato in più occasioni da questa Corte – non coincide con quello di creazione, originalità e novità assoluta … con la conseguenza che la creatività non può essere esclusa soltanto perché l'opera consiste in idee e nozioni semplici, ricomprese nel patrimonio intellettuale di persone aventi esperienza nella materia* (*Cass. 28.11.2011, no. 25173/2011; Cass. 12.03.2004, no. 5089/2004*)". Quoted from the judgement of *Cass. Civ. Sez I*, 23.03.2017, 7477/2017. See Fabbio, "La tutela autoriale del progetto di arredamento o di architettura d'interni," *Riv. dir. comm.*, 2002, II, pp. 43–53.

long-standing and highly sensitive issue of that assessment is the prerogative of the twelve IP Divisions of the local courts and regional appeal courts. The growth of industrial design and its spread into everyday life would certainly be expected to have a major impact on the interpretation of the provision, as the "artistic value" of industrial design works is always absolutely inseparable from the function for which the object is designed, if it is interpreted as the result of creative processes and innovative intellectual conceptions according to the designer's project. After abandoning efforts to provide a definition of "artistic value,"[382] the Italian Supreme Court instead attempted to summarize the subjective and objective interpretative strands of the IP Divisions of Italy's courts and legal doctrine[383] in a "Decalogue of Objectively-Oriented Criteria," to identify the so-called *quid pluris* of "high-end" design.[384]

---

382 Trib. Venezia, 02.02.2004 (ord.), *Dir. Ind.*, 2005, p. 527, commentary by Sandri (*La tutela del design e la teoria della percezione visuale, secondo cui il carattere artistico andrebbe valutato sulla base delle « emozioni » che un'opera di design tutelabile ex l.a. dovrebbe suscitare*); Trib. Milano, 29.03.2005, *AIDA*, p. 641; Trib. Milano 30.11.2004, *AIDA*, 2005, p. 590; Trib. Bologna, 3.08.2004, *AIDA*, 2005, p. 539.

383 Galli, "La revisione del codice della proprietà industriale: da un'impostazione 'proprietaria' a un approccio market-oriented," *Corriere giur.*, 2011, p. 277; Montanari, "L'industrial design tra modelli, marchi di forma e diritto d'autore," *Riv. dir. ind.*, 2010, 1, p. 7; Spada, "Industrial design e opere d'arte applicata (dialogo tra Paolo Spada e Paolo Auteri commentato da Gustavo Ghidini)," *Riv. dir. civ.*, 2002, II, pp. 271 ff.; Ghidini, *Profili evolutivi del diritto industriale*, Milan, 2001, pp. 100 ff.

See Trib. Bologna 8.9.2005, *Giur. ann. dir. ind.*, 2006, n. 4983; Trib. Bologna 10.11.2010, Trib. Venezia 10.12.2010, and Trib. Firenze 4.4.2011, *Riv. dir. ind.* 2011, p. 308; (*Lounge Chair & Ottoman* by Charles and Ray Eames): Trib. Milano 13.9.2012, *Giur. ann. dir. ind.*, 2012, n. 5895, 1029; (*Arco lamp* by Pier Giacomo Castiglioni and Achille Castiglioni): Trib. Milano 29.12.2006, Trib. Milano 8.2.2007, *Foro it.*, Rep. 2007, 130 and *Riv. dir. ind.* 2007, II, p. 42; Trib. Roma, 18.01.2011, *Giur. It.*, 2011, 11, 2314, commentary by Millano; Trib. Milano 12.9.2012, *Giur. ann. dir. ind.*, 2012, n. 5902, 1112; (*Panton Chair* by Verner Panton): Trib. Milano, 18.01.2007 (ordinance), *Riv. Dir. Ind.*, 2007, II, p. 56 and Trib. Milano, 28.11.2006 (ordinance), *Riv. Dir. Ind.*, 2006, p. 49 commentary by Sena; Trib. Milano 17.9.2012, *Giur. ann. dir. ind.*, 2012, n. 5903, 1134; (*chaise* by Le Corbusier): Trib. Monza, 15.07.2008, *Dir. Ind.*, 2008, 581 commentary by De Sapia; (jewelry reproducing Picasso, Mirò, Modigliani works of art): Trib. Venezia, 2.02.2004 (ordinance), *Dir. Ind.*, 2005, p. 527 commentary by Sandri; (Wagenfeld lamp): Trib. Firenze, 6.08.2003, *AIDA*, 2004, p. 770; (vase shape reproducing a gondola): Trib. Venezia, 21.04.2000 (ordinance), *Foro It.*, 2001, I, 1404.

384 See *Cass. Civ. Sez I*, 13.11.2015, n. 23292 *Metalco v City design*, *Dir. Ind.*, 2016, p. 527 commentary by Fittante. After the resumption of proceedings at the Venice Appeals Court, commercial section, judgment 121/2017 of 26.6.2017, the bench ruled that LIBRE by Metalco was not eligible for protection because the company City Design had registered an identical model earlier, which pre-empted copyright protection. On the artistic merit of industrial products see also Milan Appeals Court, 17.10.2006, *Giur. It.*, 2007, 10, 2241 commentary by Millanesi; Trib. Firenze, 6.8.2003, *AIDA*, 2004, p. 770, and Trib. Venezia,

The "Decalogue of Objectively-Oriented Criteria" satisfies the requirements of Article 2 (10) of Royal Decree No. 633 of 21 April 1941, and sets the following ten criteria for the cumulative protection of design works:[385] 1) the object should arouse aesthetic emotions; 2) the object should exhibit a marked subjective character in relation to the forms normally found in similar products on the market; 3) the object should be endowed with autonomous relevance; 4) the aesthetic and artistic qualities of the work should be recognized in cultural and institutional environments; 5) the work should have a recognized market value that transcends the mere functionality of the product; 6) the object should be exhibited in fairs, exhibits, museums, specialized magazines, and journals; 7) the object should be sold on the artistic, non-commercial market; 8) the work should have acquired a particularly high value on the commercial market, implying the attribution of artistic value; 9) the artist should be of note; 10) the object must have attained recognition by the community at large. As such, the assessment of eligibility is still carried out on an "artistic-legal" basis, despite the attempt to objectify the criteria. The "Decalogue of Objectively-Oriented Criteria" is clearly conditioned by various biases. To begin with, time constraints are imposed for an industrial design work to attain recognition by the community (req. 10). Another bias is the "museum-like standing" of a product design that serves as a decisive criterion for its eligibility for copyright protection.[386] Although the parameter cannot have an absolute value and must be evaluated case by case,[387] it is a discriminant against younger generations of designers who have yet to become "historicized," as well as for hybrid generative design and digital design. Similar considerations concern the fact that a design work must have been created by a well-known artist (req. 9), a requirement that brings us back to the artistic value of a work. For example, in 2015 the IP Division of the Court of Milan recognized copyright protection in the case of a peculiar bottle shape made by the famous Welsh designer Lovegrove in 2002, "a swirl of inspiration that is suddenly crystallized or frozen into an object."[388] Here it must be considered that a well-known artist

21.10.2005, *Dir. Ind.*, 2006, p. 594, commentary by Foglia. See Spada, Ghidini, Auteri, "Industrial design e opere d'arte applicate all'industria," *Riv. Dir. Civ.* 1, 2002, pp. 267 ff.

385 *Cass. Civ. Sez I*, 23.03.2017, 7477/2017, op. cit., which validates the precedent *Cass. Civ. Sez I*, 2015/23292, op. cit. *Cf* Trib. Monza 23.04.2002, cit.; Trib. Monza 16.07.2002, cit.; Trib. Bari 27.10.2003; Trib. Bologna 3.09.2004; App. Milano 21.11.2006, n. 2801.

386 Ritscher, Landolt, op. cit., p. 128.

387 Remotti commenting *Cass. Civ. Sez. I*, 29.10.2015, 22118/2015 (prayer beads and other devotional objects), *Dir. Ind.*, 2016, p. 345.

388 Trib. Milano, 1.12.2015, judgment No. 13487/2015 available at https://www.giurisprudenzadelleimprese.it.

may not always produce works of artistic value, just as, on the contrary, it is quite possible for artists who are not yet recognized as such to produce works of great value. A further and related consideration is that a design work can become an object of sale on the artistic market and not only on the purely commercial market, just as a work can acquire particularly high value on the latter (req. 7–8). Furthermore, the recourse to circumstantial criteria (req. 4–5–6: recognition in critical-specialist fields, certainly innovative traits, both in planning and implementation, early and reliable musealisation) and to subjective criteria (req. 1–2) based on an *ex ante* judgment should be properly weighed (where present) by experienced and specialized consultants, able to provide the judge with valid elements of evaluation.[389] On the other hand, under its interpretation of the "creative character" condition of Article 2(10) of the Italian copyright law, the Supreme Court assesses the "qualitatively superior character" of an object with respect to the "individual character" required by design law, which identifies the uncommon form of the design (that therefore affects the attention of the consumer), and helps make it appreciable as a "personal representation of the author," a prerequisite for identifying the author's personality,[390] although only "minimum creative freedom" is required.[391] As in the other EU legal systems, designs with features solely dictated by technical function are excluded from protection.

Therefore, to sum up, the actual practical criteria for determining protection is that of "collective recognition" by cultural and institutional environments, inferable from exhibitions, displays, prizes, reviews , and expert evaluations,[392] and that of an "added meaning" to the object, which transcends the narrow functionality of the object itself and the mere pleasantness of its forms, displaying a minimum of creative freedom. On those premises, the Arco lamp by Castiglioni 1962, distributed by Flos (Figure 28);[393] Moon Boots 1969 by Tecnica

389 Remotti, op. cit.; and Romano, *Giur. It*, 2016, 2, p. 309.

390 Trib. Torino, 17.12.2004, *AIDA*, 2005, p. 603; Trib. Milano, 29.03.2005, *AIDA*, p. 641. Trib. Venezia, 21.10.2005, *Foro it*, Rep. 2006, 111; *Cass.* 27.10.2005, 20925/2005, *Foro it.*, 2006 I, 2080 commentary by Casaburi, and *Dir ind.*, 2006, p. 290 commentary by Bonelli.

391 *Cass.* 2015/23292, cit.

392 Vanzetti, Di Cataldo, op. cit., at p. 533; Trib. Milano, 22.2.2010, *Giur. ann. dir. ind.*, 2011, n. 5636 at 219, Trib. Milano, 22.4.2010, *Giur. ann. dir. ind.*, 2011, n. 5643, at 313, Trib. Bologna, 30.8.2011, *Giur. ann. dir. ind.*, 2012, n. 5835, at 463, Trib. Bologna, 3.08.2001, *Giur. Comm.*, 2005, I, p. 82 comments by Pellegrino. *Cf* also Trib. Milano, 18.01.2007, Trib. Venezia, 13.02.2008; Sena, "Design e diritto d'autore", *Riv. Dir. Ind.*, 2001, II, p. 61; Ghidini, *Profili evolutivi del diritto industriale*, Milan, 2001, p. 105.

393 Trib. Milano, 8.02.2007, *Riv dir. Ind.*, 2007, II, p. 42; and *Foro it.*, Rep. 2007, 130; and *Riv. dir. ind.* 2007, II, p. 42.

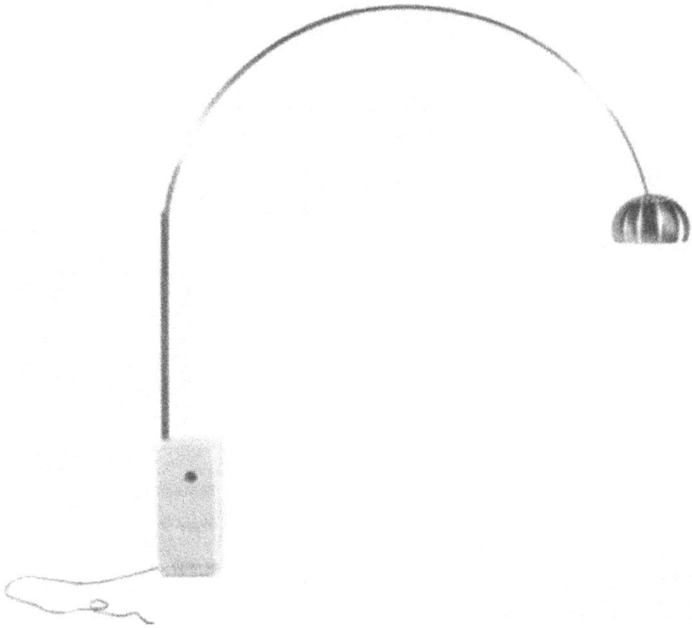

FIGURE 28 (Flos) "an expression of the post-war pursuit of a style shaped by essentiality and formal rigor, for the dynamism of its essential design, for the perfect harmony of its lines, forms, and volumes, for its absolutely innovative conception with respect to that of the classical lamp". Milan Court (IP division) 8.02.2007
TRANSL.: "ESPRESSIONE DI QUELLA RICERCA DI STILE DEL DOPOGUERRA IMPRONTATA AD ESSENZIALITÀ E RIGORE FORMALE, PER IL DINAMISMO DEL SUO DISEGNO ESSENZIALE, PER LA PERFETTA ARMONIA DEI RAPPORTI DI LINEE, FORME E VOLUMI, PER LA CONCEZIONE ASSOLUTAMENTE INNOVATIVA RISPETTO A QUELLA DELLA LAMPADA CLASSICA"

(Figure 29);[394] Panton Chair produced by Vitra (Figure 30);[395] Chaise-longue LC4 by Le Corbusier 1928;[396] and Vespa by Piaggio 1945–60 (Figure 31)[397] have

394 Trib. Milano, 12.07.2016, 8628/2016 available at https://www.giurisprudenzadelleimprese.it (accessed 9.9.2019).

395 Trib. Milano, 18.01.2007 (ord.), *Riv. Dir. Ind.*, 2007, II, p. 56; and Trib. Milano, 28.11.2006 (ord.), *Riv. Dir. Ind.*, 2006, p. 49 commentary by Sena.

396 Trib. Milano, 9.01.2014, 2311/2014 available at https://www.giurisprudenzadelleimprese.it/ (accessed 9.9.2019).

397 Trib. Torino, 6.04.2017, 1900/2017 available at https://www.giurisprudenzadelleimprese.it (accessed 9.9.2019).

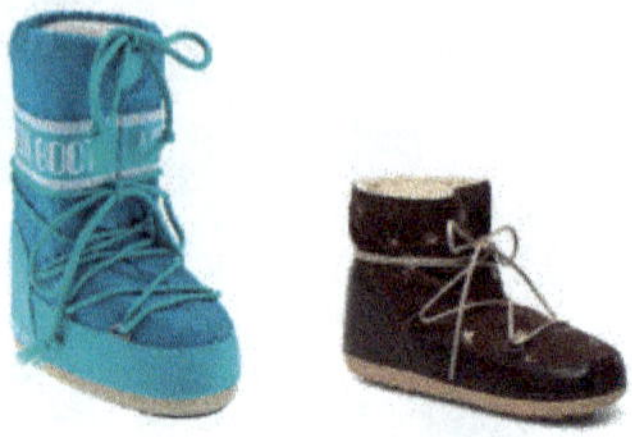

FIGURE 29 (Moon Boots) "for their particular aesthetic impact, which, when they appeared on the market, profoundly changed the aesthetic conception itself of the after-ski boot, becoming a true icon of Italian design and of their capacity to drive irreversible change in the taste of an entire historical era in relation to objects of everyday use". Milan Court (IP division) 12.07.2016
TRANSL.: "PER IL PARTICOLARE IMPATTO ESTETICO, CHE, ALLA SUA COMPARSA SUL MERCATO, HA PROFONDAMENTE MUTATO LA STESSA CONCEZIONE ESTETICA DELLO STIVALE DOPOSCI, DIVENENDO VERA E PROPRIA ICONA DEL DESIGN ITALIANO E DELLA SUA CAPACITÀ DI FARE EVOLVERE IN MODO IRREVERSIBILE IL GUSTO DI UN'INTERA EPOCA STORICA IN RELAZIONE AGLI OGGETTI D'USO QUOTIDIANO."

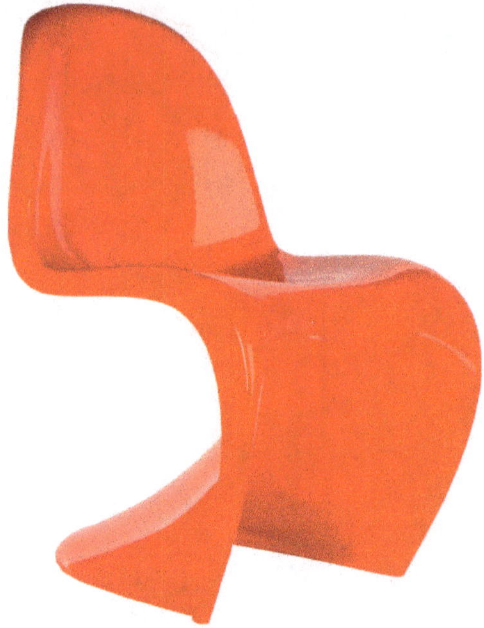

FIGURE 30 (Panton Chair) "A chair that can be considered the manifestation of a specific expressive pursuit and intuition, justified independently from its practical employment, able to exercise a particular hold on the perceptive plane". Milan Court (IP division) 18.01.2007
TRANSL.: "SEDIA CHE PUÒ CONSIDERARSI MANIFESTAZIONE DI UNA SPECIFICA RICERCA ED INTUIZIONE ESPRESSIVA, AUTONOMAMENTE GIUSTIFICATA RISPETTO ALL'IMPIEGO PRATICO, IN GRADO DI ESERCITARE UNA PARTICOLARE PRESA SUL PIANO PERCETTIVO."

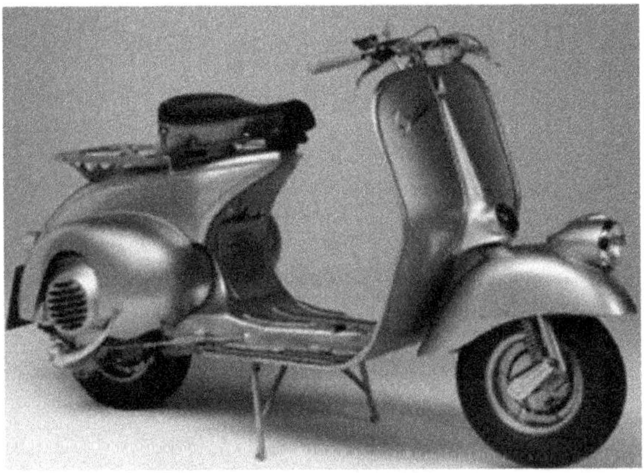

FIGURE 31 (Vespa) "The creative character and artistic character of a design work are highlighted and should be assessed by the standard of its collective recognition on the market and in artistic circles, considering its critical success, the awarding of prizes, its presence in museums, its participation in exhibitions, and its dissemination by publication in journals". Turin Court (IP division) 6.04.2017
TRANSL.: "ED INFATTI IL CARATTERE CREATIVO ED IL CARATTERE ARTISTICO DI UN'OPERA DI DESIGN VENGONO EVIDENZIATI E DEBBONO ESSERE VALUTATI ALLA STREGUA DEL RICONOSCIMENTO COLLETTIVO DI MERCATO E DEGLI AMBIENTI ARTISTICI, CONSIDERANDO IL SUCCESSO DI CRITICA, IL CONFERIMENTO DI PREMI, LA PRESENZA NEI MUSEI, LA PARTECIPAZIONE A MOSTRE, LA DIFFUSIONE DI PUBBLICAZIONI SULLE RIVISTE."

all been granted copyright by Italian "art judges"[398] on the grounds that the Louvre museum, the MoMA and others (such as the recently opened *Museo del Design Italiano* in Milan) ranked the products among the one hundred most important designs in recent history.

More recently, a turning point was reached when Italian courts granted copyright protection to several design works, irrespectively of whether they were worthy of mention by museums. In a well-known decision, the Italian

398 Ritscher, Landolt, op. cit., 128.

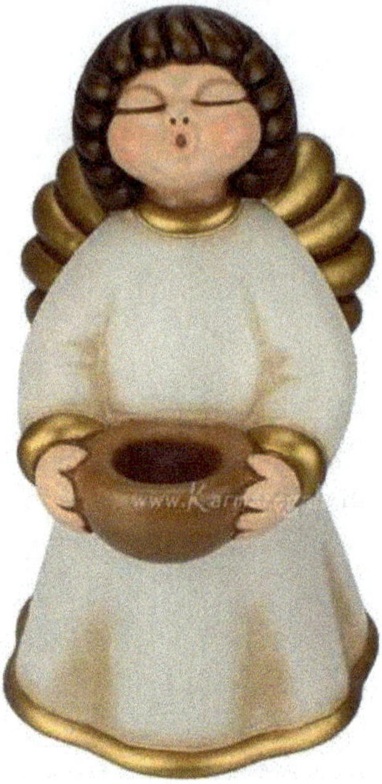

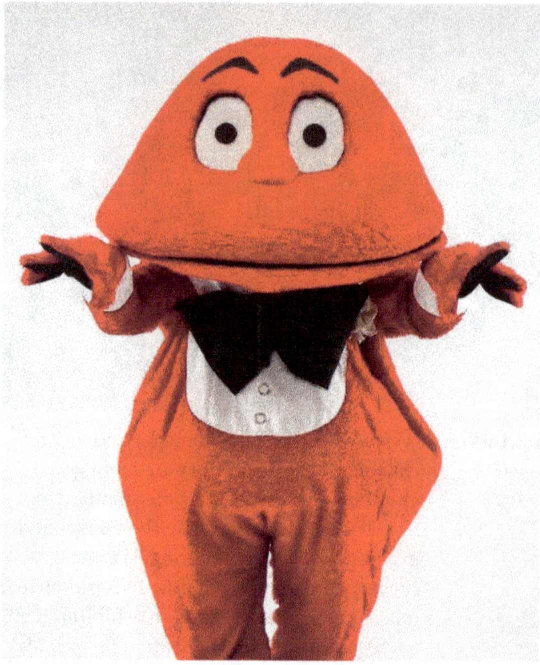

FIGURES 32–33 Ceramic figurines by the manufacturer Thun and the Gabibbo character. PHOTOS RESPECTIVELY AVAILABLE AT THUN AND STRISCIALANOTIZIA WEBSITES

Supreme Court granted copyright protection to ceramic figurines by the manufacturer Thun (Figure 32),[399] while in its decision of 6 June 2018 it granted copyright protection to the television character Gabbibo (Figure 33), against its procedural opponent, the Big Red.[400] In these cases, the Supreme Court stated that the "seriality"[401] of industrial design products does not preclude

399 *Cass. Civ. Sez I*, 23.03.2017, 7477/2017, op. cit., which overruled the decision of the Venice Appeals Court and referred the case back to the court in a different formulation: see Muià, *Dir. Ind.*, 2017, p. 235.

400 *Cass. Civ. Sez. I*, 6.06.2018, 14635/2018, which partially overruled the decision and referred the question back to the Milan Appeals Court in a different formulation for the purpose of ascertaining "evolutionary plagiarism" (*plagio evolutivo*). The judgment on merits has yet to be handed down. See also *Cass. Civ. Sez I*, 12.01.2018, 658/2018, *Euromarchi S.r.l. v. Due Esse Christmas S.r.l. et al* (on nativity figures). The Judgments of the Italian Supreme Court (*Cassazione*) are available at http://www.cortedicassazione.it/corte-di-cassazione/it/servizi_online.page.

401 Overrluing many precedents set by lower courts: Trib. Monza, 23.4.2002, *AIDA*, 2003, p. 827; Trib. Monza, 16.7.2002, *Dir. Ind.*, 2003, p. 55, commentary by Fittante, and *AIDA*, 2004, p. 668, commentary by Sarti.

their protection under copyright law, if those works are the output of a project and "that project" has the twin characteristics of being creative in character and having artistic value in itself.

Nonetheless, there is no shortage of contradictory decisions, especially in the field of fashion design, as the judgment of the Milan Appeals Court on down jackets called *The Cube* by Max Mara demonstrates.[402] In that case, the new collection *Les Plumes 2012/2013* presented by the fashion company Liu.Jo in 2012 was found not to have infringed copyright or design and model law, despite its close similarities to Max Mara's *The Cube* collection, as it was characterized by the possibility of accessorizing the down jackets with detachable buttons, buckles, belts, and cuffs, on the grounds that "modular design" is not eligible for copyright protection because "modularity lacks artistic value." The decision explains why all the most important fashion houses, including Prada, Louis Vuitton, and Gucci, pursue a "musealisation" policy, showing an increasingly widespread tendency to exhibit their fashion products in museum spaces, or in their foundations, often together with works of art.

Finally, the artistry criterion is also required by the Italian legal system through another provision at the interface of copyright and design protection, namely Article 17 of the 2002 law introducing measures to promote private enterprise and the development of competition.[403] In practice, for the application of Article 2(10) of Royal Decree No. 633 of 21 April 1941, the "disclosure" of the artistic nature of an industrial design required by Article 28 of the same Royal Decree[404] must be made to the MIBAC (Italian Ministry of Culture) before registering (or even not registering![405]) the design work. In that case, the economic exploitation rights last until the end of the twenty-fifth year after the

402 Milan Appeals Court, 5.05.2017, No. 1893, *Max Mara Fashion Group S.r.l. c. v. Liu.Jo S.p.a.*, commentary by Muià, *Dir. Ind.*, 2017, p. 433. See also Trib. Roma, 28.01.2015, *AIDA* 2015, pp. 1053 (a case dealing with stage costumes for the Italianedition of the "Dancing with the Stars" format); Trib. Roma, 15.06.2011 online database Darts IP (a case dealing with earrings designed by Delfina Delettrez).

403 "Operabilità del diritto d'autore sui disegni e modelli industriali": Article 17 of Law No. 273 of 12 December 2002, *Misure per favorire l'iniziativa privata e lo sviluppo della concorrenza*, GU Serie Generale No. 293 of 14.12.2002, Suppl. Ord. 230.

404 Article 28 of Royal Decree 1941/633: "Per acquistare il beneficio della durata normale dei diritti esclusivi di utilizzazione economica, la rivelazione deve essere fatta mediante denuncia all'ufficio della proprietà letteraria, scientifica ed artistica presso il Ministero della cultura popolare (ora Presidenza del Consiglio dei Ministri), secondo le disposizioni stabilite nel regolamento. La denuncia di rivelazione è pubblicata (...)."

405 Trib. Milano, 2.08.2012, *Vitra Patente AG ed altri v. High Tech s.r.l.*, which denied copyright protection to very famous industrial design works by Charles and Ray Eames, George Nelson Isamu Noguchi (except for the Lounge Chair and Ottoman model created by Charles and Ray Eames in 1956, which was found to transcend the designer's mere ability

death of the author.[406] Thus we see that Italian law tends to rule in favour of cumulative protection under copyright and design laws, but with considerable uncertainty. In any case, as said above, after the European Court of Justice's *Cofemel* judgment, and its rejection of any "artistic parameter," Italian courts will be required to follow the precedent.

6.1.6 *The Eclectic UK Position: Periodic Swings in Protection*

The United Kingdom has traditionally applied other criteria than the "author's own intellectual creation" or "originality" test to determine whether or not design works are eligible for copyright protection.[407] In general terms, works of applied art receive copyright protection only if they fall under the statutory categories of "artistic", or "literary" works.[408] Over the years, the law shifted from a non-cumulative stance to a cumulative one, to settle finally for partially cumulative protection. In the current UK Copyright, Designs & Patents Act 1988 (CDPA),[409] "drawings" are included under the category of "artistic works" as a type of "graphic work," irrespective of artistic quality, while "works of artistic craftsmanship," a narrower category of works of applied art, are protected "if they have an artistic quality."[410] Additionally, the act expressly provides that a three-dimensional version of an artistic work in two dimensions constitutes a reproduction of the artistic work,[411] so that an unauthorised reproduction of the three-dimensional version of a two-dimensional "artistic work" infringes copyright in relation to the two-dimensional work. However, since the statutory provision is specifically restricted to "artistic works," it follows that a three-dimensional reproduction of a "literary work" does not amount to

---

to make pleasant and functional a mass-produced product). See Alvanini, *Dir. Ind.*, 2013, p. 13.

406 Article 17(3) of Law No. 273 of 12 December 2002, cit., a provision which is in line with the Berne Convention, that provides a 25-year post-mortem term for works of applied art (Article 7(4), Berne Convention).

407 Alexander, "The concept of reproduction and the "temporary and transient" exception", *The Cambridge Law Journal*, 2009, pp. 520–523; Derclaye, "Infopaq International A/S v. Danske Dagblades Forening (C-5/08): wonderful or worrisome? The impact of the ECJ ruling in Infopaq on UK copyright law", *EIPR*, 2010, pp. 247–251; Griffiths, "Infopaq, BSA and the "Europeanisation" of United Kingdom Copyright Law", *Media & Arts Law Review*, 2011, available at SSRN: <http://papers.ssrn.com/sol3/papers.cfm?abstract_id=1777027>, accessed 6.6.2019.

408 Bently, Sherman, op. cit., pp. 679 ff.

409 Available at https://www.legislation.gov.uk/ukpga/1988/48.

410 Section 4, UK Copyright Designs and Patents Act 1988. *Cf* previous Copyright Act 1956 (4 & 5 Eliz. 2, c. 74), s. 3 (1) (c). Masiyakurinsa, "Copyright in Works of Artistic Craftsmanship: An Analysis", *Oxford Journal of Legal Studies*, 2016, pp. 506 ff; Ricketson, *The Design/Copyright Overlap* op. cit., p. 177.

411 Section 17(3), UK Copyright Designs and Patents Act 1988.

infringement of literary copyright. That means that an engineering work made in the shape or configuration of an article as depicted in a drawing, or as described in written words does not infringe copyright (under the notion of "written descriptions").[412] Similarly, a person making a rabbit dish from a recipe in Mrs Beeton's Cookery Book does not infringe copyright (under the notion of "artistic works").[413] An explanation as to why UK lawmakers have provided for such a different treatment of literary copyright may lie in the application of the axiomatic principle in copyright law that copyright protects expressions and not ideas, facts or information (the idea/expression dichotomy). In reality, the idea/expression dichotomy has no statutory basis in England, although it is considered "trite law" by judges.[414]

In the UK, therefore, the question is not whether a higher, or different level of originality applies, but whether the work falls within a protected category requiring additional conditions. In one well-known case, the House of Lords considered the very controversial concept of a "work of artistic craftsmanship."[415] The case concerned claims to copyright in a prototype for a suite of furniture designed and produced by George Hensher Ltd, and sold under the names "Denver," "Florida," and "Bronx" (with variants of the Bronx suite known as "Manhattan," "Atlantic," and "Continental"). Hensher claimed that the defendant infringed copyright by making and selling its "Amazon" suite. The appeal judges and then the House of Lords agreed that the suite of furniture was not a work of artistic craftsmanship. The case captured the imagination of many scholars because of the different approaches developed by the Lords to explain why it was not a work of artistic craftsmanship. Though the judges were unanimous in eschewing aesthetic value in deciding whether a given object is artistic or not, no agreement at all was shown in explaining what constitutes "artistic craftsmanship". Here are the opinions of their Lordships:

> There is a trend of authority with which I agree that a court ought not to be called on to make an aesthetic judgment. Judges have to be experts in the use of the English language, but they are not experts in art or aesthetics. In such a matter my opinion is of no more value than that of anyone else. But I can and must say what in my view is the meaning of the word

412 *Cf* case law reported and discussed in Wee Loon, "The Overlap between Literary Copyright and Artistic Copyright in Engineering Drawings," *Singapore Journal of Legal Studies*, 1996, pp. 524–543, p. 538.

413 See *Cuisenaire v Reed* [1963] VR 719 (making coloured rods method of teaching mathematics); *Brigid Foley Ltd v Ellott* [1982] (in accordance with the instructions in knitting guides); *Davis (J & S) (Holdings) Ltd v Wright Health* at 414.

414 *(Plastics) Ltd v Swish Products Ltd* (per Lord Hailsham of St Marylebone).

415 *Hensher v Restawile* [1976] AC 64.

artistic. (...) A work is artistic if it is genuinely admired by a section of the community by reason of the emotional or intellectual satisfaction its appearance gives; that the author was not consciously concerned to create a work of art is not determinative.

LORD REID

If it is asked whether there is artistry if there is an appeal to the eye, I would say that something more is needed. In any event, and apart from this, such questions would tend to suggest or to impose a clamp of rigidity and restriction in definition where none is needed. In deciding whether a work is one of artistic craftsmanship I consider that the work must be viewed and judged in a detached and objective way. The aim and purpose of its author may provide a pointer, but the thing produced must itself be assessed without giving decisive weight to the author's scheme of things.

LORD MORRIS OF BORTH-Y-GEST

An artistic work is no more and no less than a work of art. Every work of art is an artistic work and vice versa. (...) I do not think it is right to say that every work which has eye appeal is necessarily a work of art, though some may be. (...) The phrase works of artistic craftsmanship is made up of words in ordinary use in the English language. Unless the context otherwise requires, they must be given their ordinary and natural meaning. (...) So, in my view, it is simply a question of fact whether a work is one of artistic craftsmanship (...) Whether something is or is not artistic is a question of fact, to be decided in the light of evidence, and it is pointless to try to expound the meaning of the word.

LORD VISCOUNT DILHORNE

Work of artistic craftsmanship is a complete phrase, to be construed as a whole, and it is a mistake to consider the terms 'craftsmanship' and 'artistic in isolation from one another. The expression originates with the Copyright Act 1911, and a consideration of the social and historical backgrounds leads to the view that it was it was introduced as a result of the Art and Crafts movements associated with the names of William Morris, Ruskin and others, who held that the handicraftsman should be restored to the proper place in society and become a creative artist, while the artist should in turn be a craftsman whose aesthetic was fitness and propriety, functional efficiency and respect for the worked material, 'made for a human being by a human being'. The question is whether it is a work made by an artist-craftsman understood in that general

> sense. For that purpose, evidence is admissible and expert evidence the most cogent.
>
> LORD SIMON OF GLAISDALE

> The first essential of a work of art (which I think an artistic work must be) if it is to be distinguished from a work of craftsmanship – a distinction upon which Parliament insists – is that it shall have come into existence as the product of an author who is consciously concerned to produce a work of art [...] The word 'artistic' is for the court to interpret, not witnesses. The true test is whether the author has been consciously concerned to produce a work of art. (...) It must be possible to deduce the conscious purpose of artistic creation from the work itself or from the circumstances of its creation, but this act arises only when the question whether it is a work of art becomes one for discussion or decision by others than the author. Merit is another matter altogether (...) Whether a given object is a work of artistic craftsmanship can be posed as a question of fact, but only after the meaning of the word artistic has been determined; what that meaning is, is a question of law, since it involves a decision of what Parliament meant by the word Parliament used.
>
> LORD KILBRANDON

The CDPA lays down an exception to copyright protection in relation to drawings or preliminary models that exist specifically to be made into a particular object (to became a product of design).[416] The provision was introduced into

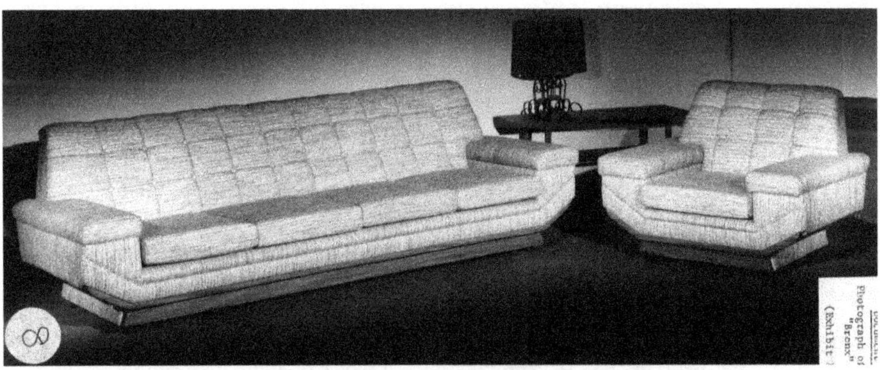

FIGURE 34 "Bronx" suite by George Hensher, Tudah Sutton and John Batchelor (1976). PHOTO AVAILABLE AT CENTRE FOR INTELLECTUAL PROPERTY AND INFORMATION LAW, HTTPS://WWW.CIPIL.LAW.CAM.AC.UK/VIRTUAL-MUSEUM/HENSHER-V-RESTAWILE-1976-AC-64

416 Section 51, UK Copyright Designs and Patents Act 1988.

the CDPA to cut back on the scope of protection enjoyed in the shape or configuration of articles in certain cases. But the interrelationship of design rights with copyright protection remains clearly evident.

The CDPA does not prevent partial cumulation, but instead seeks to exclude full cumulative protection by both design right and copyright. The case of *Lambretta Clothing Co Ltd v. Teddy Smith (UK) Ltd*[417] rekindled the debate on the issue of the nature and ambit of Section 51 of the CDPA. According to the judgment of Etherton J in the first instance, if mutual exclusivity of design right and copyright had been the intention of the drafters, then it could have been achieved by inserting an express provision. So, in the opinion of his Lordship, Section 51(1) is not just to exclude copyright protection from designs that are protected by design right. Where a third party copies, either exactly or substantially, the two-dimensional industrial drawings, the unauthorized copying is, according to Etherton J in his judgment, both an infringement of the copyright in the drawings and an infringement of any design right. The Lambretta judgment affects the interrelationship between design and copyright in many ways. If a drawing is made, although not for the purposes of creating a blueprint for the industrial manufacture of the subject matter of the drawing, then that work can have copyright protection. A drawing which sets out the shape and configuration of a useful article, although it may be based on a work which is subject to copyright protection, may be created solely with the intent that it is a blueprint for the production by an industrial process of a three-dimensional object. A final important issue in the interface between design and copyright protections concerns unregistered designs: copyright in a blueprint for a three-dimensional industrial design is not infringed where a person makes articles that embody the drawing. Accordingly, where both copyright and unregistered design coexist, copyright pre-empts the unregistered design right.[418]

Section 52 of CDPA, which limited the term of copyright protection for "artistic works" made by an industrial process (i.e. series of more than 50 copies) to 25 years, was repealed in 2016.[419] As a result, all artistic works are now

417 *Lambretta Clothing co Ltd v Teddy Smith (UK) Ltd*, [2003] EWHC 1204 Ch, *Reports of Patent, Design and Trade Mark Cases*, vol. 120, 2003, pp. 728–756. See Raj, "Flashing Badges and Design – Copyright: a case comment," *National Law School of India Review*, 2010, pp. 199–206, at pp. 205–206.

418 Bently, Sherman, op. cit., p. 800; Margoni, "Design rights and 3D Printing in the UK, Balancing Innovation and Creativity in a (dis)Harmonised and Fragmented Legal Framework," in Mendis et al. (eds.), *3D printing and beyond: Intellectual Property and Regulation*, Cheltenham and Northampton, 2019, pp. 77–98.

419 Section 52 omitted (28.7.2016) by virtue of the Enterprise and Regulatory Reform Act 2013 (c. 24), ss. 74(2) 103(3); S.I. 2016/593, arts. 2(1), 3 (with arts. 4, 5).

protected by copyright for the full term of 70 years, plus the lifetime of the author. In theory, Section 52 can apply to any type of "artistic work"[420] – graphic works, photographs, sculptures or collages, works of architecture being a model of a building, or a work of artistic craftsmanship. The difficulty with the provision is that there is no definition of such works, with the court being asked to rule in several cases whether certain works qualified for such long-term protection.

The Government stepped in to provide guidance for those who may be affected, summarizing the principles it gleaned from the case law, notably *Hensher v Restawile* of 1976 (see above). The guidance states that a work must have artistic or aesthetic quality, and must also be a work of craftsmanship, suggesting that the work must have been produced by someone who had special training, skill, and knowledge about the production of such products. In the light of the recent case law of the European Court of Justice, however, neither the traditional "skill and labour" test, nor the concept of "works of artistic craftsmanship" can be considered consistent with the European "author's own intellectual creation" standard. As such, a gradual adaptation of the author's right doctrine and lower thresholds for copyright protection for works of applied arts are expected[421] (Brexit permitting), even if, according to some authors, the practical impact of European case law on the UK copyright system will be small.[422] In fact, UK courts have already admitted that the European "author's own intellectual creation" standard restates their previous tests, but it seems that such a declaration has not substantially changed the legal situation.[423] At the moment, therefore, a work of design is protected by copyright if it is the result of the author's skills, work, judgment, and effort,[424] where the "skill and labour" test consists in the human effort involved in creating (or imitating) a work. Such a parameter is probably outdated with respect to contemporary industrial design, where more and more often the "human effort" of the designer is not so crucial.[425]

420 Bently, *Return to Industrial Copyright?*, op. cit. For details on the legislative history of the amendment see https://www.gov.uk/government/publications/copyright-protection-of-industrially-manufacturedartistic-works.

421 See Ritscher, Landolt, op. cit., p. 129.

422 Rahmatian, "Originality in UK Copyright Law: The Old "Skill and Labour" Doctrine Under Pressure," *International Review of Intellectual Property and Competition Law*, 2013, pp. 4–34.

423 *NLA v Meltwater* [2010] E.W.H.C. 3099, 81, affirmed in [2011] E.W.C.A. Civ 890.

424 *University of London Press v University Tutorial Press* [1916] 2 Ch 601, pp. 609–610 (criterion of work, formulated earlier as "sweat of the brow").

425 Domingos, *The Master Algorithm: How the Quest for the Ultimate Learning Machine Will Remake Our World*, Ney Work, 2015.

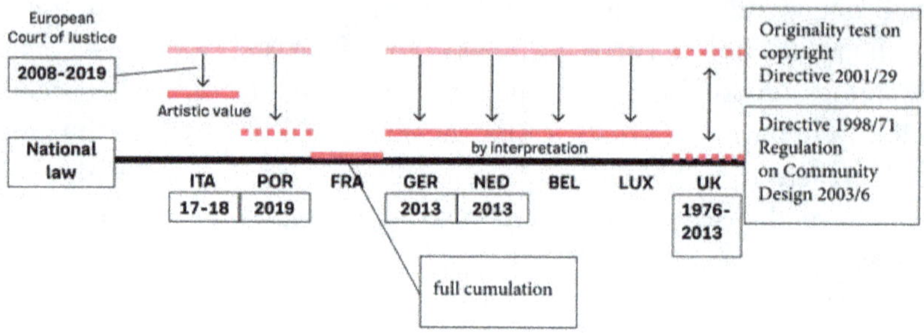

FIGURE 35 A visual representation of European measures, national laws, and court approaches, Perondi & Pasa, 2019.

6.2 The "Author": Common Usages and Design Practice

Aesthetics and Creativity Studies can contribute to our grasp of how the notions of author, co-authors, and creative processes are affected by conventions and constraints,[426] and of how they are to be treated by laws and legal systems, bearing in mind that "*this line of questioning views 'creativity' as a cause in social and intellectual endeavors, not just as an effect of individual differences, social support, or cognitive processes.*"[427] The "author's own intellectual creation" test depends largely on the day-to-day meaning of the word "original" as something proceeding directly from its source, not derivative, or imitative, but existing from the beginning, that is not a copy (Oxford and Collins English dictionaries). In Romance languages,[428] the emphasis is more on another possible meaning of "original" as something that is novel, innovative, or unique, in the sense that it departs from conventional expressions, as long as the author's personal hand is identifiable. Thus in French "original" is defined as "*qui se distingue du commun, qui sort de l'ordinaire, qui émane directement de son auteur ou de sa source, qui n'est pas une copie, une reproduction, une traduction, une refonte, etc*" (Dictionnaire de l'Académie française); in Spanish, "*que tiene carácter de novedad, que resulta de la inventiva de su autor*" (Diccionario de la

---

426 Mishra, Henriksen, *Creativity, Technology & Education: Exploring their Convergence*, Heidelberg, 2018; van Gompel, op. cit., p. 97; Testa, *La trama lucente. Che cos'è la creatività, perché ci appartiene, come funziona*, Milan, 2010; Runco, Albert, *Creativity Research: A Historical View*, in Kaufman, Sternberg (eds.), *The Cambridge Handbook of Creativity*, New York, 2010, pp. 4 ff; Sternberg, Lubart, "Investing in Creativity," *American Psychologist*, 1996, p. 677.

427 Moran, "The Roles of Creativity in Society," in Kaufman, Sternberg (eds.), *The Cambridge Handbook of Creativity*, op. cit., 2010, pp. 74 ff.

428 The modern languages that evolved from Vulgar Latin between the third and eighth centuries: see, among others, Herman, *Vulgar Latin*, (Wright transl.) Pennsylvania, 2000, pp. 96–115.

lengua espanola); in Portughese, *"não usual, extraordinário, esquisito, singular, inventado, não copiado, nem imitado ou traduzido"* (Dicionário Priberam da Língua Portuguesa); and in Italian, *"che ha una sua novità, un suo carattere proprio, che è di mano dell'autore (o fatto, dettato, diretto dall'autore), contrapposto a ciò che ne è una copia, una riproduzione, una imitazione"* (Dizionario Treccani). Such differences are not coincidental. In legal systems influenced by classical Roman law, "original" once referred to the direct origin from the extender of a document, without any connotation of "authenticity." The meaning changed when, in Mediaeval times, lawmakers searched for means of proof which, by abstracting from any symbolic signification, did not hinge on the evanescence of a simple oral affirmation, but were determined by the occurrence of precise instances traced back to a written document.[429] It was clear, on the one hand, that certainty was needed as to the direct provenance of the document, without intermediaries, while, on the other, documents needed public faith and a privileged probative force (*authenticum* ad *auctoritas*, as something that can be added, which enriches and complete the document).[430] Together, those demands marked the turning point, when the meaning of "original" changed to encompass the "authority" of the creator of the document.[431] While that applies in general, at a more technical level, definitions of the "author's intellectual creation" vary greatly in detail. This can perhaps be explained by the variety of disciplines in which creativity has been studied, including philosophy, literature and art, psychology, sociology, biology, and economics. In Aesthetics and Creativity Studies, creativity has different connotations, but what the various definitions have in common is that they involve an element of novelty and

429 For a meaningful historical and etymological investigation of the concept of authenticity with respect to that of originality, see Costamagna, "I concetti di autenticità e di originalità nella documentazione della Cancelleria genovese nel Medioevo," in *Landesherrliche Kanzleien im Spätmittelalter. Referate zum VI. Internationalen Kongreß für Diplomatik*, Munich, 1983 Silagi (ed.), 2 vol., Münich, 1984 (Münchener Beiträge zur Mediävistik und Renaissance-Forschung, 35), p. 483; Pasa, "Libertà di circolazione dei "documenti pubblici" in Europa: "autenticità" e "valore probatorio ufficiale" secondo una recente Proposta di Regolamento", in De Donno et al. (eds.), *Persona e attività economica tra libertà e regola: studi dedicati a Diego Corapi*, vol. 2, Naples, 2016, pp. 1297–1334.

430 Both terms derive from the Latin "*augere*", which expresses the concept of enrichment, growth.

431 According to Barthes, at least in literature, such authority as arising through "the prestige of the individual" culminated with capitalist ideology, which attached the greatest importance to the "person" of the "author"; see Barthes, "The Death of the Author," in *Image, Music, Text* (Heath transl.), London 1977, p. 143. According to Andina, Dante is not only author but also *auctoritas*; see Andina, *What is Art. The question of definition reloaded*, Leiden/Boston, 2017, p. 71.

TABLE 4 Mishra and Henriksen, *Creativity, Technology & Education: Exploring their Convergence*, Cham 2018, p. 19; Henriksen et al., "Novel, Effective, Whole: Toward a New Framework for Evaluations of Creative Products," *Journal of Technology and Teacher Education* 23(3), 2015, p. 455.

Creative solutions are	
Novel	Fresh, unusual, unique, surprising, startling, astonishing, astounding, germinal, trendsetting, radical, revolutionary, influential, pioneering
Effective	Valuable, important, significant, essential, necessary, logical, sensible, relevant, appropriate, adequate, functional, operable, useful, user-friendly
Whole	Organic, ordered, style, arranged, organized, formed, complete, elegant, graceful, charming, attractive, refined, complex, intricate, ornate, interesting, understandable, meaningful, clear, self-explanatory, well crafted, skillful, well made, meticulous

an element of quality (or usefulness).[432] Furthermore, they treat creativity and originality as comparative (or relative) notions;[433] that is, to be creative, a work must exhibit some sort of novel, original, or innovative outcome, either in its appearance or in its underlying ideas which are expressed in the outcome. In addition, the work must also be appropriate, that is significant, valuable, or useful, within the specific context.[434] Whether the significance of a work is evaluated retrospectively or prospectively, however, it is evident that in making the assessment, other works or processes within the same symbolic domain, or within the same genre, serve as key reference points.[435]

Another factor shaping the complexity of this issue is that the concept of authorship is actually fostered by the prestige of awards and the recognition earned from the collectivity. Prestige arises through intentional and purposeful existence, through the cultural and popular "authority" of authorship, but as it arguably shifts to the audience and social media, such as Instagram, the true dilemma becomes whether a work truly speaks for itself, or whether the brand speaks for all.[436]

432 Sternberg, Lubart, op. cit., p. 3; Sternberg, Kaufman, op. cit., p. 467.

433 Moran, op. cit., p. 75.

434 Mayer, op. cit., pp. 449–450.

435 Van Gompel, op. cit., p. 102.

436 Gibson, "'Gimme the Prize': The Author Dysfunction," *Queen Mary Journal of Intellectual Property*, 2019, pp. 127–133 at pp. 127–128.

There is a marked silence in the design field as to the notion of "author," as theories based on a common methodology are still at an embryonal stage. Ultimately, designers "are" what they practice. They work in online and offline communities, with or without technological innovation, as we saw at the beginning of Part 2. Especially in the graphic design sector, designers are also committed to "self-initiated projects"[437] – projects that are usually materialized by a studio at its own initiative (i.e. to promote its creative services), without a client setting a brief or guidelines, and for commercial purposes rather than for promotional use. The role of self-initiated projects cannot be underestimated in design practice today, certainly not in graphic design, yet they are often questioned. Part of the design world sees them as the only way to renew and develop the practice, for example by positioning objects and artefacts in specific web platforms; another part, however, see them as an unrealistic detour from the main function of design, especially graphic design, which is to act as a visual and cultural mediator between a "source" and a "receiver."[438] With self-initiated projects, the author becomes the audience, and vice versa. According to FUEL group:[439]

> The most crucial ambition we shared was to continue creating compelling and engaging graphic design. Considering a target audience is secondary to the need to make work that is interesting to us. In this sense *we are the audience*: if it works for us, hopefully it will work for others. I think this is something that has always been present, something that we could not have continued without.

Nevertheless, even in more traditional design practice, where designers work on the basis of briefs and guidelines under contractual agreements to satisfy the demands of the client, or where designers work in a corporate setting, where brand style is synchronized with product innovation in the company and the market environment,[440] the notion of "author" is changing. In

437 Printed Self-Promotion European Design. European Design Awards, available https://europeandesign.org/categories/printed-self-promotion/ (accessed 8.6.2019).

438 Sfligiotti, *Graphic Design Worlds. The double life of graphic designers. oinoi. The other way round (blog)*, 4 September 2011 available at https://oinoi.wordpress.com/testi/graphic-design-worlds-the-double-life-of-graphic-designers/ (accessed 8.6.2019); Budziňáková, *Self-Initiated Projects Need to Be Discussed*, 2012 at http://www.criticaldaily.org/index.php?project=187 (accessed 8.6.2019).

439 Murray, Sorrell, *Interview with FUEL design group*, by Butler, 21.09.2015. https://www.designboom.com/design/fuel-design-group-interview-09-20-2015/ (accessed 8.6.2019).

440 Ravasi, Lojacono, "Managing Design and Designers for Strategic Renewal", *Long Range Planning*, 2005, pp. 51–77.

companies, designers work together with engineers, product managers, and business managers among others; they conduct consumer preference tests, UX analyses, and biomechanical analyses; they develop UI tasks and make sketches and layouts in teams more often than not, coordinating and building trust and confidence across different teams (this being the function of so-called design management). Outside company settings, designers usually work with techies, planning and implementing the entire process from the gauging of customers' insights to the prototyping of products, digital interfaces, and other visual artefacts. In both cases, designers increasingly work with Artificial Intelligence and conditional generative adversarial network (CGAN) experts, working with algorithms and augmented reality or virtual reality (see Part 1, §5; Part 2, §§6 and 6.2 above). Such mathematical tools are designed to generate "new objects" according to an input vector encoding desired features and

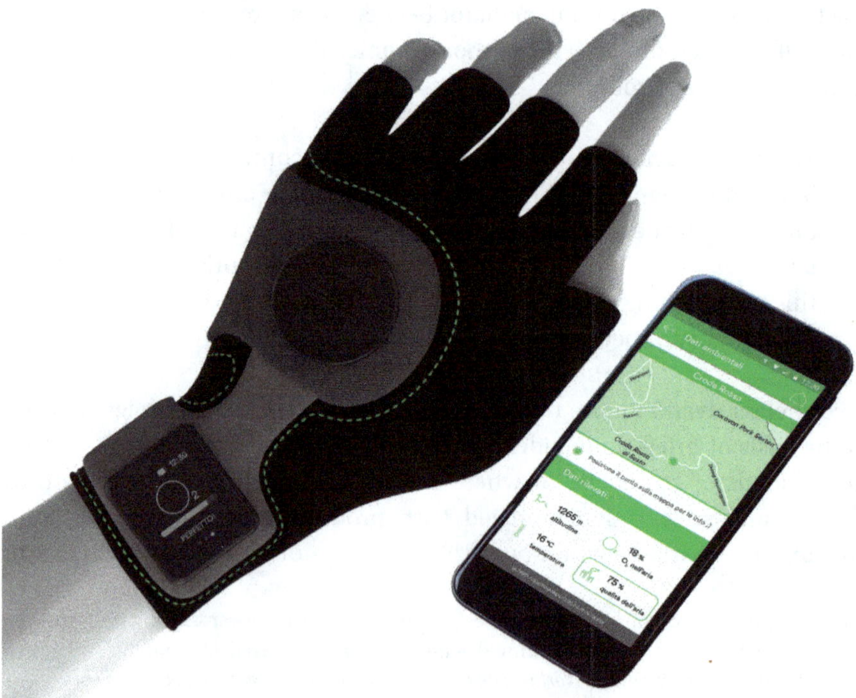

FIGURE 36 OCHÙ by Erika Coccato, Edoardo Di Pietro (Università Iuav di Venezia) is an intelligent hiking glove, designed to prevent the health dangers faced by nonprofessional hikers by tracking heartbeat, respiration, air quality, and oxygen rarefaction. In addition, it geolocates the user and, if necessary, sends emergency calls. All environmental, physiological and route data are recorded in a smartphone application. Artificial Intelligence can easily process the huge amount of data necessary for the functioning of the glove & app.

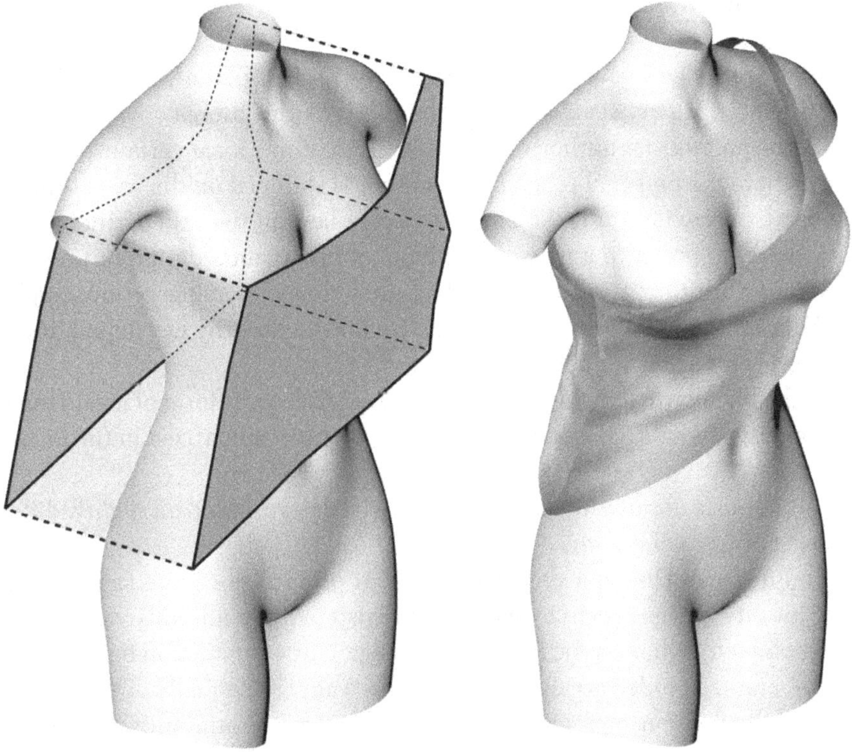

FIGURE 37 Ciammaichella, "Linea, curva, taglio, cartamodello. Il disegno nel progetto anti-effimero della moda", op. cit. Clothing simulation, which enables the drape and adherence to be studied of a garment "worn" by a 3D avatar, as it interacts with it on the different surfaces and planes.

functional type.[441] They of course affect the legal notion of "authorship" and the design/copyright interface (Figures 36-37), as machines that autonomously generate original items with realistic, aesthetic, and thoughtful attributes, and Artificial Intelligence as a source of inspiration for humans in the creative process (a sort of creative assistant)[442] are gearing up to become next generation of "young authors."

441 Deveral et al., *Using Generative Adversarial Networks to Design Shoes: The Preliminary Steps*, 2017 online at http://cs231n.stanford.edu/reports/2017/pdfs/119.pdf (accessed 8.6.2019); on parametric modelling based on generative algorithms in fashion design see Ciammaichella, "Linea, curva, taglio, cartamodello. Il disegno nel progetto anti-effimero della moda", in De Carlo, Paris (eds.), *Le linee curve per l'architettura e il design*, Milan, 2019, pp. 253-266.

442 Spai et al., *DesIGN: Design Inspiration from Generative Networks*, 2018 available at https://research.fb.com/wp-content/uploads/2018/04/design-design-inspiration-from

Conclusion

To briefly recap before concluding on the "Work" (Part 1), the "Author" (Part 2), and the interface between copyright and design protection: copyright is conceived to protect the author of intellectual creations for a certain period of time, where the personal touch of the author is stamped on the work through the creative freedom to make choices; design law, on the other hand, allows for those who invest in a new and individual ornamental design of products (jewellery, furniture, and ordinary objects including packaging, get-up, graphic symbols, and typographic typefaces) to use and exploit the developed design exclusively for a smaller period of time.

All the big "players" in the globalized market offer some form of legal protection to design works. Those forms of protection are summarized in the following points.

a) Tailored forms of protection for industrial design, based on slightly different legal notions of design.

In the European Union, a *sui generis* form of protection can be found in the "Community design" regime (where "unregistered" Community designs are also protected), whereas the USA offers design patent protection based on the utility patent, a model largely followed by the People's Republic of China.

The introduction of registered and unregistered Community design significantly boosted the attractiveness of the EU as a clever market for design protection. Both the Design Directive and the Community Design Regulation share the same legal definition of design and set an identical material threshold for protection, whereby design is protected only if it is novel, has individual character, and is not solely dictated by its technical functions and or by its interconnections (plus it cannot be contrary to public policy or to accepted principles of morality). A design is new if no other identical design has been made available to the public at the filing date, or at the date of first disclosure (unregistered design), with the major exception represented by the 12-month grace period during which disclosure is excused. A design has individual character[443]

-generative-networks.pdf (accessed 8.6.2019). According to the study, around 61% of the fashion design images generated were thought to be created by human designers, rather than by a computer, while also being considered original.

443 T-525/13, General Court (Sixth Chamber) *H&M Hennes & Mauritz BV & Co. KG v Office for Harmonisation in the Internal Market (Trade Marks and Designs) (OHIM)* [2015] on the assessment of the individual character of a design, having regard to the degree of freedom of the designer in the context of fashion items (handbags). For a similar decision in Italy see Trib. Milano 25.12.2015 on O'Bag design.

if the overall impression it produces on an informed user[444] (who is a particular user, with significant personal experience and or extensive knowledge of the sector in question)[445] is different from that produced on the same user by any previous designs made available before the date of filing (or the priority date, or before its availability to the public for unregistered designs), and only if the features of appearance of a product are not solely dictated by its technical function.[446] Industrial design protection is usually granted on the basis of a registration procedure (registered design), though under certain national laws, and after the introduction of the Community Design Regulation, design rights may also be automatically acquired by disclosing the design in a document or product (unregistered design). The requirements for protection are not examined during the application process; it is only through litigation that their fulfilment can be confirmed or denied. Owners of registered designs have exclusive rights to use the design or to licence the design to third parties for its manufacturing commercialization, importing, exporting, and distribution,[447] and, with a few exceptions,[448] can prevent third parties from using the design. Owners of unregistered designs have fewer rights, essentially only against copying, not against independent creation.[449] Furthermore, rights afforded to

444 The European Court of Justice has defined novelty and individual character through the notion of "informed user," although neither the Design Directive nor the Community Design Regulation provide a legal definition as to what constitutes an informed user: Case C-281/10 P, *PepsiCo, Inc. Grupo Promer Mon Graphic SA* [2011] E.C.R. 2011 I-10153, §§ 53, 59, after Case T-9/07, *Grupo Promer Mon Graphic SA v. OHIM – PepsiCO Inc* [2010] E.C.R. II-981.

445 The informed user is understood to be a user familiar with the sector to which the industrial design applies. In Italy, for instance, it has been interpreted as a "fluid notion": see, for example, Trib. Venezia (ord.) 13.07.2005, *Foro it.*, 128, I, 3503 commentary by Casaburi, and Trib. Napoli (ord.), 19.12.2013, *Dir. Ind.*, 2014, p. 369, commentary by Guidobaldi. Sandri introduced the doctrine of "visual perception" to grasp the overall impression of the informed user: see Sandri, "L'utilizzatore informato nel design," *Dir. Ind.*, 2006, p. 411.

446 Case C-395/16, *DOCERAM*, op. cit.

447 See the similarity with the Community patent on the type of rights conferred.

448 Private and non-commercial purposes, experimental purposes, teaching, and making citations, providing that "the source" is mentioned, meaning the designer, the design owner, and the manufacturer (see Bently, Sherman, op. cit., 760–761), or the manufacturer only at least for registered design (see Stone, op. cit., §20.74).

449 In a claim before the Irish High Court, *Karen Millen Fashions Ltd v. Dunnes Stores & Anor*, [2007] IEHC 449, Karen Millen alleged that Dunnes had infringed its unregistered design right in tops and shirts. Dunnes appealed to the Irish Supreme Court, which stayed the proceedings and referred the question to the European Court of Justice for a preliminary ruling. The decision of European Court of Justice C-345/13 *Karen Millen Fashions Ltd v. Dunnes Stores e Dunnes Stores (Limerick) Ltd* [2014], on the burden of proof for unregistered design in the sector of fashion design, stated that the holder of an unregistered

registered designs in the EU apply for a maximum of 25 years, provided that the rights-holder renews the protection every five years (for unregistered designs, only a three-year-term of protection is granted at the EU level, while in the UK, unregistered designs enjoy a maximum term of protection of 15 years). Compared to the EU approach, design patents in the USA are less promising from the designer's point of view, as they only afford 15 years of protection from issuance (which is shorter than the 20-year term from filing for US patents), and, moreover, rely on a mixed set of general and specific requirements. Design patent law derives its novelty and non-obviousness requirements (with a "prior art" test and the limited "one-year grace period" for certain disclosures made by the inventor) from utility patent rules protecting inventors, but such requirements do not really fit the purpose of industrial design which, unlike invention, is not only (or primarily) about ground-breaking innovation. US law imposes other specific requirements as well, such as ornamentality and originality, for which design protection can only cover the non-functional features of the underlying object – another cause for concern, given that industrial design purposefully combines functional and aesthetic elements.

China's stance on design protection arguably reflects its more recent decision to join international treaties on such matters[450] in response to external pressures from Western countries concerned with piracy and the free exploitation of the outcomes achieved through costly R&D investments. As stated in

---

Community design has to indicate what constitutes the individual character of that design. It is sufficient for him to indicates what in his view are the features of his design which give it individual character.

See High Court of Justice (Chancery Division) *J Choo (Jersey) Ltd. v Towerstone Ltd. & Ors* [2008] EWHC 346 (Ch) in a case concerning Towerstone's sale of a handbag at its Oxford Street store, which Jimmy Choo claimed was an imitation of its "Ramona" bag. The cause of action was an infringement of a registered and unregistered Community design right; in comparing the two bags, the High Court of Justice considered that although a detailed inspection would have revealed differences, these were trivial and the overall impression on an informed user was identical. Infringement of the registered design was therefore confirmed. To prove infringement of the unregistered designs, the claimant needed to demonstrate copying of the original design document for the handbag. Cf the reasoning of Trib. Milano, 28.03.2013, *Prada v Nau*, protecting the Prada's Postcards "SPR19M" eyewear unregistered design.

450 IP rights, and more specifically patent rights and copyright, are relatively new, as it was only in the Deng Xiaoping era that China opted to improve its IP protection to attract technological transfer and foreign investments from advanced countries. Alford, *To Steal a Book is an Elegant Offense: Intellectual Property Law in Chinese Civilization*, Stanford, 1995; Cavalieri, *L'adesione della Cina alla WTO – Implicazioni giuridiche*, Lecce, 2003; Timoteo, *La difesa di marchi e brevetti in Cina*, Turin, 2010; Devonshire, Scott, Woollard, *China Briefing: Intellectual Property Rights in China*, Berlin, 2011; Lee at al. (eds.), *Governance of Intellectual Property Rights in China and Europe*, Cheltenham/Northampton, 2016.

the Introduction, reforms to China's patent law in 2008 extended patent protection to all intellectual creations, defined as inventions, utility models, and designs.[451] To be eligible for patent protection, designs must respect "ethical rules and the public interest" (a general clause in the Chinese legal system) and be "distinctly different" from other existing designs or from the combinations of features of other existing designs; they must also be "new", in the sense that patent rights are granted only to designs that do not conflict with third party rights acquired prior to the filing date. For the purposes of Chinese patent law, "existing designs" mean designs that are known to the public both domestically and abroad before the filing date of the application: thus registration is mandatory to obtain protection in China – unlike in the EU, no protection is afforded to unregistered designs. Design patent rights last for 10 years from the application date.[452] Chinese patent law also affords exclusive rights to "utility models," which are not strictly defined in the law, but are characterized by the requirements of "novelty, inventiveness, and practical applicability."[453] While design protection covers the visual appearance of a product, utility models protect both the appearance and the functional form of the product itself, implicitly implying that design is a question of purely aesthetic appearance. Utility models can be defined as new technical solutions proposed for the shape and structure of a product, or the combination thereof, which are fit for practical use.[454] The utility model, therefore, can be defined as a protection that assigns effectiveness and convenience to a product which integrates an aesthetic innovation and, at the same time, has its own function and usefulness.[455]

451 Article 2, of the Patent Law of the People's Republic of China available at http://english.www.gov.cn/archive/laws_regulations/2014/08/23/content_281474983043612.htm (accessed 3.8.2019).

452 Articles 23 and 42 of the Patent Law of the People's Republic of China, op. cit.

453 Article 22 of the Patent Law of the People's Republic of China, op. cit.

454 De Sanctis, *Brevettare in Cina, invenzioni, modelli d'utilità, disegni industriali. Elementi di strategia aziendale*, DESK-Beijing, p. 11.

455 As is in the case of the Italian legal system, Article 82 of the Industrial Property Code. See the official English version of the Italian Industrial Property Code given by the Italian Chamber of Commerce: Article 82: "Patents for utility models may be granted for new models apt to provide particular efficacy or convenience of application or use for machines, or parts thereof, instruments, tools or functional objects in general, such as new models consisting of particular conformations, arrangements, configurations or combinations of parts." Article 40 states that: "If a design or model meets the requirements for registration and at the same time increases the utility of the object to which it refers, a simultaneous application may be made for a utility model and for the registration of a design or model, but the two types of protection may not be combined in a single title."

b) Copyright protection for industrial design for up to 70 years after the death of the creator within the Western legal tradition.

As we saw in Part 2, copyright is not fully harmonized across the EU, despite more than twenty years of efforts and many directives regarding copyright protection. Copyright covers personal and human expression as incorporated in a creative work, whether of art or literature, or works of applied art, but each Member State determines the conditions that must be met in order to obtain protection under both the Design Directive and the Community Design Regulation, which introduced the principle of a "cumulative protection" under copyright and design laws. The fundamental differences between the copyright approach (intellectual creation) and the design approach (differentiation from the existing design corpus) are: 1) the term of protection; 2) the obligation to register, for design protection; and 3) requirements such as novelty and individual character, for design protection. As said, design law is essentially modelled on patent law, but should be regarded as a genuine property right with its own space in the framework of intellectual property law.[456] Under US copyright law, at least some designs are covered by copyright protection, where they are original works set in a tangible medium of expression, incorporating pictorial, graphic, or sculptural features that can be identified separately from, and are capable of existing independently of, the utilitarian aspects of the article. Under that definition, some works of applied art, such as, for example, a table lamp base shaped to look like a female figurine, or belt buckles stylized to appear like pieces of jewellery, have been granted protection.[457] However, the "useful article doctrine" and the multifaceted notion of "conceptual separability," as variously interpreted by the appeals courts of the different circuits,[458]

456 Zentek, op. cit., p. 75; Schramm, *Der europaweite Schutz des Produktdesigns: das Gemeinschaftsgeschmacksmuster und sein Verhältnis zur Gemeinschaftsmarke*, Baden-Baden 2005, pp. 136 ff.

457 17 U.S.C. §101 and §102.

458 To be "conceptually separable," the design element must be the result of aesthetic decision-making that is independent of functional considerations, for which only designers whocan prove that they were creating the object or artefact regardless of its utilitarian benefits and for the sake of creating something artistic have any real chance of being protected under US copyright law. Such a requirement is paradoxical, because design is the result of utilitarian considerations as well as appearance. See Nimmer, Nimmer, *Nimmer on Copyright*, New York, continually updated resource [from 1985]. See also Magliocca, "Ornamental Design and incremental Innovation," *Marquette Law Review*, 2003, pp. 844–894; Afori, "Reconcpetualizing Property in Designs", *Cardozo Arts and Entertainment*, 2007–2008, pp. 1105–1178; Dinwoodie, "The Protection of Design under US Law", *IPRinfo* 04/2008, pp. 1–12 online. For an overview, see Hua, "Copyright Protection of Works of Applied Art: Rethinking Conceptual Separability and the Aesthetic Requirement," *Journal of Intellectual Property Law & Practice*, 2017, pp. 673–684.

diminish the chances of obtaining copyright protection for designs and set a highly unpredictable framework under which US courts are called to decide on alleged infringement. The differentiation between functional and aesthetic elements is at stake, but the US courts have been unable to develop a consistent and coherent case law on the issue.[459] Especially in cases of design features that could not be physically separated from a useful article, outcomes have been very divergent and sometimes quite pedantic.[460] The Federal Supreme Court established its position on the application of the separability test in *Star Athletica* 2017,[461] when it eliminated certain components of the analysis that had been adopted based on the Copyright Act's legislative history, such as the distinction between physical and conceptual separability; at the same time, however, it did not require that the article remain fully functional after separating its aesthetic features, suggesting, *e contrario*, that design features may be protectable even when they are partially functional.[462] Nevertheless, it is still controversial how the lower courts will apply the *Star Athletica* decision to aesthetic elements of designs works outside the fashion industry.[463] Furthermore, in the USA, registration of a work with the Copyright Office (within three months of first publicizing) is essential for the copyright owner to qualify for the additional entitlements of being able to sue and collect statutory damages for infringement, and to recover the legal expenses incurred through the lawsuit.

---

459 Ginsburg, "Courts Have Twisted Themselves into Knots (and the Twisted Knots Remain to Untangle): US Copyright Protection for Applied Art after Star Athletics," in Derclaye (ed.), *The copyright/design interface* op. cit., p. 297.

460 U.S. Court of Appeals, Second Circuit, Case No. 1351 – *Kieselstein-Cord v. Accessories By Pearl, Inc* 632 F.2d 989, 993 [2nd Cir. 1980 (sculptural elements of belt buckle are conceptually separable from their utilitarian function)]; *Pivot Point International Inc. Charlene Products, Inc.* 372 F.3d 913 (7th Cir. 2004); *Universal Furniture International, Inc. v. Collezione Europa USA, Inc.* 618 F.3d 418 (4th Cir. 2010). *Brandir Int'l, Inc. u. Cascade Pac. Lumber Co.*, 834 F.2d 1142, 1145 (2nd Cir. 1987): "Where design elements can be identified as reflecting the designer's artistic judgment exercised independently of functional influences, conceptual separability exists."

461 US Supreme Court No. 15–866 of 22 March 2017 – *Star Athletica, LLC v. Varsity Brands, Inc.* Liebenau, "Star Athletica v. Varsity Brands – U.S. Copyright Protection for Applied Art" *GRUR Int.*, 1, 2017, p. 843.

462 "Of course, to qualify as a pictorial, graphic, or sculptural work on its own, the feature cannot itself be a useful article or '[a]n article that is normally a part of a useful article' (which is itself considered a useful article)" 197 L. Ed. 2d at 367 (citations omitted).

463 See Ginsburg, *Courts Have Twisted* op. cit. pp. 297 ff: the approach in *Star Athletica* only offers an effective way to discern the separability of pre-existing artworks applied to useful articles but identifies difficulties in the case of artistic designs created as useful articles (as a whole). According to Liebenau, op. cit., p. 844, the decision merely answers the narrow question about the separability of surface decorations from their utilitarian base.

In China, no overlapping protection between copyright law and design patent law is admitted,[464] which means that copyright protection is strictly an alternative to design patent protection. Only designs that qualify as "works of applied art" are eligible for copyright protection, which lasts for 50 years after the death of the creator. At first, however, Chinese law, did not explain what the expression "works of applied art" meant,[465] defining it only later on[466] as "works which carry both practical uses and aesthetic meanings." As a result, many Chinese courts initially granted design works legal protection as "works of fine art," defined as "two- or three-dimensional works created in lines, colours or other medium [*sic*] which, when being viewed, impart aesthetic effect, such as paintings, works of calligraphy, sculptures and works of architecture."[467] Courts across China have interpreted the provision subjectively, without clarifying what level of creative or aesthetic value is required to classify an object as a "work of fine art."[468] For the most part, decisions have looked to past judgments, from which four key parameters can be outlined: 1) Originality (a common standard for all copyrightable works, but in the case of works of applied art it carries the additional requirements of being an "independent creation" and expressing the "creativity" of the author); 2) Reproducibility (a common characteristic of copyrightable works); 3) Practical applicability (unlike their Western counterparts, Chinese courts only afford protection to objects that blend aesthetic value *and* function); and 4) Aesthetic value (which can be confusing, because by applying this requirement courts tend to mistake design for works of fine art).[469]

---

464 As was the case in UK law and the US laws at the beginning of the XX century: see Ladas, op. cit., vol. II, p. 836.

465 The term entered into the Chinese legal system after the PRC signed the Berne Convention for the Protection of Literary and Artistic Works in 1992.

466 See the Copyright Law amendment of Article 3 (July 6, 2012) that added "works of applied art" to the list of copyrightable "works".

467 Article 4(7) of the Regulations for the Implementation of the Copyright Law of the People's Republic of China: for the full text see http://www.wipo.int/edocs/lexdocs/laws/en/cn/cn009en.pdf (accessed 2.9.2019).

468 Cozzolino, *The protection of industrial design as works of applied art in Italy and China*, Final Thesis, Master's Degree Programme in Languages, Economics and Institutions of Asia and North Africa, Academic Year 2017/2018, on line at http://dspace.unive.it/bitstream/handle/10579/13780/865808–1221351.pdf?sequence=2 (accessed 2.9.2019).

469 Furthermore, Chinese judges enjoy little independence and autonomy, since the courts are subordinate, vertically and horizontally, to political power.

c) Trademark protection for two-dimensional designs and three-dimensional designs in the USA and Europe, but not in China.[470]
In China, trademark protection applies to designs only if the three-dimensional product shape (i.e., the product configuration) does not serve any functional purposes at all, and only if it has acquired a distinctiveness (or the product's appearance has secondary meaning[471]) identifying the brand of the product. By contrast, trademark protection in the USA covers the classic Coca-Cola bottle shape, for instance.

Europe is different again, however, as trademark protection is of more limited reach under the three indents of Article 7(1)(e)i–iii of Regulation (EU) 2017/1001 on the European Union trade mark,[472] as emerged in rulings on the shape of the *Tripp Trapp* chair by Stokke,[473] the specific form of the *Bang &*

470 Under Article 25 of the Chinese Patent Law, as amended after the third reform in 2008, overlapping protection is no longer contemplated for elements that normally form labels and which can be protected by copyright or by trademark law if they have distinctive character.

471 Cf §43(a) Lanham Act 1946, the so-called "trade dress" protection of both product packaging and product design. Product design, unlike product packaging, can never be inherently distinctive, for which the design owner has to show there is "secondary meaning," by proving, through customer surveys, that the relevant public associates the design with a particular source or producer because the product has been properly advertised. Until secondary meaning is established, the design is not protected under federal trademark law. Dinwoodie, Janis, *Trade Dress and Design Law*, 1st ed., New York, 2010.

472 OJEU, 16.6.2017, L 154/1. In the interests of clarity and reason, since the decision, Council Regulation (EC) No 40/94, which was codified in 2009 as Regulation (EC) No 207/2009, and Directive 89/104/EEC, which was codified as Directive 2008/95/EC, have been substantially amended several times. Kur, *Too Pretty to Protect? Trademark law and the Enigma of Aesthetic Functionality*, Max Planck Institute for Intellectual Property and Competition Law research paper No. 11–16, 2011 (online).

473 On the first indent (previously Article 7(1)(e) Regulation No 40/94, a provision which was essentially identical to Article 3(1)(e) of the Trademarks Directive No 89/104), see C-205/13, *Hauck GmbH & Co. KG v Stokke A/S, Stokke Nederland BV, Peter Opsvik, Peter Opsvik A/S* [2014]: §25 "When applying the first indent, (…) you also have to take account of the fact that the concept of a 'shape which results from the nature of the goods themselves' means that shapes with essential characteristics which are inherent to the generic function or functions of such goods must, in principle, also be denied registration. The reservation of such characteristics to a single economic operator would make it difficult for competing undertakings to give their goods a shape which would be suited to the use for which those goods are intended – these being the essential characteristics that consumers look for in the products of competitors, given that they are intended to perform an identical or similar function."

Olufsen loudspeaker,[474] and *Lego* bricks.[475] Such limitation is unfortunate from a company's point of view, because trademark protection can be renewed indefinitely for periods of ten years at a time and has a broad scope of protection, preventing any use that is likely to cause "confusion," thus favouring company reputation and popularity.[476] In practice, combined protection (cumulative design and trademark protection, or trademark after design) requires certain prerequisites in the EU. In particular, designs must meet the strict criteria of both design and trademark laws. Over the last decade, the Court of Justice of the European Union has sought to clarify the direct assessment required by the "global impression" test, taking into account both the notion of "informed user" developed in design law, and the notion of "pertinent public" developed

474 On the third indent (previously Article 7(1)(e) Regulation No 40/94, a provision which was essentially identical to Article 3(1)(e) of the trademarks Directive No 89/104), see General Court (Eighth Chamber), T-508/08, *Bang & Olufsen v OHIM* [2011]. A trademark application is to be rejected also when the shape is the substantial value of the good: §§74–76 "Indeed, the shape for which registration was sought reveals a very specific design and the applicant itself admits, ..., that that design is an essential element of its branding and increases the appeal of the product at issue, that is to say, its value. Furthermore, it is apparent from the evidence referred to at point 33 of the decision of the First Board of Appeal of OHIM of 10 September 2008 (Case R 497/2005-1), namely extracts from distributors' websites and on-line auction or second-hand websites, that the aesthetic characteristics of that shape are emphasised first and that the shape is perceived as a kind of pure, slender, timeless sculpture for music reproduction, which makes it an important selling point. It does not therefore appear that, in the present case, the Board of Appeal committed any error in holding that, independently of the other characteristics of the goods at issue, the shape in respect of which registration was sought gives substantial value to the goods concerned". Thus the European Court confirmed that aesthetic shapes that are specifically marketed for their attractiveness are not protectable under trademark law, regardless of what factors customers base their buying decisions on (§§70–73).

475 On the second indent (previously Article 7(1)(e) Regulation No 40/94, a provision which was essentially identical to Article 3(1)(e) of the trademarks Directive No 89/104) see C-48/09 P, *Lego Juris A/S v Office for Harmonisation in the Internal Market (Trade Marks and Designs) (OHIM)* [2010], (Appeal Case before the General Court T-270/06): §41: "(...) signs which consist exclusively of the shape of goods which are necessary to obtain a technical result are not to be registered" and §60 "(...) If the three-dimensional sign consisting of such a shape were registered as a trade mark, it would be difficult for the competitors of the proprietor of that mark to place on the market shapes of goods constituting a real alternative, that is to say, shapes which are not similar and which are nevertheless attractive to the consumer from a functional perspective."

476 R 395/1999-3, *Salvatore Ferragamo v OHIM*, decision of 3 May 2000, demonstrates that sometimes fashion undertakings can register 3D trademarks, as happened with Ferragamo's square buckle for shoes. However, against the registration of 3D trademark in the fashion industry see R-371/2012-1, *Max Mara v OHIM* of 13 December 2012 (down jacket) and the Joined Cases T-409/10 and T-410/10, *Bottega Veneta v OHIM*, Judgment of the General Court of 22 March 2013 (shape of a handbag).

in trademark law. In any case, "functionality" remains a valid defence against claims of infringement of both trademark and design rights.

d) Cross-over protection under patent law (only in China) and under utility model rules, which are a 'second-tier' form of protection for minor innovations, generally less known and not implemented in all countries;[477] and protection under unfair competition laws, to avoid servile imitation.

Jurisprudence and the legal literature have long dealt with the interface of design protection with other forms of protection, such as copyright, trademark, and patent protection. Ultimately, intellectual property rights are not mutually exclusive, but rather they coexist in the same object or artefact, although structured differently in many respects.[478] To their credit, the European Design Directive and the Community Design Regulation have been successful in eliminating the barriers to cumulative protection, whereby a work of design/applied art that formerly could be protected *either* by copyright *or* by industrial design (so called separability) can now be protected by *both*. According to European Court of Justice case law, the "author's own intellectual creation" standard (i.e., originality) does not require any special "artistic value" to be assessed positively; moreover, the test applies to all copyrightable works and, by virtue of Directive 2001/29/EC, to all utilitarian objects. Member States which still permit only partial cumulation (where the level of originality implied by the "author's own intellectual creation" standard is particularly high, as with the "artistic value" required by Italian and Portuguese laws) will thus have to adapt accordingly. Indeed, cases such as *Donner*[479] and *Cassina*[480] provide clear evidence of the problems arising for cross-border trade in design objects when they are protected by copyright in certain EU Member States, but not in others which require a higher threshold for protection. The majority of EU Member States (see Part 2, §6.2 and Figure 35 above), however, already require a rather low standard for originality.[481] Nevertheless, the "freedom" of the designer is essential, and when designers can prove – by way of sketches,

---

477 Harrison, *Patents and Utility Models*, in Wilkof, Basheer (eds.), op. cit., pp. 105–117, at 106 shows a list of countries applying utility models laws. A proposal for a European utility model directive was presented in 1997, but was dropped after meeting some criticism: IP/99/433, available at https://ec.europa.eu/commission/presscorner/detail/en/IP_99_433 (accessed 10.11.2019).

478 Ritscher, Landolt, op. cit., p. 126; Ritscher, "Global Protection of Product Designs from a Practitioner's Point of View," in de Werra (ed.), op. cit., pp. 129–141; Geier, *Schutzkumulationen: Angriff auf die Gemein freiheit oder legitimer Schutz Geistigen Eigentums?*, Tübingen, 2015.

479 C-5/11, *Donner*, op. cit.

480 C-456/06, *Peek & Cloppenburg v Cassina*, [2008] E.C.R. 2008 I-02731.

481 C-145/10, *Eva-Maria Painer*, op. cit., §93.

maquettes, and properly archived designs – they were able to express their creativity throughout the entire design process by making free and creative choices,[482] their work deserves to be protected against piracy and copying. Thus, it is advisable for designers to learn to document their creative freedom, substantiating the processes underpinning their developments and choices. In infringement proceedings, such a documentary evidence would likely be a valuable means to enforcing designers' copyright claims based.[483]

In general terms, special standards such as the "artistic value" of a design work lack any basis of legitimation.[484] The notion of "design work" within the meaning of copyright law should therefore be detached from its presence in museums, or from art-historical evaluations from relevant circles. A "successful exhibition" should not be a *vademecum* for a judge, nor "artistic character" a benchmark for a work of design.

Design works come in a vast array of forms and flavours, as the images included in this essay serve to show (Figures 1, 6, 8–25, 26–33, 67 above). As suggested by the European Copyright Society, a common denominator in identifying design objects and artefacts could be that they are a "means of communication" between the designer and the public. The fact that many utilitarian objects, such as furniture, fashion, or tableware, are displayed in museums all over the world may certainly provide evidence of their aesthetic merits,[485] but a design work – just like other categories of work – can still reflect the "author's personality" even without staking its place in a museum. Thus, the practice by some national courts of denying copyright protection to mass-produced objects of common use on the grounds that they lack "artistic value" is disputable.[486] Similarly disputable from the point of view of design works

482 C-145/10, *Eva-Maria Painer*, op. cit., §88; see also Metzger, "Der Einfluss des EuGH auf die gegenwärtige Entwicklung des Urheberrechts," *GRUR*, 2012, pp. 118 ff: p. 122; Stromholm, "Was bleibt vom Erbe übrig? Uberlegungen zur Entwicklung des heutigen Urheberrechts," *GRUR Int.*, 1989, p. 15.

483 Just recently, for example, the pop star Ed Sheeran used video footage documenting the creation process of his song *Shape of You* as a defensive argument in copyright infringement proceedings (14 August 2018).

484 Ritscher, Landolt, op. cit., p. 132; Schaefer, Nordemann, "Die Neubestimmung des Schutzumfangs urheberrechtlich geschützter Werke der angewandten Kunst nach den Entscheidungen Seilzirkus und Geburtstagszug," in Dreier, Pfeifer, Specht (eds.), *Anwalt des Urheberrechts, Festschrift für Gernot Schulze zum 70. Geburtstag*, 2017, pp. 39, 42 ff.

485 European Copyright Society, op. cit.

486 Auteri, "La futura disciplina europea del design tra tutela del diritto di autore e concorrenza," *Contr. impr. Europa*, 1998, pp. 229–258 at p. 232; Sarti, "Osservazioni in tema di industrial design e diritto d'autore," *AIDA*, 2004, p. 673; Guizzardi, *La tutela d'autore del*

is a key conception underpinning copyright protection, as it has been theorized over the centuries. The theory of the uniqueness of the mechanical body (the object), to which a plurality of mystical bodies correspond (form as one of the different "functions" of the same object)[487] may well stand when "*the only truly necessary entity is God*," to quote Ockham, but it does not help us understand the complexity of design today, its sequential (and sometimes disruptive) innovation process, and its vertical integration into business innovation processes.[488] According to some authors, copyright cases are primarily about thwarting competition, not about protecting artistic or creative achievement.[489] If designers and manufacturers cannot rely on design protection because they failed to fulfil the formalities required for acquiring or maintaining design rights, or because the 25-year term has expired, they can always fall back on copyright protection, which lasts the author's lifetime plus 70 years, thus hampering competition, they say. Yet, in almost fifty years of EU competition case law, only once has the Court of Justice found that the exploitation of copyright had given rise to abuse of a dominant position.[490] As such, it could be excluded that an indulgent protection of design works under copyright law (*de facto* one hundred-year protection) would result in the excessive monopolization of everyday utility goods or ultimately hamper the creative process. Cumulative protection is often implemented by inserting non-preemption clauses in intellectual property laws, which expressly provide that the protection of a design work under the applicable law does not preempt, or affect protection of the same work by other laws that might be applicable. Such an approach is recommended by the WIPO Model Law on Industrial Designs.[491]

---

disegno industriale, incentivi all'innovazione e regime circolatorio, Milan, 2005, p. 76. *Cf* Fittante, "Disegni e modelli: carattere creativo e valore artistico," *Dir. Ind.* 2003, pp. 55–61 at p. 60.

487 Paul of Tarsus, *Epistle to the Romans* 12, 4–5; the theory was developed in Medieval times by William of Ockham, an English Franciscan friar and theologian to support Christian theology. The legal transplant of his theory is not been investigated, but arguably it could be useful for understanding copyright protection for contemporary design.

488 Bessen, Maskin, "Sequential Innovation, Patents Imitations," *RAND Journal of Economics*, 2009, p. 611.

489 van Gompel, op. cit., p. 118. The threat of monopolization was addressed very early on by the German BGH, see BGH, *GRUR* 1958, 562 (564) – *Candida-Schrift*; Schack, op. cit., §237; Kriesel, op. cit., p. 34.

490 Scordamaglia (*Direttore Generale h.c. del Consiglio dell'Unione Europea*), "Il diritto d'autore sulle opere del disegno industriale secondo la L. n. 46/2007," *Dir. Ind.*, 2008, p. 81.

491 Available at https://www.wipo.int/publications/en/details.jsp?id=3173&plang=EN.

In terms of *sui generis* design protection, the rule which excludes "design features which are solely dictated by their technical function" (see Part 1, §3.3.2, and Part 2 §§ 6.2 above) clashes with the "coherent unit" which is the work of design, as it is perceived by the observer. That is explained by the "Navon effect,"[492] where first we perceive the "global configuration" of an object, and only afterwards the "details," for which it is always a matter of making an overall evaluation at a glance, maintaining a certain physical distance from the design work. Alternative features are always possible from the point of view of the designer.[493] At the same time, it is also true that creative processes are contingent on many external factors. Cultural productions are usually made with audiences in mind and individual creators operate within social, technical, and institutional environments with numerous constraints, which implies that, in reality, the autonomy of an author to make free and creative choices is *de facto* limited – especially when design works are the result of complex collaborative processes in both offline and online communities, or the outcome of conditional generative adversarial networks (CGAN) and the like (see Part 2, especially §6.2 above). But the real point here is not the authors' freedom of choice. Rather, design protection must be consistent with the fact that technical (functional) and aesthetic features are not divisible,[494] because even the appearance of a design object or artefact is indispensable in achieving the object's functional purpose, even in relation to the chosen technical features, because otherwise Design, in practice, would become little more than a mere "cosmetic exercise." In the vast majority of cases, aesthetic features are of primary relevance in serving the functional outcome, otherwise it would simply be bad design. Whether there should be differing levels of protection, depending on the role played by aesthetics and by functionality in a design work, is thus a matter to be addressed, as is, more importantly, the way in which design protection overlaps with other forms of protection as a result. A promising solution could lie in the spread of utility model protection (see the Introduction and this Conclusion), but – as we have observed – utility model law has yet to be harmonized in Europe or elsewhere.

492 Navon, "Forest before Trees: the Precedence of Global Features in Visual Perception," *Cognitive Psichology* 9/1977, p. 353. The human eye is not a calculator; any methodology that isolates the details and focuses on them to highlight differences is wrong.

493 See the German BGH with regards to unfair competition law, BGH, *GRUR*, 2012, 58 – *Seilzirkus* and the Judgements of the Swiss Federal Supreme Court regarding 3D-marks, BGE of 3 July 2012, 4A20/2012 and BGE 129 III 514 of 2 July 2002 quoted in Ritscher, Landolt, op. cit., p. 133.

494 Romano, op. cit., p. 309.

Finally, the cause of design protection would probably be better served if contracting parties enjoyed greater freedom in negotiating ate least some layers of protection. Under the principle of cumulation, five different regimes are available, more often than not affording overlapping protection for the same object,[495] which parties to the contract could therefore tailor to their intents. Of course, adequate safeguards would be needed, so as to prevent unfair competition, by artificially prolonging, for instance, the protection enjoyed by an economic asset which the law envisages should be in the public domain within a certain term. Such issues clearly involve policy decisions, balancing the conflicting interests of big manufacturers, small and medium enterprises, designers, and consumers at large.[496] Ultimately, the recognition of IP rights is about the distribution of market power. One error is to presume that because a rightsholder has a potential monopoly, it follows that it can control the market. As said, EU competition case law since the mid-1970s demonstrates that is not the case. Preventing unfair monopolistic behaviour and competition litigation is by far the least attractive premise for the protection of design works, also because competition rules arguably put the regulation of the market in the hands of the participants with the deepest pockets.[497] Self-regulation is fashionable, but is unable to assess the public interest adequately. It is evident that any reconceptualization of IP law demands the engagement of the manufacturing and business communities, as well as the scientific community of programmers, computer scientists, and neuroscientists for digital issues, for a new design right governance framework to be achieved.

The IP field, however, is notoriously hard to re-conceptualize. Design works display a significant correlation between creativity and technology, while the relationship between design rights and copyright protection is not linear, especially now that digital technology has flooded the design world. It is not just a question of different cultures underpinning intellectual property laws, such as the Anglo-American conception of copyright or the Continental European

495 Margoni, *Design rights and 3D Printing in the UK*, op. cit.

496 DG Growth, *Legal Review on Industrial Design Protection in Europe*, Final Report 2016, MARKT2014/083/D available at http://ec.europa.eu/growth/content/legal-review-industrial-designprotectioneurope-0_en, p. 140. In the Italian literature: Galli, "Proprietà intellettuale, un diritto per il futuro," *Dir. Ind.*, 2011, p. 105; Grossi, *Itinerari dell'impresa, Quaderni fiorentini per la storia del pensiero giuridico moderno*, XXVIII, 1999, p. 999. As Tullio Ascarelli has written: "intellectual property arises from the individual creative act, but is destined to be promptly socialized," Ascarelli, *Teoria della concorrenza e dei beni immateriali*, Milan, 1960.

497 McQueen, op. cit., p. 94.

approach.[498] Even if it is true that Continental European law originally saw exclusive copyright as a natural right granted to the author of an intellectual work, whereas the Anglo-American tradition intended copyright more as a utilitarian incentive,[499] in both cases contentious debate persists over the competing interests of authors, publishers and typesetters, employers, and the general public.[500] The same is true when it comes to the design/copyright interface and in all the other cases of overlapping protections, where any re-conceptualization of IP will have to strike a balance between the conflicting interests of all the players involved. Issues concerning the originator, copyist, and user are not necessarily clear-cut, and the public interest argument invariably does not favour authors.[501] A plurality of often uncoordinated, and largely overlapping, intellectual property rights has been identified in the literature as inefficient, costly, and the cause of legal uncertainty.[502] Such pluralism is, however, also a resource that generates positive outcomes. Balancing innovation and creativity with efforts to avoid building barriers for newcomers to specific market sectors is certainly a hard task, but it is one that design protection would do well to grapple with. Another comes from the consideration that the most audacious design projects today rely on data and information (Figures 16–33, 36-37 above) – information that, as with any other anticommon,[503] can only be enhanced through its use,[504] suggesting that the next challenge for design protection will be the interface with privacy and data protection laws. Contemporary issues concerning the global role of intellectual property show that IP law can constantly be reinvented as different conceptions of knowledge surface among legal elites and ordinary citizens.

---

498 Wilf (ed.), *Intellectual Property Law and History*, New York, 2012.

499 Ginsburg, A *Tale of Two Copyrights* op. cit., pp. 27 ff.

500 Stokes, "Copyrighting American History: International Copyright and the Periodization of the Nineteenth Century," in Wilf (ed.), *Intellectual Property Law and History*, op. cit. pp. 181 ff.

501 McQueen, op. cit., p. 102.

502 Margoni, *The Harmonisation* op. cit.

503 What is usually referred to as "the tragedy of the anticommons" is a type of coordination breakdown, in which a single resource (information in this case) has numerous rights-holders, who prevent others from using it, frustrating what would be a socially desirable outcome. See *ex pluris*, Heller, *The Gridlock Economy: How too much ownership wrecks markets, stops innovation, and costs lives*, New York, 2008. In Italy, Gambaro, "Dalla new property alle new properties," in Scalisi (ed.), *Scienza e insegnamento del diritto civile in Italia*, Milan, 2004, pp. 686 ff; Ramello, "Il diritto d'autore nella prospettiva *law and economics*," *Economia della cultura*, 2003, p. 207; Nivarra, "Anticommons and Legal Standards," *AIDA* 2013, pp. 260–276.

504 Donolo, "Reti come beni comuni," *Parolechiave* 34/2005.

Acknowledgments

In writing this work I benefited from the suggestions and opinions of various colleagues; in no particular order of gratitude, I wish thank Medardo Chiapponi, Massimiliano Ciammaichella, Martina Frausin, Raimonda Riccini, Laura Badalucco, Pietro Costa, Andrea Ciotti, Luca Casarotto, Luciano Perondi, Maximiliano Romero, and the students of my Intellectual Property course for the Department of Architecture and Arts at the Università Iuav di Venezia.

www.ingramcontent.com/pod-product-compliance
Lightning Source LLC
Chambersburg PA
CBHW071349230926
51846CB00002B/484
* 9 7 8 9 0 0 4 4 3 0 3 0 3 *